The National Curriculum

Handbook for secondary teachers in England
Key stages 3 and 4

Foreword

The National Curriculum lies at the heart of our policies to raise standards. It sets out a clear, full and statutory entitlement to learning for all pupils. It determines the content of what will be taught, and sets attainment targets for learning. It also determines how performance will be assessed and reported. An effective National Curriculum therefore gives teachers, pupils, parents, employers and their wider community a clear and shared understanding of the skills and knowledge that young people will gain at school. It allows schools to meet the individual learning needs of pupils and to develop a distinctive character and ethos rooted in their local communities. And it provides a framework within which all partners in education can support young people on the road to further learning.

Getting the National Curriculum right presents difficult choices and balances. It must be robust enough to define and defend the core of knowledge and cultural experience which is the entitlement of every pupil, and at the same time flexible enough to give teachers the scope to build their teaching around it in ways which will enhance its delivery to their pupils.

The focus of this National Curriculum, together with the wider school curriculum, is therefore to ensure that pupils develop from an early age the essential literacy and numeracy skills they need to learn; to provide them with a guaranteed, full and rounded entitlement to learning; to foster their creativity; and to give teachers discretion to find the best ways to inspire in their pupils a joy and commitment to learning that will last a lifetime.

An entitlement to learning must be an entitlement for all pupils. This National Curriculum includes for the first time a detailed, overarching statement on inclusion which makes clear the principles schools must follow in their teaching right across the curriculum, to ensure that all pupils have the chance to succeed, whatever their individual needs and the potential barriers to their learning may be.

Equality of opportunity is one of a broad set of common values and purposes which underpin the school curriculum and the work of schools. These also include a commitment to valuing ourselves, our families and other relationships, the wider groups to which we belong, the diversity in our society and the environment in which we live. Until now, ours was one of the few national curricula not to have a statement of rationale setting out the fundamental principles underlying the curriculum. The handbooks for primary and secondary teachers include for the first time such a statement.

This is also the first National Curriculum in England to include citizenship, from September 2002, as part of the statutory curriculum for secondary schools. Education in citizenship and democracy will provide coherence in the way in which all pupils are helped to develop a full understanding of their roles and responsibilities as citizens in a modern democracy. It will play an important role, alongside other aspects of the curriculum and school life, in helping pupils to deal with difficult moral and social questions that arise in their lives and in society. The handbooks also provide for the first time a national framework for the teaching of personal, social and health education. Both elements reflect the fact that education is also about helping pupils to develop the knowledge, skills and understanding they need to live confident, healthy, independent lives, as individuals, parents, workers and members of society.

Rt Hon David Blunkett
Secretary of State for Education
and Employment

Sir William Stubbs
Chairman, Qualifications
and Curriculum Authority

4

About this handbook

This handbook:

- sets out the legal requirements of the National Curriculum in England for pupils aged 11 to 16
- provides information to help teachers implement the National Curriculum in their schools.

It has been written for secondary teachers. Parents, governors and all those with an interest in education will also find it useful.

The National Curriculum for pupils aged five to 11 is set out in the handbook for primary teachers. There are also separate booklets for the 12 National Curriculum subjects.

All these publications and related materials can be found on the National Curriculum web site at www.nc.uk.net.

Contents

Teaching requirements for each subject

Guidelines

The National Curriculum attainment targets

The school curriculum and the National Curriculum: values, aims and purposes

The school curriculum and the National Curriculum: values, aims and purposes

The school curriculum comprises all learning and other experiences that each school plans for its pupils. The National Curriculum is an important element of the school curriculum.

Values and purposes underpinning the school curriculum

Education influences and reflects the values of society, and the kind of society we want to be. It is important, therefore, to recognise a broad set of common values and purposes that underpin the school curriculum and the work of schools.[1]

Foremost is a belief in education, at home and at school, as a route to the spiritual, moral, social, cultural, physical and mental development, and thus the well-being, of the individual. Education is also a route to equality of opportunity for all, a healthy and just democracy, a productive economy, and sustainable development. Education should reflect the enduring values that contribute to these ends. These include valuing ourselves, our families and other relationships, the wider groups to which we belong, the diversity in our society and the environment in which we live. Education should also reaffirm our commitment to the virtues of truth, justice, honesty, trust and a sense of duty.

At the same time, education must enable us to respond positively to the opportunities and challenges of the rapidly changing world in which we live and work. In particular, we need to be prepared to engage as individuals, parents, workers and citizens with economic, social and cultural change, including the continued globalisation of the economy and society, with new work and leisure patterns and with the rapid expansion of communication technologies.

Aims for the school curriculum

If schools are to respond effectively to these values and purposes, they need to work in collaboration with families and the local community, including church and voluntary groups, local agencies and business, in seeking to achieve two broad aims through the curriculum. These aims provide an essential context within which schools develop their own curriculum.

[1] In planning their curriculum, schools may wish to take account of the statement of values finalised after widespread consultation by the National Forum for Values in Education and the Community (May 1997). These are reproduced on pages 197–199 of this handbook.

**Aim 1: The school curriculum should aim to provide opportunities
for all pupils to learn and to achieve.**

The school curriculum should develop enjoyment of, and commitment to,
learning as a means of encouraging and stimulating the best possible progress and
the highest attainment for all pupils. It should build on pupils' strengths, interests
and experiences and develop their confidence in their capacity to learn and work
independently and collaboratively. It should equip them with the essential learning
skills of literacy, numeracy, and information and communication technology,
and promote an enquiring mind and capacity to think rationally.

The school curriculum should contribute to the development of pupils'
sense of identity through knowledge and understanding of the spiritual, moral,
social and cultural heritages of Britain's diverse society and of the local, national,
European, Commonwealth and global dimensions of their lives. It should
encourage pupils to appreciate human aspirations and achievements in aesthetic,
scientific, technological and social fields, and prompt a personal response
to a range of experiences and ideas.

By providing rich and varied contexts for pupils to acquire, develop and
apply a broad range of knowledge, understanding and skills, the curriculum
should enable pupils to think creatively and critically, to solve problems and to
make a difference for the better. It should give them the opportunity to become
creative, innovative, enterprising and capable of leadership to equip them
for their future lives as workers and citizens. It should also develop their
physical skills and encourage them to recognise the importance of pursuing
a healthy lifestyle and keeping themselves and others safe.

**Aim 2: The school curriculum should aim to promote pupils' spiritual, moral,
social and cultural development and prepare all pupils for the opportunities,
responsibilities and experiences of life.**

The school curriculum should promote pupils' spiritual, moral, social and cultural
development and, in particular, develop principles for distinguishing between right
and wrong. It should develop their knowledge, understanding and appreciation
of their own and different beliefs and cultures, and how these influence individuals
and societies. The school curriculum should pass on enduring values, develop
pupils' integrity and autonomy and help them to be responsible and caring citizens
capable of contributing to the development of a just society. It should promote
equal opportunities and enable pupils to challenge discrimination and stereotyping.
It should develop their awareness and understanding of, and respect for, the
environments in which they live, and secure their commitment to sustainable
development at a personal, local, national and global level. It should also equip
pupils as consumers to make informed judgements and independent decisions
and to understand their responsibilities and rights.

The school curriculum should promote pupils' self-esteem and emotional well-
being and help them to form and maintain worthwhile and satisfying relationships,
based on respect for themselves and for others, at home, school, work and in the
community. It should develop their ability to relate to others and work for the
common good.

It should enable pupils to respond positively to opportunities, challenges and responsibilities, to manage risk and to cope with change and adversity. It should prepare pupils for the next steps in their education, training and employment and equip them to make informed choices at school and throughout their lives, enabling them to appreciate the relevance of their achievements to life and society outside school, including leisure, community engagement and employment.

The interdependence of the two aims

These two aims reinforce each other. The personal development of pupils, spiritually, morally, socially and culturally, plays a significant part in their ability to learn and to achieve. Development in both areas is essential to raising standards of attainment for all pupils.

The national framework and the purposes of the National Curriculum

The two broad aims for the school curriculum are reflected in section 351 of the Education Act 1996, which requires that all maintained schools provide a balanced and broadly based curriculum that:

- promotes the spiritual, moral, cultural, mental and physical development of pupils at the school and of society
- prepares pupils at the school for the opportunities, responsibilities and experiences of adult life.

The Act requires the Secretary of State, local authorities and the governing body and headteacher to take steps to achieve these requirements. The Secretary of State meets his responsibilities in this area by providing a national framework which incorporates the National Curriculum, religious education and other statutory requirements. This framework is designed to enable all schools to respond effectively to national and local priorities, to meet the individual learning needs of all pupils and to develop a distinctive character and ethos rooted in their local communities.

The four main purposes of the National Curriculum

To establish an entitlement

The National Curriculum secures for all pupils, irrespective of social background, culture, race, gender, differences in ability and disabilities, an entitlement to a number of areas of learning and to develop knowledge, understanding, skills and attitudes necessary for their self-fulfilment and development as active and responsible citizens.

To establish standards

The National Curriculum makes expectations for learning and attainment explicit to pupils, parents, teachers, governors, employers and the public, and establishes national standards for the performance of all pupils in the subjects it includes. These standards can be used to set targets for improvement, measure progress towards those targets, and monitor and compare performance between individuals, groups and schools.

To promote continuity and coherence

The National Curriculum contributes to a coherent national framework that promotes curriculum continuity and is sufficiently flexible to ensure progression in pupils' learning. It facilitates the transition of pupils between schools and phases of education and provides a foundation for lifelong learning.

To promote public understanding

The National Curriculum increases public understanding of, and confidence in, the work of schools and in the learning and achievements resulting from compulsory education. It provides a common basis for discussion of educational issues among lay and professional groups, including pupils, parents, teachers, governors and employers.

Developing the school curriculum

While these four purposes do not change over time, the curriculum itself cannot remain static. It must be responsive to changes in society and the economy, and changes in the nature of schooling itself. Teachers, individually and collectively, have to reappraise their teaching in response to the changing needs of their pupils and the impact of economic, social and cultural change. Education only flourishes if it successfully adapts to the demands and needs of the time.

The school curriculum and the National Curriculum: about key stages 3 and 4

The school curriculum and the National Curriculum: about key stages 3 and 4

Where and when the National Curriculum applies

The National Curriculum applies to pupils of compulsory school age in community and foundation schools, including community special schools and foundation special schools, and voluntary aided and voluntar controlled schools. It is organised on the basis of four key stages[1], as shown here.

	Key stage 1	Key stage 2	Key stage 3	Key stage 4	
Age	5–7	7–11	11–14	14–16	
Year groups	1–2	3–6	7–9	10–11	
English	■	■	■	■	National Curriculum core subjects
Mathematics	■	■	■	●	
Science	■	■	■	●	
Design and technology	■	■	■	●	National Curriculum non-core foundation subjects
Information and communication technology	■	■	■	■	
History	■	■	■		
Geography	■	■	■		
Modern foreign languages			■	●	
Art and design	■	■	■		
Music	■	■	■		
Physical education	■	■	■	●	
Citizenship			▶	▶	

■ Statutory from August 2000
● Statutory from August 2001
▶ Statutory from August 2002

Schools have some discretion over when to start teaching the key stage programmes of study, as the law requires that programmes of study should be taught during the key stage, not that they be introduced at a particular time.

[1] The four key stages are defined precisely in section 355(1) a–d of the Education Act 1996.

Physical education

The Government believes that two hours of physical activity a week, including the National Curriculum for physical education and extra-curricular activities, should be an aspiration for all schools. This applies throughout all key stages.

Competitive games activities are compulsory throughout key stages 1 to 3. At key stage 4, although pupils can choose other activities instead of competitive team and individual games, the Government expects schools to continue to provide these for pupils who wish to take up this option.

Design and technology at key stage 3

The Government believes that schools should be encouraged to look for opportunities to teach both food and textiles as part of the range of contrasting materials that pupils should use as part of the key stage 3 programme of study.

Mathematics at key stage 4

In mathematics there are two programmes of study – foundation and higher. Pupils may be taught either the foundation or the higher programme of study. The higher programme of study is designed for pupils who have attained a secure level 5 at the end of key stage 3.

Science at key stage 4

In science there are two programmes of study – single science and double science. Pupils may be taught either the single or the double science programme of study. The requirements of either option would also be met by pupils taking GCSE courses in all three of the separate sciences of biology, chemistry and physics. The Government firmly believes that double science or the three separate sciences should be taken by the great majority of pupils. Single science is intended for a minority of pupils who have good reason to spend more time on other subjects.

Possible modifications at key stage 4

Regulations under section 363 of the 1996 Education Act allow schools to make exceptional provision to meet a wider range of individual pupils' needs.

From September 2000, regulations will allow schools to meet the statutory requirement for pupils to study design and technology, modern foreign languages or science by providing courses leading to a specified range of qualifications, not all of which will fully cover the programmes of study. The range of qualifications will be separately specified in the annual DfEE circular listing qualifications approved under section 400 of the 1996 Education Act.

Schools may disapply, for any one pupil, up to two National Curriculum subjects, in order to:

- provide wider opportunities for work-related learning than are possible alongside the full statutory requirement by disapplying up to two of design and technology, modern foreign languages and science (from September 1998)
- allow pupils making significantly less progress than their peers to study fewer National Curriculum subjects in order to consolidate their learning across the curriculum by disapplying design and technology and/or modern foreign languages (from September 2000)

- respond to pupils' individual strengths and talents by allowing them to emphasise a particular curriculum area by exchanging a statutory subject for a further course in that curriculum area, by disapplying design and technology and/or modern foreign languages (from September 2000).

In order to disapply National Curriculum subjects for these purposes, schools and their governors must satisfy themselves that they have met the regulations and the criteria within them and inform QCA of their plans. Guidance is available in: *Disapplication of the National Curriculum at key stage 4 using section 363 of the 1996 Education Act for a wider focus on work-related learning* (order ref QCA/98/215). Further guidance will be available in spring 2000.

The structure of the National Curriculum

For each subject and for each key stage, programmes of study set out what pupils should be taught, and attainment targets set out the expected standards of pupils' performance. It is for schools to choose how they organise their school curriculum to include the programmes of study.

Programmes of study

The programmes of study[2] set out what pupils should be taught in each subject at each key stage, and provide the basis for planning schemes of work. When planning, schools should also consider the four general teaching requirements (pages 32–42) that apply across the programmes of study.

The exemplar schemes of work jointly published by the DfEE and QCA, show how the programmes of study and attainment targets can be translated into practical, manageable teaching plans.

Attainment targets and level descriptions

An attainment target sets out the 'knowledge, skills and understanding which pupils of different abilities and maturities are expected to have by the end of each key stage'[3]. Except in the case of citizenship[4], attainment targets consist of eight level descriptions of increasing difficulty, plus a description for exceptional performance above level 8. Each level description describes the types and range of performance that pupils working at that level should characteristically demonstrate.

The level descriptions provide the basis for making judgements about pupils' performance at the end of key stages 1, 2 and 3. At key stage 4, national qualifications are the main means of assessing attainment in National Curriculum subjects.

Range of levels within which the great majority of pupils are expected to work		Expected attainment for the majority of pupils at the end of the key stage	
Key stage 1	**1–3**	at age 7	**2**
Key stage 2	**2–5**	at age 11	**4**
Key stage 3	**3–7**	at age 14	**5/6**[5]

[2] The Education Act 1996, section 353b, defines a programme of study as the 'matters, skills and processes' that should be taught to pupils of different abilities and maturities during the key stage.

[3] As defined bt the Education Act 1996, section 353a.

[4] In citizenship, expected performance for the majority of pupils at the end of key stages 3 and 4 is set out in end of key stage descriptions.

[5] Including modern foreign languages.

Using level descriptions

Assessing attainment at the end of key stage 3

In deciding on a pupil's level of attainment at the end of key stage 3, teachers should judge which description best fits the pupil's performance. When doing so, each description should be considered alongside descriptions for adjacent levels.

Arrangements for statutory assessment at the end of key stage 3 are set out in detail in QCA's annual booklets about assessment and reporting arrangements.

The level descriptions are not designed to assess individual pieces of work. They list aspects of attainment, based on the programmes of study, which teachers need to assess to build up a picture of a pupil's performance over time in a range of contexts.

Planning

Teachers' planning for schemes of work should start from the programmes of study and the needs and abilities of their pupils. Level descriptions can help to determine the degree of challenge and progression for work across each year of a key stage.

Reporting

Teachers are required to report annually to parents on pupils' progress. Although not designed to be used at the end of each year across the key stage, the level descriptions can be used as a basis to describe pupils' progress.

Target setting

To support target setting for pupils who achieve significantly below age-related expectations, performance criteria have been developed in English and mathematics leading to level 1 and within levels 1 and 2. In addition, performance criteria have been developed for pupils' personal and social development. These criteria were published in *Supporting the target setting process* (DfEE/QCA 1998).

Links with qualifications

Scales used in approved national qualifications build on pupils' prior learning as set out in the programmes of study at key stage 3 and the level descriptions. Qualifications used by pupils of compulsory school age, whether in school, college or workplace, must be approved under section 400 of the Education Act 1996. Approved qualifications are listed in a DfEE circular sent annually to schools and colleges. Pupils may be offered courses leading to the following qualifications:

- GCSE
- GCSE (short course)
- Part One GNVQ at foundation and intermediate level
- GNVQ (or GNVQ units) at foundation, intermediate and advanced level
- NVQ (or NVQ units) at levels 1 and 2 (approved titles only)
- key skills unit in information technology
- entry level qualifications
- GCE AS level
- other approved qualifications.

Other requirements

Religious education

Under the Education Act 1996 schools must provide religious education for all registered pupils, although parents can choose to withdraw their children. Schools, other than voluntary aided schools and those of a religious character, must teach religious education according to the locally agreed syllabus. Each agreed syllabus should reflect the fact that the religious traditions in Great Britain are in the main Christian, while taking account of the teachings and practices of the other principal religions represented in Great Britain.

Religious education makes a distinctive contribution to the school curriculum by developing pupils' knowledge and understanding of religion, religious beliefs, practices, language and traditions and their influence on individuals, communities, societies and cultures. It enables pupils to consider and respond to a range of important questions related to their own spiritual development, the development of values and attitudes and fundamental questions concerning the meaning and purpose of life.

Sex education

Secondary schools must provide sex education for their pupils. It must include teaching about AIDS, HIV and other sexually transmitted infections and be given in such a way as to encourage pupils to have due regard to moral considerations and the value of family life. The detailed content and nature of sex education is for schools to decide. Parents can choose to withdraw their children from all or part of sex education.

Careers education

All schools must provide a programme of careers education for pupils during years 9, 10 and 11 and an appropriate range of careers information. They must also allow officers from the careers service access to pupils at key decision-making points during their education. Schools are encouraged to provide careers education for pupils before year 9 and for those in the sixth form.

Careers education contributes to the school curriculum by helping pupils manage progression in their learning and work as they move through school and beyond. Careers education helps pupils to choose and prepare for opportunities, responsibilities and experiences in education, training and employment that will contribute to their own fulfilment and to the well-being of others, including the wider society and economy.

Careers education contributes to pupils' personal effectiveness through its emphasis on transferable skills such as decision-making, handling information critically, self-awareness, action planning and review, negotiating and self-presentation. Pupils can use these skills to manage their self-development and career exploration as well as their career plans, decisions and routes.

DfEE circulars 5/97 and 5/98 provide guidance for schools on meeting the statutory requirements. QCA has published guidance for schools and colleges, *Learning outcomes from careers education and guidance* (QCA/99/359), to complement the DfEE circulars.

Learning across the National Curriculum[6]

Promoting spiritual, moral, social and cultural development across the National Curriculum

All National Curriculum subjects provide opportunities to promote pupils' spiritual, moral, social and cultural development. Explicit opportunities to promote pupils' development in these areas are provided in religious education, citizenship and the non-statutory framework for personal, social and health education[7] (PSHE) at key stages 3 and 4. A significant contribution is also made by school ethos, effective relationships throughout the school, collective worship, and other curriculum activities.

- Pupils' *spiritual development* involves the growth of their sense of self, their unique potential, their understanding of their strengths and weaknesses, and their will to achieve. As their curiosity about themselves and their place in the world increases, they try to answer for themselves some of life's fundamental questions. They develop the knowledge, skills, understanding, qualities and attitudes they need to foster their own inner lives and non-material well-being.

- Pupils' *moral development* involves pupils acquiring an understanding of the difference between right and wrong and of moral conflict, a concern for others and the will to do what is right. They are able and willing to reflect on the consequences of their actions and learn how to forgive themselves and others. They develop the knowledge, skills, understanding, qualities and attitudes they need in order to make responsible moral decisions and to act on them.

- Pupils' *social development* involves pupils acquiring an understanding of the responsibilities and rights of being members of families and communities (local, national and global), and an ability to relate to others and to work with others for the common good. They display a sense of belonging and an increasing willingness to participate. They develop the knowledge, skills, understanding, qualities and attitudes they need to make an active contribution to the democratic process in each of their communities.

- Pupils' *cultural development* involves pupils acquiring an understanding of cultural traditions and an ability to appreciate and respond to a variety of aesthetic experiences. They acquire a respect for their own culture and that of others, an interest in others' ways of doing things and curiosity about differences. They develop the knowledge, skills, understanding, qualities and attitudes they need to understand, appreciate and contribute to culture.

Promoting personal, social and health education

Guidelines are provided in this handbook to help schools establish coherence and consistency, and to promote curriculum continuity and progression in pupils' learning in PSHE. These complement the statutory requirements for citizenship, which will be introduced in 2002.

---

[6] Additional information on opportunities to promote learning across the National Curriculum is included in the subject booklets.

[7] Guidelines for the non-statutory framework are included on pages 190–196 of this handbook.

Promoting skills across the National Curriculum

At all key stages, pupils learn, practise, combine, develop and refine a wide range of skills in their work across the National Curriculum. Some of these skills are subject specific (painting in art and design), some are common to several subjects (enquiry skills in science, history and geography).

Some skills are universal, for example the skills of communication, improving own learning and performance, and creative thinking. These skills are also embedded in the subjects of the National Curriculum and are essential to effective learning.

Opportunities for teaching and learning all these skills across the key stages can be identified when planning. Pupils can be encouraged to reflect on what and on how they learn, and how these skills can be applied to different subjects, different problems and real-life situations.

Key skills

Six skill areas are described as key skills because they help learners to improve their learning and performance in education, work and life. These key skills are embedded in the National Curriculum.

Communication

The key skill of communication includes skills in speaking, listening, reading and writing. Skills in speaking and listening include the ability to speak effectively for different audiences; to listen, understand and respond appropriately to others; and to participate effectively in group discussion. Skills in reading and writing include the ability to read fluently a range of literary and non-fiction texts and to reflect critically on what is read; and the ability to write fluently for a range of purposes and audiences, including critical analysis of their own and others' writing. Opportunities for developing this key skill are provided through English in particular and through pupils' use of language across the curriculum.

Application of number

The key skill of application of number includes developing a range of mental calculation skills and the ability to apply them within a variety of contexts. Skills include developing the understanding and use of mathematical language related to numbers and calculations in order to process data, solve increasingly complex problems and explain the reasoning used. Pupils need to be able to apply calculation skills and the understanding of number to problems in other National Curriculum subjects and to real-life situations. Opportunities for developing this key skill are provided explicitly in mathematics.

Information technology

The key skill of information technology includes the ability to use a range of information sources and ICT tools to find, analyse, interpret, evaluate and present information for a range of purposes. Skills include the ability to make critical and informed judgements about when and how to use ICT for maximum benefit in accessing information, in solving problems or for expressive work. The ability to use ICT information sources includes enquiry and decision-making skills, as well as information-processing and creative thinking skills and the ability to review, modify and evaluate work with ICT. Opportunities for developing this key skill are provided explicitly through the subject of ICT and through pupils' use of ICT across the curriculum.

Working with others

The key skill of working with others includes the ability to contribute to small-group and whole-class discussion, and to work with others to meet a challenge. If pupils are to work with others they must develop social skills and a growing awareness and understanding of others' needs. All subjects provide opportunities for pupils to cooperate and work effectively with others in formal and informal settings, to appreciate the experience of others and consider different perspectives, and to benefit from what others think, say and do.

Improving own learning and performance

The key skill of improving own learning and performance involves pupils reflecting on and critically evaluating their work and what they have learnt, and identifying ways to improve their learning and performance. They need to be able to identify the purposes of learning, to reflect on the processes of learning, to assess progress in learning, to identify obstacles or problems in learning and to plan ways to improve learning. All subjects provide opportunities for pupils to review their work and discuss ways to improve their learning.

Problem solving

The key skill of problem solving involves pupils developing the skills and strategies that will help them to solve the problems they face in learning and in life. Problem solving includes the skills of identifying and understanding a problem, planning ways to solve a problem, monitoring progress in tackling a problem and reviewing solutions to problems. All subjects provide pupils with opportunities to respond to the challenge of problems and to plan, test, modify and review the progress needed to achieve particular outcomes.

Thinking skills

By using thinking skills pupils can focus on 'knowing how' as well as 'knowing what' – learning how to learn. The following thinking skills complement the key skills and are embedded in the National Curriculum.

Information-processing skills

These enable pupils to locate and collect relevant information, to sort, classify, sequence, compare and contrast, and to analyse part/whole relationships.

Reasoning skills

These enable pupils to give reasons for opinions and actions, to draw inferences and make deductions, to use precise language to explain what they think, and to make judgements and decisions informed by reasons or evidence.

Enquiry skills

These enable pupils to ask relevant questions, to pose and define problems, to plan what to do and how to research, to predict outcomes and anticipate consequences, and to test conclusions and improve ideas.

Creative thinking skills

These enable pupils to generate and extend ideas, to suggest hypotheses, to apply imagination, and to look for alternative innovative outcomes.

Evaluation skills

These enable pupils to evaluate information, to judge the value of what they read, hear and do, to develop criteria for judging the value of their own and others' work or ideas, and to have confidence in their judgements.

Promoting other aspects of the school curriculum

Financial capability

Financial capability is about making competent decisions in relation to managing money and planning finances for the future. It helps pupils to make independent and informed decisions about budgeting, spending, saving and investing, using credit, avoiding debt, and obtaining value for money. It helps pupils to understand their own and others' needs and to consider the effects of their decisions on individuals, groups, families, and communities and at a national level. Pupils should be able to understand the financial implications of their choices and to leave school prepared to be confident and knowledgeable consumers, aware of their responsibilities and rights.

There are opportunities for pupils to develop financial capability within the school curriculum, in particular in their work in mathematics, PSHE and citizenship, as well as through involvement in other school activities such as work with business and the community.

Enterprise and entrepreneurial skills

Changing patterns of work mean that many young people will consider self-employment at some point in their working lives. Pupils should therefore develop skills and attitudes that will prepare them for this as a career option. Many aspects of the curriculum at all key stages provide opportunities for developing enterprise and entrepreneurial skills.

Enterprise can be associated with a set of attributes, skills and attitudes that enable people to create and thrive on change. Enterprise education enables pupils to develop confidence, self-reliance and willingness to embrace change. Through participation in mini-enterprises pupils can practise risk management, learning from mistakes and being innovative.

Entrepreneurialism is the creation of wealth through the development of new and small businesses. Opportunities can be provided for pupils to learn about and explore the role of individuals in sustaining and developing the economy and society and to develop the entrepreneurial characteristics of tenacity, independence, innovation, imagination, risk-taking, creativity, intuition and leadership.

Work-related learning

The school curriculum provides opportunities for all pupils to prepare for working life by developing basic understanding of the diversity of workplace opportunities and requirements. A coordinated framework for work-related learning will enable schools to identify the intended learning outcomes and to recognise how different elements of the curriculum relate to these outcomes.

Work-related learning results from planned activities that use work as a context for learning or to illustrate aspects of working life. 'Learning through work', such as enterprise activities and work experience, can raise standards by using contexts that improve motivation and attainment. 'Learning about work' through, for example, visits to places of work, career-related activities and vocational courses, can improve young people's understanding of themselves and opportunities at work. 'Learning for work' through, for example, the development of key skills and career-management skills, can improve the transition of young people to adult and working life. QCA has published guidance for schools on the development of work-related learning: *Preparation for working life: Guidance on developing a coordinated approach to work-related learning at key stage 4* (QCA/99/384), and *Learning through work-related contexts: A guide to successful practice* (QCA/98/310).

Education for sustainable development

Education for sustainable development enables pupils to develop the knowledge, skills, understanding and values to participate in decisions about the way we do things individually and collectively, both locally and globally, that will improve the quality of life now without damaging the planet for the future. There are opportunities for pupils to develop their understanding of sustainable development within the school curriculum, in particular in their work in geography, science, PSHE and citizenship.

The National Curriculum programmes of study

A common structure and design for all subjects

The programmes of study

The National Curriculum programmes of study have been given a common structure and a common design.

In each subject, at each key stage, the main column **1** contains the programme of study, which sets out two sorts of requirements:

- **Knowledge, skills and understanding 2** – what has to be taught in the subject during the key stage
- **Breadth of study 3** – the contexts, activities, areas of study and range of experiences through which the **Knowledge, skills and understanding** should be taught.

Schools are not required by law to teach the content in grey type. This includes the examples in the main column **4** [printed inside square brackets], all text in the margins **5** and information and examples in the inclusion statement. In the programmes of study *italic type* is used to emphasise options, where schools and teachers can choose between requirements.

The programmes of study for English, mathematics and science

The programmes of study for English and science contain sections that correspond directly to the attainment targets for each subject. In mathematics this one-to-one correspondence does not hold for all key stages – see the mathematics programme of study for more information. In English, the three sections of the programme of study each contain **Breadth of study** requirements. In mathematics and science there is a single, separate set of **Breadth of study** requirements for each key stage.

The programmes of study in the non-core foundation subjects

In these subjects (except for citizenship) the programme of study simply contains two sets of requirements – **Knowledge, skills and understanding** and **Breadth of study**. The programmes of study for citizenship contain no **Breadth of study** requirements.

Information in the margins

At the start of each key stage, the margin begins with a summary **6** of the main things that pupils will learn during the key stage. The margins also contain four other types of non-statutory information:

- notes giving key information that should be taken into account when teaching the subject
- notes giving definitions of words and phrases in the programmes of study
- suggested opportunities for pupils to use information and communication technology (ICT) as they learn the subject
- some key links with other subjects indicating connections between teaching requirements, and suggesting how a requirement in one subject can build on the requirements in another in the same key stage.

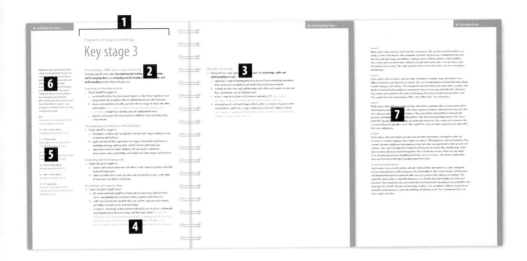

The referencing system

References work as follows:

A reference in ...	... reads ...	... and means ...
Physical education key stage 2	11a, 11b → links to other subjects These requirements build on Gg/2c.	Physical education key stage 2, requirements 11a and 11b build on geography (key stage 2), paragraph 2, requirement c.
Art and design key stage 1	4a → links to other subjects This requirement builds on Ma3/2a, 2c, 2d.	Art and design key stage 1, requirement 4a builds on mathematics (key stage 1), Ma3 Shape, space and measures, paragraph 2, requirements a, c and d.
Citizenship key stage 3	1a → links to other subjects This requirement builds on Hi/10, 13.	Citizenship key stage 3, requirement 1a builds on history (key stage 3) paragraphs 10 and 13.

The attainment targets

The attainment targets **7** are at the end of this handbook. They can be read alongside the programmes of study by folding out the booklet.

General teaching requirements

Inclusion: providing effective learning opportunities for all pupils

Schools have a responsibility to provide a broad and balanced curriculum for all pupils. The National Curriculum is the starting point for planning a school curriculum that meets the specific needs of individuals and groups of pupils. This statutory inclusion statement on providing effective learning opportunities for all pupils outlines how teachers can modify, as necessary, the National Curriculum programmes of study to provide all pupils with relevant and appropriately challenging work at each key stage[1]. It sets out three principles that are essential to developing a more inclusive curriculum:

A Setting suitable learning challenges

B Responding to pupils' diverse learning needs

C Overcoming potential barriers to learning and assessment for individuals and groups of pupils.

Applying these principles should keep to a minimum the need for aspects of the National Curriculum to be disapplied for a pupil.

Schools are able to provide other curricular opportunities outside the National Curriculum to meet the needs of individuals or groups of pupils such as speech and language therapy and mobility training.

Three principles for inclusion

In planning and teaching the National Curriculum, teachers are required to have due regard to the following principles.

A Setting suitable learning challenges

1 Teachers should aim to give every pupil the opportunity to experience success in learning and to achieve as high a standard as possible. The National Curriculum programmes of study set out what most pupils should be taught at each key stage – but teachers should teach the knowledge, skills and understanding in ways that suit their pupils' abilities. This may mean choosing knowledge, skills and understanding from earlier or later key stages so that individual pupils can make progress and show what they can achieve. Where it is appropriate for pupils to make extensive use of content from an earlier key stage, there may not be time to teach all aspects of the age-related programmes of study. A similarly flexible approach will be needed to take account of any gaps in pupils' learning resulting from missed or interrupted schooling [for example, that may be experienced by travellers, refugees, those in care or those

[1] Additional information about inclusion is included in the subject booklets.

with long-term medical conditions, including pupils with neurological problems, such as head injuries, and those with degenerative conditions].

2   For pupils whose attainments fall significantly below the expected levels at a particular key stage, a much greater degree of differentiation will be necessary. In these circumstances, teachers may need to use the content of the programmes of study as a resource or to provide a context, in planning learning appropriate to the age and requirements of their pupils.[2]

3   For pupils whose attainments significantly exceed the expected level of attainment within one or more subjects during a particular key stage, teachers will need to plan suitably challenging work. As well as drawing on materials from later key stages or higher levels of study, teachers may plan further differentiation by extending the breadth and depth of study within individual subjects or by planning work which draws on the content of different subjects.[3]

B Responding to pupils' diverse learning needs

1   When planning, teachers should set high expectations and provide opportunities for all pupils to achieve, including boys and girls, pupils with special educational needs, pupils with disabilities, pupils from all social and cultural backgrounds, pupils of different ethnic groups including travellers, refugees and asylum seekers, and those from diverse linguistic backgrounds. Teachers need to be aware that pupils bring to school different experiences, interests and strengths which will influence the way in which they learn. Teachers should plan their approaches to teaching and learning so that all pupils can take part in lessons fully and effectively.

2   To ensure that they meet the full range of pupils' needs, teachers should be aware of the requirements of the equal opportunities legislation that covers race, gender and disability.[4]

3   Teachers should take specific action to respond to pupils' diverse needs by:
    a   creating effective learning environments
    b   securing their motivation and concentration
    c   providing equality of opportunity through teaching approaches
    d   using appropriate assessment approaches
    e   setting targets for learning.

Examples for B/3a – creating effective learning environments
Teachers create effective learning environments in which:
- the contribution of all pupils is valued
- all pupils can feel secure and are able to contribute appropriately
- stereotypical views are challenged and pupils learn to appreciate and view positively differences in others, whether arising from race, gender, ability or disability

[2] Teachers may find QCA's guidance on planning work for pupils with learning difficulties a helpful companion to the programmes of study.
[3] Teachers may find QCA's guidance on meeting the requirements of gifted and talented pupils a helpful companion to the programmes of study.
[4] The Sex Discrimination Act 1975, the Race Relations Act 1976, the Disability Discrimination Act 1995.

- pupils learn to take responsibility for their actions and behaviours in school and in the wider community
- all forms of bullying and harassment, including racial harassment, are
- pupils are enabled to participate safely in clothing appropriate to the beliefs, particularly in subjects such as science, design and technology physical education.

Examples for B/3b – securing motivation and concentration

Teachers secure pupils' motivation and concentration by:

- using teaching approaches appropriate to different learning styles
- using, where appropriate, a range of organisational approaches, such as setting, grouping or individual work, to ensure that learning needs are properly addressed
- varying subject content and presentation so that this matches their learning needs
- planning work which builds on their interests and cultural experiences
- planning appropriately challenging work for those whose ability and understanding are in advance of their language skills
- using materials which reflect social and cultural diversity and provide positive images of race, gender and disability
- planning and monitoring the pace of work so that they all have a chance to learn effectively and achieve success
- taking action to maintain interest and continuity of learning for pupils who may be absent for extended periods of time.

Examples for B/3c – providing equality of opportunity

Teaching approaches that provide equality of opportunity include:

- ensuring that boys and girls are able to participate in the same curriculum, particularly in science, design and technology and physical education
- taking account of the interests and concerns of boys and girls by using a range of activities and contexts for work and allowing a variety of interpretations and outcomes, particularly in English, science, design and technology, ICT, art and design, music and physical education
- avoiding gender stereotyping when organising pupils into groups, assigning them to activities or arranging access to equipment, particularly in science, design and technology, ICT, music and physical education
- taking account of pupils' specific religious or cultural beliefs relating to the representation of ideas or experiences or to the use of particular types of equipment, particularly in science, design and technology, ICT and art and design
- enabling the fullest possible participation of pupils with disabilities or particular medical needs in all subjects, offering positive role models and making provision, where necessary, to facilitate access to activities with appropriate support, aids or adaptations. (See **Overcoming potential barriers to learning and assessment for individuals and groups of pupils.**)

Examples for B/3d – using appropriate assessment approaches

Teachers use appropriate assessment approaches that:

- allow for different learning styles and ensure that pupils are given the chance and encouragement to demonstrate their competence and attainment through appropriate means
- are familiar to the pupils and for which they have been adequately prepared
- use materials which are free from discrimination and stereotyping in any form
- provide clear and unambiguous feedback to pupils to aid further learning.

Examples for B/3e – setting targets for learning

Teachers set targets for learning that:

- build on pupils' knowledge, experiences, interests and strengths to improve areas of weakness and demonstrate progression over time
- are attainable and yet challenging and help pupils to develop their self-esteem and confidence in their ability to learn.

C Overcoming potential barriers to learning and assessment for individuals and groups of pupils

A minority of pupils will have particular learning and assessment requirements which go beyond the provisions described in sections A and B and, if not addressed, could create barriers to learning. These requirements are likely to arise as a consequence of a pupil having a special educational need or disability or may be linked to a pupil's progress in learning English as an additional language.

1   Teachers must take account of these requirements and make provision, where necessary, to support individuals or groups of pupils to enable them to participate effectively in the curriculum and assessment activities. During end of key stage assessments, teachers should bear in mind that special arrangements are available to support individual pupils.

Pupils with special educational needs

2   Curriculum planning and assessment for pupils with special educational needs must take account of the type and extent of the difficulty experienced by the pupil. Teachers will encounter a wide range of pupils with special educational needs, some of whom will also have disabilities (see paragraphs C/4 and C/5). In many cases, the action necessary to respond to an individual's requirements for curriculum access will be met through greater differentiation of tasks and materials, consistent with school-based intervention as set out in the SEN Code of Practice. A smaller number of pupils may need access to specialist equipment and approaches or to alternative or adapted activities, consistent with school-based intervention augmented by advice and support from external specialists as described in the SEN Code of Practice, or, in exceptional circumstances, with a statement of special educational need.

Teachers should, where appropriate, work closely with representatives of other agencies who may be supporting the pupil.

3   Teachers should take specific action to provide access to learning for pupils with special educational needs by:

   a   providing for pupils who need help with communication, language and literacy

   b   planning, where necessary, to develop pupils' understanding through the use of all available senses and experiences

   c   planning for pupils' full participation in learning and in physical and practical activities

   d   helping pupils to manage their behaviour, to take part in learning effectively and safely, and, at key stage 4, to prepare for work

   e   helping individuals to manage their emotions, particularly trauma or stress, and to take part in learning.

Examples for C/3a – helping with communication, language and literacy
Teachers provide for pupils who need help with communication, language and literacy through:

- using texts that pupils can read and understand
- using visual and written materials in different formats, including large print, symbol text and Braille
- using ICT, other technological aids and taped materials
- using alternative and augmentative communication, including signs and symbols
- using translators, communicators and amanuenses.

Examples for C/3b – developing understanding
Teachers develop pupils' understanding through the use of all available senses and experiences, by:

- using materials and resources that pupils can access through sight, touch, sound, taste or smell
- using word descriptions and other stimuli to make up for a lack of first-hand experiences
- using ICT, visual and other materials to increase pupils' knowledge of the wider world
- encouraging pupils to take part in everyday activities such as play, drama, class visits and exploring the environment.

Examples for C/3c – planning for full participation
Teachers plan for pupils' full participation in learning and in physical and practical activities through:

- using specialist aids and equipment
- providing support from adults or peers when needed
- adapting tasks or environments
- providing alternative activities, where necessary.

Examples for C/3d – managing behaviour

Teachers help pupils to manage their behaviour, take part in learning effectively and safely, and, at key stage 4, prepare for work by:

- setting realistic demands and stating them explicitly
- using positive behaviour management, including a clear structure of rewards and sanctions
- giving pupils every chance and encouragement to develop the skills they need to work well with a partner or a group
- teaching pupils to value and respect the contribution of others
- encouraging and teaching independent working skills
- teaching essential safety rules.

Examples for C/3e – managing emotions

Teachers help individuals manage their emotions and take part in learning through:

- identifying aspects of learning in which the pupil will engage and plan short-term, easily achievable goals in selected activities
- providing positive feedback to reinforce and encourage learning and build self-esteem
- selecting tasks and materials sensitively to avoid unnecessary stress for the pupil
- creating a supportive learning environment in which the pupil feels safe and is able to engage with learning
- allowing time for the pupil to engage with learning and gradually increasing the range of activities and demands.

Pupils with disabilities

4   Not all pupils with disabilities will necessarily have special educational needs. Many pupils with disabilities learn alongside their peers with little need for additional resources beyond the aids which they use as part of their daily life, such as a wheelchair, a hearing aid or equipment to aid vision. Teachers must take action, however, in their planning to ensure that these pupils are enabled to participate as fully and effectively as possible within the National Curriculum and the statutory assessment arrangements. Potential areas of difficulty should be identified and addressed at the outset of work, without recourse to the formal provisions for disapplication.

5   Teachers should take specific action to enable the effective participation of pupils with disabilities by:

   a   planning appropriate amounts of time to allow for the satisfactory completion of tasks
   b   planning opportunities, where necessary, for the development of skills in practical aspects of the curriculum
   c   identifying aspects of programmes of study and attainment targets that may present specific difficulties for individuals.

Examples for C/5a – planning to complete tasks

Teachers plan appropriate amounts of time to allow pupils to complete tasks satisfactorily through:

- taking account of the very slow pace at which some pupils will be able to record work, either manually or with specialist equipment, and of the physical effort required
- being aware of the high levels of concentration necessary for some pupils when following or interpreting text or graphics, particularly when using vision aids or tactile methods, and of the tiredness which may result
- allocating sufficient time, opportunity and access to equipment for pupils to gain information through experimental work and detailed observation, including the use of microscopes
- being aware of the effort required by some pupils to follow oral work, whether through use of residual hearing, lip reading or a signer, and of the tiredness or loss of concentration which may occur.

Examples for C/5b – developing skills in practical aspects

Teachers create opportunities for the development of skills in practical aspects of the curriculum through:

- providing adapted, modified or alternative activities or approaches to learning in physical education and ensuring that these have integrity and equivalence to the National Curriculum and enable pupils to make appropriate progress
- providing alternative or adapted activities in science, art and design and design and technology for pupils who are unable to manipulate tools, equipment or materials or who may be allergic to certain types of materials
- ensuring that all pupils can be included and participate safely in geography fieldwork, local studies and visits to museums, historic buildings and sites.

Examples for C/5c – overcoming specific difficulties

Teachers overcome specific difficulties for individuals presented by aspects of the programmes of study and attainment targets through:

- using approaches to enable hearing impaired pupils to learn about sound in science and music
- helping visually impaired pupils to learn about light in science, to access maps and visual resources in geography and to evaluate different products in design and technology and images in art and design
- providing opportunities for pupils to develop strength in depth where they cannot meet the particular requirements of a subject, such as the visual requirements in art and design and the singing requirements in music
- discounting these aspects in appropriate individual cases when required to make a judgement against level descriptions.

Pupils who are learning English as an additional language

6   Pupils for whom English is an additional language have diverse needs in terms of support necessary in English language learning. Planning should take account of such factors as the pupil's age, length of time in this country, previous educational experience and skills in other languages. Careful monitoring of each pupil's progress in the acquisition of English language skills and of subject knowledge and understanding will be necessary to confirm that no learning difficulties are present.

7   The ability of pupils for whom English is an additional language to take part in the National Curriculum may be ahead of their communication skills in English. Teachers should plan learning opportunities to help pupils develop their English and should aim to provide the support pupils need to take part in all subject areas.

8   Teachers should take specific action to help pupils who are learning English as an additional language by:

   a   developing their spoken and written English

   b   ensuring access to the curriculum and to assessment.

Examples for C/8a – developing spoken and written English

Teachers develop pupils' spoken and written English through:

- ensuring that vocabulary work covers both the technical and everyday meaning of key words, metaphors and idioms
- explaining clearly how speaking and writing in English are structured to achieve different purposes, across a range of subjects
- providing a variety of reading material [for example, pupils' own work, the media, ICT, literature, reference books] that highlight the different ways English is used, especially those that help pupils to understand society and culture
- ensuring that there are effective opportunities for talk and that talk is used to support writing in all subjects
- where appropriate, encouraging pupils to transfer their knowledge, skills and understanding of one language to another, pointing out similarities and differences between languages
- building on pupils' experiences of language at home and in the wider community, so that their developing uses of English and other languages support one another.

Examples for C/8b – ensuring access

Teachers make sure pupils have access to the curriculum and to assessment through:

- using accessible texts and materials that suit pupils' ages and levels of learning
- providing support by using ICT or video or audio materials, dictionaries and translators, readers and amanuenses
- using home or first language, where appropriate.

Use of language across the curriculum

1   Pupils should be taught in all subjects to express themselves correctly and appropriately and to read accurately and with understanding. Since standard English, spoken and written, is the predominant language in which knowledge and skills are taught and learned, pupils should be taught to recognise and use standard English.

Writing

2   In writing, pupils should be taught to use correct spelling and punctuation and follow grammatical conventions. They should also be taught to organise their writing in logical and coherent forms.

Speaking

3   In speaking, pupils should be taught to use language precisely and cogently.

Listening

4   Pupils should be taught to listen to others, and to respond and build on their ideas and views constructively.

Reading

5   In reading, pupils should be taught strategies to help them read with understanding, to locate and use information, to follow a process or argument and summarise, and to synthesise and adapt what they learn from their reading.

6   Pupils should be taught the technical and specialist vocabulary of subjects and how to use and spell these words. They should also be taught to use the patterns of language vital to understanding and expression in different subjects. These include the construction of sentences, paragraphs and texts that are often used in a subject [for example, language to express causality, chronology, logic, exploration, hypothesis, comparison, and how to ask questions and develop arguments].

Use of information and communication technology across the curriculum

1   Pupils should be given opportunities[1] to apply and develop their ICT capability through the use of ICT tools to support their learning in all subjects (with the exception of physical education at key stages 1 and 2).

2   Pupils should be given opportunities to support their work by being taught to:

   a   find things out from a variety of sources, selecting and synthesising the information to meet their needs and developing an ability to question its accuracy, bias and plausibility

   b   develop their ideas using ICT tools to amend and refine their work and enhance its quality and accuracy

   c   exchange and share information, both directly and through electronic media

   d   review, modify and evaluate their work, reflecting critically on its quality, as it progresses.

[1] At key stage 1, there are no statutory requirements to teach the use of ICT in the programmes of study for the non-core foundation subjects. Teachers should use their judgement to decide where it is appropriate to teach the use of ICT across these subjects at key stage 1. At other key stages, there are statutory requirements to use ICT in all subjects, except physical education.

Health and safety

1   This statement applies to science, design and technology, information and communication technology, art and design, and physical education.

2   When working with tools, equipment and materials, in practical activities and in different environments, including those that are unfamiliar, pupils should be taught:

   a   about hazards, risks and risk control

   b   to recognise hazards, assess consequent risks and take steps to control the risks to themselves and others

   c   to use information to assess the immediate and cumulative risks

   d   to manage their environment to ensure the health and safety of themselves and others

   e   to explain the steps they take to control risks.

Teaching requirements for each subject

Six Views Of A Waterfall

When the river threw itself off the cliff
It spun a twist of rope
So as not to lose touch with itself

'Poem' is deliberately meant to confuse and disorientate people who may be looking for traditional, archaic, 'proper' poetry. By giving it a title that does not relate to anything, Armitage sets out to challenge expectation of British poetry. The poem is written in a traditional, rhyming structure, but this only increases its ambiguity. Starting the poem with 'and' suggests that this is not really the beginning, and that the reader is 'listening in' on a longer monologue.

Humanlife on One

The human crouches in the shadows, patiently awaiting his victim. His sharp, darting eyes watch every movement, his ears listening and alert. A fellow predator, an enemy from another pack, catches his eye. He is also watching for the same prey. They both try to reach the best spot, while simultaneously attempting to look inconspicuous. His weapon, deadly to his prey, hidden in his pouch, is ready to be whipped out at any second. A tiny movement within the hunted's safe-haven causes the hunter to become stone-still, ready to pounce when the time is right. The entry of the victim's habitat opens. A small face peeks out, clad in sunglasses and baseball cap, the face barely visible. The pitiful disguise is unsuccessful: the hunter is not discouraged. He remains perfectly still, waiting for the right moment. The prey glances around suspiciously, but assured she is not being watched, the face becomes a full body, creeping out into the open. Only now does the predator spring into action, leaping from the shadows, whipping out his camera and, before the victim can scream, "NO PHOTOS," the deed is done, the exclusive photo taken. The A-list celebrity is indeed becoming an endangered species.

The value of English in the curriculum? What can I say? Without English, nothing. And without good English, nothing very well.

Anne Fine, Author

English is the language of the future, the language of the computer. English is the most important tool you'll ever need, no matter what career you choose. You have the right to English. Make it your right!

Benjamin Zephaniah, Poet, Writer, Actor, TV & Radio Presenter

A good book, studied with a good English teacher, takes you on a journey in search of answers to the crucial questions in life you didn't even know you wanted (or needed) to ask.

Professor Lisa Jardine, Queen Mary & Westfield College, University of London

Studying English literature at school was my first, and probably my biggest, step towards mental freedom and independence. It was like falling in love with life.

Ian McEwan, Novelist

English

The importance of English

English is a vital way of communicating in school, in public life and internationally. Literature in English is rich and influential, reflecting the experience of people from many countries and times.

In studying English pupils develop skills in speaking, listening, reading and writing. It enables them to express themselves creatively and imaginatively and to communicate with others effectively. Pupils learn to become enthusiastic and critical readers of stories, poetry and drama as well as non-fiction and media texts. The study of English helps pupils understand how language works by looking at its patterns, structures and origins. Using this knowledge pupils can choose and adapt what they say and write in different situations.

Programme of study: English

Key stages 3 & 4

In English, during key stage 3 pupils develop confidence in speaking and writing for public and formal purposes. They also develop their ability to evaluate the way language is used. They read classic and contemporary texts and explore social and moral issues.

In English, during key stage 4 pupils learn to use language confidently, both in their academic studies and for the world beyond school. They use and analyse complex features of language. They are keen readers who can read many kinds of text and make articulate and perceptive comments about them.

Speaking and listening: during key stages 3 and 4 pupils learn to speak and listen confidently in a wide variety of contexts. They learn to be flexible, adapting what they say and how they say it to different situations and people. When they speak formally or to people they do not know, they are articulate and fluent in their use of spoken standard English. They learn how to evaluate the contributions they, and others, have made to discussions and drama activities. They take leading and other roles in group work.

Teaching should ensure that work in **speaking and listening**, **reading** and **writing** is integrated.

En1 Speaking and listening

Knowledge, skills and understanding

Speaking

1   To speak fluently and appropriately in different contexts, adapting their talk for a range of purposes and audiences, including the more formal, pupils should be taught to:

  a   structure their talk clearly, using markers so that their listeners can follow the line of thought

  b   use illustrations, evidence and anecdote to enrich and explain their ideas

  c   use gesture, tone, pace and rhetorical devices for emphasis

  d   use visual aids and images to enhance communication

  e   vary word choices, including technical vocabulary, and sentence structure for different audiences

  f   use spoken standard English fluently in different contexts

  g   evaluate the effectiveness of their speech and consider how to adapt it to a range of situations.

Listening

2   To listen, understand and respond critically to others, pupils should be taught to:

  a   concentrate on and recall the main features of a talk, reading, radio or television programme

  b   identify the major elements of what is being said both explicitly and implicitly

  c   distinguish features of presentation where a speaker aims to explain, persuade, amuse or argue a case

  d   distinguish tone, undertone, implications and other signs of a speaker's intentions

  e   recognise when a speaker is being ambiguous or deliberately vague, glosses over points, uses and abuses evidence and makes unsubstantiated statements

  f   ask questions and give relevant and helpful comments.

Group discussion and interaction

3   To participate effectively as members of different groups, pupils should be taught to:

  a   make different types of contributions to groups, adapting their speech to their listeners and the activity

  b   take different views into account and modify their own views in the light of what others say c   sift, summarise and use the most important points

d   take different roles in the organisation, planning and sustaining of groups

e   help the group to complete its tasks by varying contributions appropriately, clarifying and synthesising others' ideas, taking them forward and building on them to reach conclusions, negotiating consensus or agreeing to differ.

Drama

4   To participate in a range of drama activities and to evaluate their own and others' contributions, pupils should be taught to:

a   use a variety of dramatic techniques to explore ideas, issues, texts and meanings

b   use different ways to convey action, character, atmosphere and tension when they are scripting and performing in plays [for example, through dialogue, movement, pace]

c   appreciate how the structure and organisation of scenes and plays contribute to dramatic effect

d   evaluate critically performances of dramas that they have watched or in which they have taken part.

Standard English

5   Pupils should be taught to use the vocabulary, structures and grammar of spoken standard English fluently and accurately in informal and formal situations.

Language variation

6   Pupils should be taught about how language varies, including:

a   the importance of standard English as the language of public communication nationally and often internationally

b   current influences on spoken and written language

c   attitudes to language use

d   the differences between speech and writing

e   the vocabulary and grammar of standard English and dialectal variation

f   the development of English, including changes over time, borrowings from other languages, origins of words, and the impact of electronic communication on written language.

Note on standard English
The paragraphs on **standard English**, **language variation**, **language structure** and **language structure and variation** in **speaking and listening**, **reading** and **writing** provide a coherent basis for language study.

Note for 5
When teaching **standard English** it is helpful to bear in mind the most common non-standard usages in England:
- subject–verb agreement (they was)
- formation of past tense (have fell, I done)
- formation of negatives (ain't)
- formation of adverbs (come quick)
- use of demonstrative pronouns (them books)
- use of pronouns (me and him went)
- use of prepositions (out the door).

Note for 10
Interaction may be face-to-face or by electronic means.

Breadth of study

7 During the key stage, pupils should be taught the **Knowledge, skills and understanding** through the following range of activities, contexts and purposes.

Speaking

8 The range of purposes should include:

a describing, narrating, explaining, arguing, persuading, entertaining

and pupils should be given opportunities to make:

b extended contributions to talk in different contexts and groups

c presentations to different audiences.

Listening

9 The range should include listening to and watching:

a live talks and presentations

b recordings [for example, radio, television, film]

c discussions in which pupils respond straight away.

Group discussion and interaction

10 The range of purposes should include:

a exploring, hypothesising, debating, analysing

and pupils should be given opportunities to:

b take different roles in groups [for example, roles in organising or leading discussion, supporting others, enabling focused talk].

Drama activities

11 The range should include:

a improvisation and working in role

b devising, scripting and performing in plays

c discussing and reviewing their own and others' performances.

En2 Reading

Knowledge, skills and understanding

Reading: during key stages 3 and 4 pupils read a wide range of texts independently, both for pleasure and for study. They become enthusiastic, discriminating and responsive readers, understanding layers of meaning and appreciating what they read on a critical level.

Understanding texts

1   To develop understanding and appreciation of texts, pupils should be taught:

   Reading for meaning

   a   to extract meaning beyond the literal, explaining how the choice of language and style affects implied and explicit meanings

   b   to analyse and discuss alternative interpretations, ambiguity and allusion

   c   how ideas, values and emotions are explored and portrayed

   d   to identify the perspectives offered on individuals, community and society

   e   to consider how meanings are changed when texts are adapted to different media

   f   to read and appreciate the scope and richness of complete novels, plays and poems

   Understanding the author's craft

   g   how language is used in imaginative, original and diverse ways

   h   to reflect on the writer's presentation of ideas and issues, the motivation and behaviour of characters, the development of plot and the overall impact of a text

   i   to distinguish between the attitudes and assumptions of characters and those of the author

   j   how techniques, structure, forms and styles vary

   k   to compare texts, looking at style, theme and language, and identifying connections and contrasts.

English literary heritage

2   Pupils should be taught:

   a   how and why texts have been influential and significant [for example, the influence of Greek myths, the Authorised Version of the Bible, the Arthurian legends]

   b   the characteristics of texts that are considered to be of high quality

   c   the appeal and importance of these texts over time.

Texts from different cultures and traditions

3   Pupils should be taught:

   a   to understand the values and assumptions in the texts

   b   the significance of the subject matter and the language

   c   the distinctive qualities of literature from different traditions

   d   how familiar themes are explored in different cultural contexts [for example, how childhood is portrayed, references to oral or folk traditions]

   e   to make connections and comparisons between texts from different cultures.

Printed and ICT-based information texts

4   To develop their reading of print and ICT-based information texts, pupils should be taught to:

a   select, compare and synthesise information from different texts

b   evaluate how information is presented

c   sift the relevant from the irrelevant, and distinguish between fact and opinion, bias and objectivity

d   identify the characteristic features, at word, sentence and text level, of different types of texts.

Media and moving image texts

5   Pupils should be taught:

a   how meaning is conveyed in texts that include print, images and sometimes sounds

b   how choice of form, layout and presentation contribute to effect [for example, font, caption, illustration in printed text, sequencing, framing, soundtrack in moving image text]

c   how the nature and purpose of media products influence content and meaning [for example, selection of stories for a front page or news broadcast]

d   how audiences and readers choose and respond to media.

Language structure and variation

6   Pupils should be taught to draw on their knowledge of grammar and language variation to develop their understanding of texts and how language works.

Breadth of study

7   During the key stage, pupils should be taught the **Knowledge, skills and understanding** through the following ranges of literature and non-fiction and non-literary texts.

Literature

8   The range should include:

a   plays, novels, short stories and poetry from the English literary heritage, including:

  i   two plays by Shakespeare, one of which should be studied in key stage 3

  ii   drama by major playwrights

  iii   works of fiction by two major writers published before 1914 selected from the list on page 51

  iv   two works of fiction by major writers published after 1914

  v   poetry by four major poets published before 1914 selected from the list on page 51

  vi   poetry by four major poets published after 1914

b   recent and contemporary drama, fiction and poetry written for young people and adults

c   drama, fiction and poetry by major writers from different cultures and traditions.

Non-fiction and non-literary texts

9   The range should include:

a   literary non-fiction

b   print and ICT-based information and reference texts

c   media and moving image texts [for example, newspapers, magazines, advertisements, television, films, videos].

Examples of major playwrights
William Congreve, Oliver Goldsmith, Christopher Marlowe, Sean O'Casey, Harold Pinter, J B Priestley, Peter Shaffer, G B Shaw, R B Sheridan, Oscar Wilde.

List of major writers published before 1914 (see requirement 8a iii on page 50)
Jane Austen, Charlotte Brontë, Emily Brontë, John Bunyan, Wilkie Collins, Joseph Conrad, Daniel Defoe, Charles Dickens, Arthur Conan Doyle, George Eliot, Henry Fielding, Elizabeth Gaskell, Thomas Hardy, Henry James, Mary Shelley, Robert Louis Stevenson, Jonathan Swift, Anthony Trollope, H G Wells.

Examples of fiction by major writers after 1914
E M Forster, William Golding, Graham Greene, Aldous Huxley, James Joyce, D H Lawrence, Katherine Mansfield, George Orwell, Muriel Spark, William Trevor, Evelyn Waugh.

List of major poets published before 1914 (see requirement 8a v on page 50)
Matthew Arnold, Elizabeth Barrett Browning, William Blake, Emily Brontë, Robert Browning, Robert Burns, Lord Byron, Geoffrey Chaucer, John Clare, Samuel Taylor Coleridge, John Donne, John Dryden, Thomas Gray, George Herbert, Robert Herrick, Gerard Manley Hopkins, John Keats, Andrew Marvell, John Milton, Alexander Pope, Christina Rossetti, William Shakespeare (sonnets), Percy Bysshe Shelley, Edmund Spenser, Alfred Lord Tennyson, Henry Vaughan, William Wordsworth, Sir Thomas Wyatt.

Examples of major poets after 1914
W H Auden, Gillian Clarke, Keith Douglas, T S Eliot, U A Fanthorpe, Thomas Hardy, Seamus Heaney, Ted Hughes, Elizabeth Jennings, Philip Larkin, Wilfred Owen, Sylvia Plath, Stevie Smith, Edward Thomas, R S Thomas, W B Yeats.

Examples of recent and contemporary drama, fiction and poetry
Drama: Alan Ayckbourn, Samuel Beckett, Alan Bennett, Robert Bolt, Brian Friel, Willis Hall, David Hare, Willie Russell, R C Sherriff, Arnold Wesker.

Fiction: J G Ballard, Berlie Doherty, Susan Hill, Laurie Lee, Joan Lingard, Bill Naughton, Alan Sillitoe, Mildred Taylor, Robert Westall.

Poetry: Simon Armitage, James Berry, Douglas Dunn, Liz Lochhead, Adrian Mitchell, Edwin Muir, Grace Nichols, Jo Shapcott.

Examples of drama, fiction and poetry by major writers from different cultures and traditions
Drama: Athol Fugard, Arthur Miller, Wole Soyinka, Tennessee Williams.

Fiction: Chinua Achebe, Maya Angelou, Willa Cather, Anita Desai, Nadine Gordimer, Ernest Hemingway, H H Richardson, Doris Lessing, R K Narayan, John Steinbeck, Ngugi wa Thiong'o.

Poetry: E K Brathwaite, Emily Dickinson, Robert Frost, Robert Lowell, Les Murray, Rabindranath Tagore, Derek Walcott.

Examples of non-fiction and non-literary texts
Personal record and viewpoints on society: Peter Ackroyd, James Baldwin, John Berger, James Boswell, Vera Brittain, Lord Byron, William Cobbett, Gerald Durrell, Robert Graves, Samuel Johnson, Laurie Lee, Samuel Pepys, Flora Thompson, Beatrice Webb, Dorothy Wordsworth.

Travel writing: Jan Morris, Freya Stark, Laurens Van Der Post.

Reportage: James Cameron, Winston Churchill, Alistair Cooke, Dilys Powell.

The natural world: David Attenborough, Rachel Carson, Charles Darwin, Steve Jones.

En3 Writing

Writing: during key stages 3 and 4 pupils develop confidence in writing for a range of purposes. They develop their own distinctive styles and recognise the importance of writing with commitment and vitality. They learn to write correctly, using different formats, layouts and ways of presenting their work.

Note for 1d
The variety of narrative structures includes the use of words, sound and images.

1h → ICT opportunity
Pupils could make choices of font style and size and whether to use bold, italics or bullets in presenting their work.

Note for 2a
Planning and revising can be done simultaneously when working on screen.

En3 Writing

Knowledge, skills and understanding

Composition

1   Pupils should be taught to draw on their reading and knowledge of linguistic and literary forms when composing their writing. Pupils should be taught to:

Writing to imagine, explore, entertain

a   draw on their experience of good fiction, of different poetic forms and of reading, watching and performing in plays

b   use imaginative vocabulary and varied linguistic and literary techniques

c   exploit choice of language and structure to achieve particular effects and appeal to the reader

d   use a range of techniques and different ways of organising and structuring material to convey ideas, themes and characters

Writing to inform, explain, describe

e   form sentences and paragraphs that express connections between information and ideas precisely [for example, cause and effect, comparison]

f   use formal and impersonal language and concise expression

g   consider what the reader needs to know and include relevant details

h   present material clearly, using appropriate layout, illustrations and organisation

Writing to persuade, argue, advise

i   develop logical arguments and cite evidence

j   use persuasive techniques and rhetorical devices

k   anticipate reader reaction, counter opposing views and use language to gain attention and sustain interest

Writing to analyse, review, comment

l   reflect on the nature and significance of the subject matter

m   form their own view, taking into account a range of evidence and opinions

n   organise their ideas and information, distinguishing between analysis and comment

o   take account of how well the reader knows the topic.

Planning and drafting

2   To improve and sustain their writing, pupils should be taught to:

a   plan, draft, redraft and proofread their work on paper and on screen

b   judge the extent to which any or all of these processes are needed in specific pieces of writing

c   analyse critically their own and others' writing.

Punctuation

3 Pupils should be taught to use the full range of punctuation marks correctly to signal sentence structure, and to help the reader.

Spelling

4 Pupils should be taught to:

a increase their knowledge of regular patterns of spelling, word families, roots of words and derivations, including stem, prefix, suffix, inflection

b apply their knowledge of word formation

c spell increasingly complex polysyllabic words that do not conform to regular patterns

d check their spelling for errors and use a dictionary when necessary

e use different kinds of dictionary, thesaurus and spellchecker.

Handwriting and presentation

5 Pupils should be taught to write with fluency and, when required, speed. In presenting final polished work, pupils should be taught to:

a ensure that work is neat and clear

b write legibly, if their work is handwritten

c make full use of different presentational devices where appropriate.

Standard English

6 Pupils should be taught about the variations in written standard English and how they differ from spoken language, and to distinguish varying degrees of formality, selecting appropriately for a task.

Language structure

7 Pupils should be taught the principles of sentence grammar and whole-text cohesion and use this knowledge in their writing. They should be taught:

a word classes or parts of speech and their grammatical functions

b the structure of phrases and clauses and how they can be combined to make complex sentences [for example, coordination and subordination]

c paragraph structure and how to form different types of paragraph

d the structure of whole texts, including cohesion, openings and conclusions in different types of writing [for example, through the use of verb tenses, reference chains]

e the use of appropriate grammatical terminology to reflect on the meaning and clarity of individual sentences [for example, nouns, verbs, adjectives, prepositions, conjunctions, articles].

Note for 4e

Using spellcheckers involves understanding both their uses and their limitations.

5c → ICT opportunity

Pupils could use a variety of ways to present their work, including using pictures and moving images as well as print.

Note for 9

Written texts are shaped by choices of purpose, form and reader. These elements are interdependent so that, for example, forms are adapted to the writer's aim and the intended reader.

Breadth of study

8   During the key stage, pupils should be taught the **Knowledge, skills and understanding** through addressing the following range of purposes, readers and forms of writing.

9   The range of purposes for writing should include:

     a   to imagine, explore and entertain, focusing on creative, aesthetic and literary uses of language. The forms for such writing should be drawn from different kinds of stories, poems, playscripts, autobiographies, screenplays, diaries

     b   to inform, explain and describe, focusing on conveying information and ideas clearly. The forms for such writing should be drawn from memos, minutes, accounts, information leaflets, prospectuses, plans, records, summaries

     c   to persuade, argue and advise, focusing on presenting a case and influencing the reader. The forms for such writing should be drawn from brochures, advertisements, editorials, articles and letters conveying opinions, campaign literature, polemical essays

     d   to analyse, review and comment, focusing on considered and evaluative views of ideas, texts and issues. The forms for such writing should be drawn from reviews, commentaries, articles, essays, reports.

10   Pupils should also be taught to use writing for thinking and learning [for example, for hypothesising, paraphrasing, summarising, noting].

11   The range of readers for writing should include specific, known readers, a large, unknown readership and the pupils themselves.

The huge number project

How long would a traffic jam be with 1,000,000 cars in it?

First of all we measured Mr Jones's Ford Orion, it came out at 4.15 metres.

$$
\begin{array}{r}
4.15 \\
\times\ 1,000,000 \\
\hline
4,150,000 \\
\hline
\end{array}
$$

We worked out that 1,000,000 Ford Orions would be 4,150,000 m.

We needed to change that into km. So we divided it by 1,000.

$$
\begin{array}{r}
4,150,000 \\
\div\quad 1,000 \\
\hline
4,150\ \text{km} \\
\hline
\end{array}
$$

Then we hit a problem. We realised that there would be a gap in between the cars of about 1 m.

So that would add on 1,000,000 m

$$
\begin{array}{r}
5,150,000 \\
\div\quad 1000 \\
\hline
5,150\ \text{km} \\
\hline
\end{array}
$$

Then we used an atlas to see what countries the first car would have reached by the time the last one left London.

The importance of mathematics
Mathematics equips pupils with a uniquely powerful set of tools to understand and change the world. These tools include logical reasoning, problem-solving skills, and the ability to think in abstract ways. Mathematics is important in everyday life, many forms of employment, science and technology, medicine, the economy, the environment and development, and in public decision-making.

Different cultures have contributed to the development and application of mathematics. Today, the subject transcends cultural boundaries and its importance is universally recognised. Mathematics is a creative discipline. It can stimulate moments of pleasure and wonder when a pupil solves a problem for the first time, discovers a more elegant solution to that problem, or suddenly sees hidden connections.

Mathematics

Maths is the study of patterns abstracted from the world around us – so anything we learn in maths has literally thousands of applications, in arts, sciences, finance, health and leisure!
Professor Ruth Lawrence, University of Michigan

Mathematics is not just a collection of skills, it is a way of thinking. It lies at the core of scientific understanding, and of rational and logical argument.
Dr Colin Sparrow, Lecturer in Mathematics, University of Cambridge

Maths is the truly global language. With it, we convey ideas to each other that words can't handle – and bypass our spoken Tower of Babel.
Professor Alison Wolf, Head of Mathematical Sciences Group, Institute of Education, University of London

If you want to take part in tomorrow's world, you'll need mathematics and statistics just as much as grammar and syntax.
Professor Robert Worcester, Chairman, Market Opinion Research International

Since the age of ten, I've been hooked on mathematical problems as intellectual challenges. However, nobody has to worry that pure mathematics won't be used. Mathematics – even some of the most abstruse mathematics that we thought would never be used – is now used every time you use your credit card, every time you use your computer.
Professor Andrew Wiles, Princeton University

The cars would have reached:
1) Greenland   5) Chad   9) Russia
2) Mauritania   6) Libya   10) Finland
3) Mali   7) Egypt   11) Norway
4) Niger   8) Turkey

Programme of study: mathematics

Key stage 3

Knowledge, skills and understanding

Teaching should ensure that appropriate connections are made between the sections on **number and algebra, shape, space and measures**, and **handling data**.

Ma2 Number and algebra

Using and applying number and algebra

1   Pupils should be taught to:

   Problem solving

   a   explore connections in mathematics to develop flexible approaches to increasingly demanding problems; select appropriate strategies to use for numerical or algebraic problems

   b   break down a complex calculation into simpler steps before attempting to solve it

   c   use alternative approaches to overcome difficulties and evaluate the effectiveness of their strategies

   d   select efficient techniques for numerical calculation and algebraic manipulation

   e   make mental estimates of the answers to calculations; use checking procedures to monitor the accuracy of their results

   Communicating

   f   represent problems and solutions in algebraic or graphical forms; move from one form of representation to another to get different perspectives on the problem; present and interpret solutions in the context of the original problem

   g   develop correct and consistent use of notation, symbols and diagrams when solving problems

   h   examine critically, improve, then justify their choice of mathematical presentation; present a concise, reasoned argument

   Reasoning

   i   explore, identify, and use pattern and symmetry in algebraic contexts, investigating whether particular cases can be generalised further and understanding the importance of a counter-example; identify exceptional cases when solving problems; make conjectures and check them for new cases

   j   show step-by-step deduction in solving a problem; explain and justify how they arrived at a conclusion

   k   distinguish between a practical demonstration and a proof

   l   recognise the importance of assumptions when deducing results; recognise the limitations of any assumptions that are made and the effect that varying the assumptions may have on the solution to a problem.

During key stage 3 pupils take increasing responsibility for planning and executing their work. They extend their calculating skills to fractions, percentages and decimals, and begin to understand the importance of proportional reasoning. They are beginning to use algebraic techniques and symbols with confidence. They generate and solve simple equations and study linear functions and their corresponding graphs. They begin to use deduction to manipulate algebraic expressions. Pupils progress from a simple understanding of the features of shape and space to using definitions and reasoning to understand geometrical objects. As they encounter simple algebraic and geometric proofs, they begin to understand reasoned arguments. They communicate mathematics in speech and a variety of written forms, explaining their reasoning to others. They study handling data through practical activities and are introduced to a quantitative approach to probability. Pupils work with increasing confidence and flexibility to solve unfamiliar problems. They develop positive attitudes towards mathematics and increasingly make connections between different aspects of mathematics.

Note

This programme of study covers the attainment range for this key stage. Teachers are expected to plan work drawing on all the numbered sub-sections of the programme of study. For some groups of pupils, all or part of particular lettered paragraphs may not be appropriate.

Note about sections

There is no separate section of the programme of study numbered Ma1 that corresponds to the first attainment target, **using and applying mathematics**. Teaching requirements relating to this attainment target are included within the other sections of the programme of study.

Numbers and the number system

2   Pupils should be taught to:

Integers

a   use their previous understanding of integers and place value to deal with
arbitrarily large positive numbers and round them to a given power of 10;
understand and use negative numbers, both as positions and translations
on a number line; order integers; use the concepts and vocabulary of factor
(divisor), multiple, common factor, highest common factor, least common
multiple, prime number and prime factor decomposition

Powers and roots

b   use the terms square, positive and negative square root (knowing that the
square root sign denotes the positive square root), cube, cube root; use index
notation for small integer powers and index laws for multiplication and
division of positive integer powers

Fractions

c   use fraction notation; understand equivalent fractions, simplifying a fraction
by cancelling all common factors; order fractions by rewriting them with
a common denominator

Decimals

d   use decimal notation and recognise that each terminating decimal is
a fraction [for example, $0.137 = \frac{137}{1000}$]; order decimals

Percentages

e   understand that 'percentage' means 'number of parts per 100' and use this
to compare proportions; interpret percentage as the operator 'so many
hundredths of' [for example, 10% means 10 parts per 100 and 15% of Y
means $\frac{15}{100} \times Y$]

Ratio and proportion

f   use ratio notation, including reduction to its simplest form and its various
links to fraction notation

g   recognise where fractions or percentages are needed to compare proportions;
identify problems that call for proportional reasoning, and choose the
correct numbers to take as 100%, or as a whole.

1f → links to other subjects
This requirement builds on En1/1d
and En3/1n.

1h → links to other subjects
This requirement builds on En1/1e,
3b and En3/1f, 1i.

Note for 3b

Pupils do not need to know the names of these laws.

Calculations

3   Pupils should be taught to:

Number operations and the relationships between them

a   add, subtract, multiply and divide integers and then any number; multiply or divide any number by powers of 10, and any positive number by a number between 0 and 1; find the prime factor decomposition of positive integers [for example, $8000 = 2^6 \times 5^3$]

b   use brackets and the hierarchy of operations; know how to use the commutative, associative and distributive laws to do mental and written calculations more efficiently

c   calculate a given fraction of a given quantity, expressing the answer as a fraction; express a given number as a fraction of another; add and subtract fractions by writing them with a common denominator; perform short division to convert a simple fraction to a decimal

d   understand and use unit fractions as multiplicative inverses [for example, by thinking of multiplication by $\frac{1}{5}$ as division by 5, or multiplication by $\frac{6}{7}$ as multiplication by 6 followed by division by 7 (or vice versa)]; multiply and divide a given fraction by an integer, by a unit fraction and by a general fraction

e   convert simple fractions of a whole to percentages of the whole and vice versa, then understand the multiplicative nature of percentages as operators [for example, 20% discount on £150 gives a total calculated as £(0.8×150)]

f   divide a quantity in a given ratio [for example, share £15 in the ratio 1:2]

Mental methods

g   recall all positive integer complements to 100 [for example, $37 + 63 = 100$]; recall all multiplication facts to 10×10, and use them to derive quickly the corresponding division facts; recall the cubes of 2, 3, 4, 5 and 10, and the fraction-to-decimal conversion of familiar simple fractions [for example, $\frac{1}{2}, \frac{1}{4}, \frac{1}{5}, \frac{1}{10}, \frac{1}{100}, \frac{1}{3}, \frac{2}{3}, \frac{1}{8}$]

h   round to the nearest integer and to one significant figure; estimate answers to problems involving decimals

i   develop a range of strategies for mental calculation; derive unknown facts from those they know [for example, estimate $\sqrt{85}$]; add and subtract mentally numbers with up to two decimal places [for example, $13.76 - 5.21$, $20.08 + 12.4$]; multiply and divide numbers with no more than one decimal digit [for example, 14.3×4, $56.7 \div 7$], using factorisation when possible

Written methods

j   use standard column procedures for addition and subtraction of integers
    and decimals

k   use standard column procedures for multiplication of integers and decimals,
    understanding where to position the decimal point by considering what
    happens if they multiply equivalent fractions [for example, $0.6 \times 0.7 = 0.42$
    since $\frac{6}{10} \times \frac{7}{10} = \frac{42}{100} = 0.42$]; solve a problem involving division by a decimal
    by transforming it to a problem involving division by an integer

l   use efficient methods to calculate with fractions, including cancelling
    common factors before carrying out the calculation, recognising that, in
    many cases, only a fraction can express the exact answer

m   solve simple percentage problems, including increase and decrease
    [for example, simple interest, VAT, discounts, pay rises, annual rate of
    inflation, income tax, discounts]

n   solve word problems about ratio and proportion, including using informal
    strategies and the unitary method of solution [for example, given that m
    identical items cost £y, then one item costs £$\frac{y}{m}$ and n items cost £$(n \times \frac{y}{m})$,
    the number of items that can be bought for £z is $z \times \frac{m}{y}$]

Calculator methods

o   use calculators effectively and efficiently: know how to enter complex
    calculations using brackets [for example, for negative numbers, or the
    division of more than one term], know how to enter a range of calculations,
    including those involving measures [for example, time calculations in which
    fractions of an hour need to be entered as fractions or decimals]

p   use the function keys for reciprocals, squares, square roots, powers, fractions
    (and how to enter a fraction as a decimal); use the constant key

q   understand the calculator display, interpreting it correctly [for example,
    in money calculations, and when the display has been rounded by the
    calculator], and knowing not to round during the intermediate steps
    of a calculation.

Solving numerical problems

4   Pupils should be taught to:

a   draw on their knowledge of the operations and the relationships between
    them, and of simple integer powers and their corresponding roots, to solve
    problems involving ratio and proportion, a range of measures and
    compound measures, metric units, and conversion between metric
    and common imperial units, set in a variety of contexts

b   select appropriate operations, methods and strategies to solve number problems, including trial and improvement where a more efficient method to find the solution is not obvious

c   use a variety of checking procedures, including working the problem backwards, and considering whether a result is of the right order of magnitude

d   give solutions in the context of the problem to an appropriate degree of accuracy, recognising limitations on the accuracy of data and measurements.

Equations, formulae and identities

5   Pupils should be taught to:

Use of symbols

a   distinguish the different roles played by letter symbols in algebra, knowing that letter symbols represent definite unknown numbers in equations [for example, $x^3 + 1 = 65$], defined quantities or variables in formulae [for example, $V = IR$], general, unspecified and independent numbers in identities [for example, $3x + 2x = 5x$, or $3(a + b) = 3a + 3b$, or $(x + 1)(x - 1) = x^2 - 1$] and in functions they define new expressions or quantities by referring to known quantities [for example, $y = 2 - 7x$]

b   understand that the transformation of algebraic expressions obeys and generalises the rules of arithmetic; simplify or transform algebraic expressions by collecting like terms [for example, $x^2 + 3x + 5 - 4x + 2x^2 = 3x^2 - x + 5$], by multiplying a single term over a bracket, by taking out single term common factors [for example, $x^2 + x = x(x + 1)$], and by expanding the product of two linear expressions including squaring a linear expression [for example, $(x + 1)^2 = x^2 + 2x + 1$, $(x - 3)(x + 2) = x^2 - x - 6$]; distinguish in meaning between the words 'equation', 'formula', 'identity' and 'expression'

Index notation

c   use index notation for simple integer powers, and simple instances of index laws; substitute positive and negative numbers into expressions such as $3x^2 + 4$ and $2x^3$

Equations

d   set up simple equations [for example, find the angle a in a triangle with angles a, $a + 10$, $a + 20$]; solve simple equations [for example, $5x = 7$, $3(2x + 1) = 8$, $2(1 - x) = 6(2 + x)$, $4x^2 = 36$, $3 = \frac{12}{x}$], by using inverse operations or by transforming both sides in the same way

Linear equations

e   solve linear equations, with integer coefficients, in which the unknown
    appears on either side or on both sides of the equation; solve linear
    equations that require prior simplification of brackets, including those
    that have negative signs occurring anywhere in the equation, and those
    with a negative solution

5f → ICT opportunity
Pupils could use a spreadsheet to construct
formulae to model situations.

Formulae

f   use formulae from mathematics and other subjects [for example, formulae
    for the area of a triangle, the area enclosed by a circle,
    density = mass/volume]; substitute numbers into a formula; derive a formula
    and change its subject [for example, convert temperatures between degrees
    Fahrenheit and degrees Celsius, find the perimeter of a rectangle given its
    area A and the length l of one side]

Direct proportion

g   set up and use equations to solve word and other problems involving direct
    proportion, and relate their algebraic solutions to graphical representations
    of the equations

Simultaneous linear equations

h   link a graphical representation of an equation to its algebraic solution; find
    an approximate solution of a pair of linear simultaneous equations by
    graphical methods, then find the exact solution by eliminating one variable;
    consider the graphs of cases that have no solution, or an infinite number
    of solutions

Inequalities

i   solve simple linear inequalities in one variable, and represent the solution
    set on a number line

Numerical methods

j   use systematic trial and improvement methods with ICT tools to find
    approximate solutions of equations where there is no simple analytical
    method [for example, $x^3 + x = 100$].

Sequences, functions and graphs

6   Pupils should be taught to:

Sequences

a   generate common integer sequences (including sequences of odd or even
    integers, squared integers, powers of 2, powers of 10, triangular numbers)

b   find the first terms of a sequence given a rule arising naturally from a
    context [for example, the number of ways of paying in pence using only 1p
    and 2p coins, or from a regularly increasing spatial pattern]; find the rule
    (and express it in words) for the nth term of a sequence

6g → ICT opportunity
Pupils could use a spreadsheet to generate points and plot graphs.

c   generate terms of a sequence using term-to-term and position-to-term definitions of the sequence; use linear expressions to describe the nth term of an arithmetic sequence, justifying its form by referring to the activity or context from which it was generated

Functions

d   express simple functions, at first in words and then in symbols; explore the properties of simple polynomial functions

e   use the conventions for coordinates in the plane; plot points in all four quadrants; recognise (when values are given for m and c) that equations of the form $y = mx + c$ correspond to straight-line graphs in the coordinate plane; plot graphs of functions in which y is given explicitly in terms of x [for example, $y = 2x + 3$], or implicitly [for example, $x + y = 7$]

f   construct linear functions arising from real-life problems and plot their corresponding graphs; discuss and interpret graphs arising from real situations [for example, distance–time graph for an object moving with constant speed]

g   generate points and plot graphs of simple quadratic and cubic functions [for example, $y = x^2$, $y = 3x^2 + 4$, $y = x^3$]

Gradients

h   find the gradient of lines given by equations of the form $y = mx + c$ (when values are given for m and c); investigate the gradients of parallel lines and lines perpendicular to these lines [for example, knowing that $y = 5x$ and $y = 5x - 4$ represent parallel lines, each with gradient 5 and that the graph of any line perpendicular to these lines has gradient $-\frac{1}{5}$].

Ma3 Shape, space and measures

Using and applying shape, space and measures

1   Pupils should be taught to:

Problem solving

a   select problem-solving strategies and resources, including ICT, to use in geometrical work, and monitor their effectiveness

b   select and combine known facts and problem-solving strategies to solve complex problems

c   identify what further information is needed to solve a problem; break complex problems down into a series of tasks

Communication

d   interpret, discuss and synthesise geometrical information presented in a variety of forms

e   communicate mathematically, making use of geometrical diagrams and related explanatory text

f   use precise language and exact methods to analyse geometrical configurations

g   review and justify their choices of mathematical presentation

Reasoning

h   distinguish between practical demonstration, proof, conventions, facts, definitions and derived properties

i   explain and justify inferences and deductions using mathematical reasoning

j   explore connections in geometry; pose conditional constraints of the type 'If … then …'; and ask questions 'What if …?' or 'Why?'

k   show step-by-step deduction in solving a geometrical problem

l   state constraints and give starting points when making deductions

m   recognise the limitations of any assumptions that are made; understand the effects that varying the assumptions may have on the solution

n   identify exceptional cases when solving geometrical problems.

Geometrical reasoning

2   Pupils should be taught to:

Angles

a   recall and use properties of angles at a point, angles on a straight line (including right angles), perpendicular lines, and opposite angles at a vertex

b   distinguish between acute, obtuse, reflex and right angles; estimate the size of an angle in degrees

Properties of triangles and other rectilinear shapes

c   use parallel lines, alternate angles and corresponding angles; understand the properties of parallelograms and a proof that the angle sum of a triangle is 180 degrees; understand a proof that the exterior angle of a triangle is equal to the sum of the interior angles at the other two vertices

1d → links to other subjects
This requirement builds on En1/3b and En2/1a.

1e → links to other subjects
This requirement builds on En1/1d and En3/1f.

1f → links to other subjects
This requirement builds on En3/1f.

1g → links to other subjects
This requirement builds on En1/1e, 3b and En3/1i, 1n.

d   use angle properties of equilateral, isosceles and right-angled triangles; understand congruence, recognising when two triangles are congruent; explain why the angle sum of any quadrilateral is 360 degrees

e   use their knowledge of rectangles, parallelograms and triangles to deduce formulae for the area of a parallelogram, and a triangle, from the formula for the area of a rectangle

f   recall the essential properties of special types of quadrilateral, including square, rectangle, parallelogram, trapezium and rhombus; classify quadrilaterals by their geometric properties

g   calculate and use the sums of the interior and exterior angles of quadrilaterals, pentagons and hexagons; calculate and use the angles of regular polygons

h   understand, recall and use Pythagoras' theorem

Properties of circles

i   recall the definition of a circle and the meaning of related terms, including centre, radius, chord, diameter, circumference, tangent, arc, sector and segment; understand that the tangent at any point on a circle is perpendicular to the radius at that point; explain why the perpendicular from the centre to a chord bisects the chord; understand that inscribed regular polygons can be constructed by equal division of a circle

3-D shapes

j   explore the geometry of cuboids (including cubes), and shapes made from cuboids

k   use 2-D representations of 3-D shapes and analyse 3-D shapes through 2-D projections and cross-sections, including plan and elevation.

Transformations and coordinates

3   Pupils should be taught to:

Specifying transformations

a   understand that rotations are specified by a centre and an (anticlockwise) angle; use right angles, fractions of a turn or degrees to measure the angle of rotation; understand that reflections are specified by a mirror line, translations by a distance and direction, and enlargements by a centre and positive scale factor

Properties of transformations

b   recognise and visualise rotations, reflections and translations, including reflection symmetry of 2-D and 3-D shapes, and rotation symmetry of 2-D shapes; transform 2-D shapes by translation, rotation and reflection, recognising that these transformations preserve length and angle, so that any figure is congruent to its image under any of these transformations

c   recognise, visualise and construct enlargements of objects using positive integer scale factors greater than one, then positive scale factors less than one; understand from this that any two circles and any two squares are mathematically similar, while, in general, two rectangles are not

d   recognise that enlargements preserve angle but not length; identify the scale factor of an enlargement as the ratio of the lengths of any two corresponding line segments and apply this to triangles; understand the implications of enlargement for perimeter; use and interpret maps and scale drawings; understand the implications of enlargement for area and for volume

Coordinates

e   understand that one coordinate identifies a point on a number line, two coordinates identify a point in a plane and three coordinates identify a point in space, using the terms '1-D', '2-D' and '3-D'; use axes and coordinates to specify points in all four quadrants; locate points with given coordinates; find the coordinates of points identified by geometrical information [for example, find the coordinates of the fourth vertex of a parallelogram with vertices at (2, 1) (–7, 3) and (5, 6)]; find the coordinates of the midpoint of the line segment AB, given points A and B, then calculate the length AB.

Measures and construction

4   Pupils should be taught to:

Measures

a   interpret scales on a range of measuring instruments, including those for time and mass; know that measurements using real numbers depend on the choice of unit; recognise that measurements given to the nearest whole unit may be inaccurate by up to one half in either direction; convert measurements from one unit to another; know rough metric equivalents of pounds, feet, miles, pints and gallons; make sensible estimates of a range of measures in everyday settings

b   understand angle measure, using the associated language [for example, use bearings to specify direction]

c   understand and use compound measures, including speed and density

Construction

d   measure and draw lines to the nearest millimetre, and angles to the nearest degree; draw triangles and other 2-D shapes using a ruler and protractor, given information about their side lengths and angles; understand, from their experience of constructing them, that triangles satisfying SSS, SAS, ASA and RHS are unique, but SSA triangles are not; construct cubes, regular tetrahedra, square-based pyramids and other 3-D shapes from given information

Note for 3d
Enlargement of triangles is fundamental to work in trigonometry in the higher programme of study for key stage 4 Ma3/2g.

e use straight edge and compasses to do standard constructions, including an equilateral triangle with a given side, the midpoint and perpendicular bisector of a line segment, the perpendicular from a point to a line, the perpendicular from a point on a line, and the bisector of an angle

Mensuration

f find areas of rectangles, recalling the formula, understanding the connection to counting squares and how it extends this approach; recall and use the formulae for the area of a parallelogram and a triangle; find the surface area of simple shapes using the area formulae for triangles and rectangles; calculate perimeters and areas of shapes made from triangles and rectangles

g find volumes of cuboids, recalling the formula and understanding the connection to counting cubes and how it extends this approach; calculate volumes of right prisms and of shapes made from cubes and cuboids

h find circumferences of circles and areas enclosed by circles, recalling relevant formulae

i convert between area measures, including cm^2 and m^2, and volume measures, including cm^3 and m^3

Loci

j find loci, both by reasoning and by using ICT to produce shapes and paths [for example, equilateral triangles].

Ma4 Handling data

Using and applying handling data

1 Pupils should be taught to:

Problem solving

a carry out each of the four aspects of the handling data cycle to solve problems:

   i specify the problem and plan: formulate questions in terms of the data needed, and consider what inferences can be drawn from the data; decide what data to collect (including sample size and data format) and what statistical analysis is needed

   ii collect data from a variety of suitable sources, including experiments and surveys, and primary and secondary sources

   iii process and represent the data: turn the raw data into usable information that gives insight into the problem

   iv interpret and discuss the data: answer the initial question by drawing conclusions from the data

b identify what further information is required to pursue a particular line of enquiry

c select and organise the appropriate mathematics and resources to use for a task

d review progress as they work; check and evaluate solutions

Communicating

e interpret, discuss and synthesise information presented in a variety of forms

f communicate mathematically, making use of diagrams and related explanatory text

g examine critically, and justify, their choice of mathematical presentation of problems involving data

Reasoning

h apply mathematical reasoning, explaining and justifying inferences and deductions

i explore connections in mathematics and look for cause and effect when analysing data

j recognise the limitations of any assumptions, and the effects that varying the assumptions could have on conclusions drawn from the data analysis.

Specifying the problem and planning

2 Pupils should be taught to:

a see that random processes are unpredictable

b identify questions that can be addressed by statistical methods

c discuss how data relate to a problem; identify possible sources of bias and plan to minimise it

1e → links to other subjects
This requirement builds on En1/3b and En2/1a

1f → ICT opportunity
Pupils could use presentation software to communicate their findings and display the data.

1f → links to other subjects
This requirement builds on En1/1d and En3/1f.

1g → links to other subjects
This requirement builds on En1/1e, 3b and En3/1i, 1n.

5c → ICT opportunity
Pupils could use databases to
present their findings.

d   identify which primary data they need to collect and in what format
(including grouped data, considering appropriate equal class intervals)

e   design an experiment or survey; decide what secondary data to use.

Collecting data

3   Pupils should be taught to:

a   design and use data-collection sheets for grouped discrete and continuous
data; collect data using various methods including observation, controlled
experiment, data logging, questionnaires and surveys

b   gather data from secondary sources, including printed tables and lists
from ICT-based sources

c   design and use two-way tables for discrete and grouped data.

Processing and representing data

4   Pupils should be taught to:

a   draw and produce, using paper and ICT, pie charts for categorical data and
diagrams for continuous data, including line graphs for time series, scatter
graphs, frequency diagrams and stem-and-leaf diagrams

b   calculate mean, range and median of small data sets with discrete then
continuous data; identify the modal class for grouped data

c   understand and use the probability scale

d   understand and use estimates or measures of probability from theoretical
models, including equally likely outcomes, or from relative frequency

e   list all outcomes for single events, and for two successive events, in a
systematic way

f   identify different mutually exclusive outcomes and know that the sum
of the probabilities of all these outcomes is 1

g   find the median for large data sets and calculate an estimate of the mean
for large data sets with grouped data

h   draw lines of best fit by eye, understanding what these represent.

Interpreting and discussing results

5   Pupils should be taught to:

a   relate summarised data to the initial questions

b   interpret a wide range of graphs and diagrams and draw conclusions

c   look at data to find patterns and exceptions

d   compare distributions and make inferences, using the shapes of distributions
and measures of average and range

e   evaluate and check results, answer questions, and modify their approach
if necessary

f   have a basic understanding of correlation

g   use lines of best fit

h   use the vocabulary of probability in interpreting results involving
uncertainty and prediction

i   compare experimental data and theoretical probabilities

j   understand that if they repeat an experiment, they may – and usually will –
get different outcomes, and that increasing sample size generally leads to
better estimates of probability and population characteristics.

Breadth of study

1   During the key stage, pupils should be taught the **Knowledge, skills and
understanding** through:

a   activities that ensure they become familiar with and confident using
standard procedures for a range of problems, including ratio and proportion

b   activities that enable them to understand that algebra is an extension
of number

c   solving familiar and unfamiliar problems, including multi-step problems,
in a range of numerical, algebraic and graphical contexts and in open-ended
and closed form

d   activities that develop short chains of deductive reasoning and concepts of
proof in algebra and geometry

e   activities focused on geometrical definitions in which they do practical work
with geometrical objects to develop their ability to visualise these objects
and work with them mentally

f   practical work in which they draw inferences from data and consider how
statistics are used in real life to make informed decisions

g   a sequence of activities that address increasingly demanding statistical problems

h   tasks focused on using appropriate ICT [for example, spreadsheets,
databases, geometry or graphic packages], using calculators correctly and
efficiently, and knowing when it is not appropriate to use a particular form
of technology.

Programme of study: mathematics foundation

Key stage 4

During key stage 4 (foundation) pupils consolidate their understanding of basic mathematics, which will help them to tackle unfamiliar problems in the workplace and everyday life and develop the knowledge and skills they need in the future. They become more fluent in making connections between different areas of mathematics and its application in the world around them. They become increasingly proficient in calculating fractions, percentages and decimals, and use proportional reasoning in simple contexts. Building on their understanding of numbers, they make generalisations using letters, manipulate simple algebraic expressions and apply basic algebraic techniques to solve problems. They extend their use of mathematical vocabulary to talk about numbers and geometrical objects. They begin to understand and follow a short proof, and use geometrical properties to find missing angles and lengths, explaining their reasoning with increasing confidence. They collect data, learn statistical techniques to analyse data and use ICT to present and interpret the results.

Note

This programme of study is intended for those pupils who have not attained a secure level 5 at the end of key stage 3. Teachers are expected to plan work drawing on all the numbered sub-sections of the programme of study.

For some groups of pupils, all or part of particular lettered paragraphs may not be appropriate.

Note about sections

There is no separate section of the programme of study numbered Ma1 that corresponds to the first attainment target, **using and applying mathematics**. Teaching requirements relating to this attainment target are included within the other sections of the programme of study.

Knowledge, skills and understanding

Teaching should ensure that appropriate connections are made between the sections on **number and algebra**, **shape, space and measures**, and **handling data**.

Ma2 Number and algebra

Using and applying number and algebra

1   Pupils should be taught to:

Problem solving

a   select and use suitable problem-solving strategies and efficient techniques to solve numerical and algebraic problems

b   break down a complex calculation into simpler steps before attempting to solve it

c   use algebra to formulate and solve a simple problem – identifying the variable, setting up an equation, solving the equation and interpreting the solution in the context of the problem

d   make mental estimates of the answers to calculations; use checking procedures, including use of inverse operations; work to stated levels of accuracy

Communicating

e   interpret and discuss numerical and algebraic information presented in a variety of forms

f   use notation and symbols correctly and consistently within a given problem

g   use a range of strategies to create numerical, algebraic or graphical representations of a problem and its solution; move from one form of representation to another to get different perspectives on the problem

h   present and interpret solutions in the context of the original problem

i   review and justify their choice of mathematical presentation

Reasoning

j   explore, identify, and use pattern and symmetry in algebraic contexts [for example, using simple codes that substitute numbers for letters], investigating whether particular cases can be generalised further, and understanding the importance of a counter-example; identify exceptional cases when solving problems

k   show step-by-step deduction in solving a problem

l   distinguish between a practical demonstration and a proof

m   recognise the importance of assumptions when deducing results; recognise the limitations of any assumptions that are made and the effect that varying the assumptions may have on the solution to a problem.

Numbers and the number system

2 Pupils should be taught to:

Integers

a use their previous understanding of integers and place value to deal with arbitrarily large positive numbers and round them to a given power of 10; understand and use positive numbers, both as positions and translations on a number line; order integers; use the concepts and vocabulary of factor (divisor), multiple and common factor

Powers and roots

b use the terms square, positive square root, cube; use index notation for squares, cubes and powers of 10; express standard index form both in conventional notation and on a calculator display

Fractions

c understand equivalent fractions, simplifying a fraction by cancelling all common factors; order fractions by rewriting them with a common denominator

Decimals

d use decimal notation and recognise that each terminating decimal is a fraction [for example, $0.137 = \frac{137}{1000}$]; order decimals

Percentages

e understand that 'percentage' means 'number of parts per 100' and use this to compare proportions; interpret percentage as the operator 'so many hundredths of' [for example, 10% means 10 parts per 100 and 15% of Y means $\frac{15}{100} \times$ Y]; use percentage in real-life situations [for example, commerce and business, including rate of inflation, VAT and interest rates]

Ratio

f use ratio notation, including reduction to its simplest form and its various links to fraction notation [for example, in maps and scale drawings, paper sizes and gears].

Calculations

3 Pupils should be taught to:

Number operations and the relationships between them

a add, subtract, multiply and divide integers and then any number; multiply or divide any number by powers of 10, and any positive number by a number between 0 and 1

b use brackets and the hierarchy of operations

1e → links to other subjects
This requirement builds on En1/3b and En2/1a.

1h, 1i → links to other subjects
These requirements build on En1/1d, 1e and En3/1f, 1i, 1n.

Note for 3i
Pupils do not need to know the names of the laws.

c   calculate a given fraction of a given quantity [for example, for scale drawings and construction of models, down payments, discounts], expressing the answer as a fraction; express a given number as a fraction of another; add and subtract fractions by writing them with a common denominator; perform short division to convert a simple fraction to a decimal

d   understand and use unit fractions as multiplicative inverses [for example, by thinking of multiplication by $\frac{1}{5}$ as division by 5, or multiplication by $\frac{6}{7}$ as multiplication by 6 followed by division by 7 (or vice versa)]; multiply and divide a fraction by an integer, and multiply a fraction by a unit fraction

e   convert simple fractions of a whole to percentages of the whole and vice versa [for example, analysing diets, budgets or the costs of running, maintaining and owning a car], then understand the multiplicative nature of percentages as operators [for example, 30% increase on £150 gives a total calculated as £(1.3×150) while a 20% discount gives a total calculated as £(0.8×150)]

f   divide a quantity in a given ratio [for example, share £15 in the ratio of 1:2]

Mental methods

g   recall all positive integer complements to 100 [for example, $37 + 63 = 100$]; recall all multiplication facts to 10×10, and use them to derive quickly the corresponding division facts; recall the cubes of 2, 3, 4, 5 and 10, and the fraction-to-decimal conversion of familiar simple fractions [for example, $\frac{1}{2}, \frac{1}{4}, \frac{1}{5}, \frac{1}{10}, \frac{1}{100}, \frac{1}{3}, \frac{2}{3}, \frac{1}{8}$]

h   round to the nearest integer and to one significant figure; estimate answers to problems involving decimals

i   develop a range of strategies for mental calculation; derive unknown facts from those they know [for example, estimate $\sqrt{85}$]; add and subtract mentally numbers with up to two decimal places [for example, $13.76 - 5.21$, $20.08 + 12.4$]; multiply and divide numbers with no more than one decimal digit, [for example, 14.3×4, $56.7 \div 7$] using the commutative, associative, and distributive laws and factorisation where possible, or place value adjustments

Written methods

j   use standard column procedures for addition and subtraction of integers and decimals

k   use standard column procedures for multiplication of integers and decimals, understanding where to position the decimal point by considering what happens if they multiply equivalent fractions; solve a problem involving division by a decimal (up to two places of decimals) by transforming it to a problem involving division by an integer

l   use efficient methods to calculate with fractions, including cancelling common factors before carrying out the calculation, recognising that, in many cases, only a fraction can express the exact answer m solve simple percentage problems, including increase and decrease [for example, VAT, annual rate of inflation, income tax, discounts]

n solve word problems about ratio and proportion, including using informal strategies and the unitary method of solution [for example, given that m identical items cost $£y$, then one item costs $£\frac{y}{m}$ and n items cost $£(n \times \frac{y}{m})$, the number of items that can be bought for $£z$ is $z \times \frac{m}{y}$]

Calculator methods

o use calculators effectively and efficiently: know how to enter complex calculations and use function keys for reciprocals, squares and powers

p enter a range of calculations, including those involving standard index form and measures [for example, time calculations in which fractions of an hour must be entered as fractions or as decimals]

q understand the calculator display, interpreting it correctly [for example, in money calculations, or when the display has been rounded by the calculator], and knowing not to round during the intermediate steps of a calculation.

Solving numerical problems

4 Pupils should be taught to:

a draw on their knowledge of the operations and the relationships between them, and of simple integer powers and their corresponding roots, to solve problems involving ratio and proportion, a range of measures and compound measures, metric units, and conversion between metric and common imperial units, set in a variety of contexts

b select appropriate operations, methods and strategies to solve number problems, including trial and improvement where a more efficient method to find the solution is not obvious

c use a variety of checking procedures, including working the problem backwards, and considering whether a result is of the right order of magnitude

d give solutions in the context of the problem to an appropriate degree of accuracy, interpreting the solution shown on a calculator display, and recognising limitations on the accuracy of data and measurements.

5f → ICT opportunity

Pupils could use a spreadsheet to construct formulae to model situations.

Equations, formulae and identities

5   Pupils should be taught to:

Use of symbols

a   distinguish the different roles played by letter symbols in algebra, knowing that letter symbols represent definite unknown numbers in equations [for example, $5x + 1 = 16$], defined quantities or variables in formulae [for example, $V = IR$], general, unspecified and independent numbers in identities [for example, $3x + 2x = 5x$, $(x + 1)^2 = x^2 + 2x + 1$ for all values of x] and in functions they define new expressions or quantities by referring to known quantities [for example, $y = 2x$]

b   understand that the transformation of algebraic expressions obeys and generalises the rules of arithmetic; manipulate algebraic expressions by collecting like terms, by multiplying a single term over a bracket, and by taking out single term common factors [for example, $x + 5 - 2x - 1 = 4 - x$; $5(2x + 3) = 10x + 15$; $x^2 + 3x = x(x + 3)$]; distinguish in meaning between the words 'equation', 'formula', 'identity' and 'expression'

Index notation

c   use index notation for simple integer powers, and simple instances of index laws; substitute positive and negative numbers into expressions such as $3x^2 + 4$ and $2x^3$

Inequalities

d   solve simple linear inequalities in one variable, and represent the solution set on the number line

Linear equations

e   solve linear equations, with integer coefficients, in which the unknown appears on either side or on both sides of the equation; solve linear equations that require prior simplification of brackets, including those that have negative signs occurring anywhere in the equation, and those with a negative solution

Formulae

f   use formulae from mathematics and other subjects expressed initially in words and then using letters and symbols [for example, formulae for the area of a triangle, the area enclosed by a circle, wage earned = hours worked × rate per hour]; substitute numbers into a formula; derive a formula and change its subject [for example, convert temperatures between degrees Fahrenheit and degrees Celsius, find the perimeter of a rectangle given its area A and the length l of one side, use $V = IR$ to generate a formula for R in terms of V and I].

Sequences, functions and graphs

6   Pupils should be taught to:

Sequences

a   generate terms of a sequence using term-to-term and position-to-term definitions of the sequence; use linear expressions to describe the nth term of an arithmetic sequence, justifying its form by referring to the activity or context from which it was generated

Graphs of linear functions

b   use the conventions for coordinates in the plane; plot points in all four quadrants; recognise (when values are given for m and c) that equations of the form $y = mx + c$ correspond to straight-line graphs in the coordinate plane; plot graphs of functions in which y is given explicitly in terms of x [for example, $y = 2x + 3$], or implicitly [for example, $x + y = 7$]

c   construct linear functions from real-life problems and plot their corresponding graphs; discuss and interpret graphs arising from real situations; understand that the point of intersection of two different lines in the same two variables that simultaneously describe a real situation is the solution to the simultaneous equations represented by the lines; draw line of best fit through a set of linearly related points and find its equation

Gradients

d   find the gradient of lines given by equations of the form $y = mx + c$ (when values are given for m and c); investigate the gradients of parallel lines

Interpret graphical information

e   interpret information presented in a range of linear and non-linear graphs [for example, graphs describing trends, conversion graphs, distance–time graphs, graphs of height or weight against age, graphs of quantities that vary against time, such as employment].

6d → ICT opportunity
Pupils could use a spreadsheet to calculate points and draw graphs to explore the effects of varying m and c in the graph of $y=mx+c$.

1d → links to other subjects
This requirement builds on En1/3b
and En2/1a.

1e → links to other subjects
This requirement builds on En1/1d
and En3/1f.

1f → links to other subjects
This requirement builds on En1/1e
and En3/1f.

1g → links to other subjects
This requirement builds on En3/1i, 1n.

Ma3 Shape, space and measures

Using and applying shape, space and measures

1   Pupils should be taught to:

Problem solving

a   select problem-solving strategies and resources, including ICT tools,
to use in geometrical work, and monitor their effectiveness

b   select and combine known facts and problem-solving strategies to solve
complex problems

c   identify what further information is needed to solve a geometrical problem;
break complex problems down into a series of tasks

Communicating

d   interpret, discuss and synthesise geometrical information presented in
a variety of forms

e   communicate mathematically, by presenting and organising results and
explaining geometrical diagrams

f   use geometrical language appropriately

g   review and justify their choices of mathematical presentation

Reasoning

h   distinguish between practical demonstrations and proofs

i   apply mathematical reasoning, explaining and justifying inferences and
deductions

j   show step-by-step deduction in solving a geometrical problem

k   state constraints and give starting points when making deductions

l   recognise the limitations of any assumptions that are made; understand
the effects that varying the assumptions may have on the solution

m   identify exceptional cases when solving geometrical problems.

Geometrical reasoning

2   Pupils should be taught to:

Angles

a   recall and use properties of angles at a point, angles on a straight line
(including right angles), perpendicular lines, and opposite angles at a vertex

b   distinguish between acute, obtuse, reflex and right angles; estimate the size
of an angle in degrees

Properties of triangles and other rectilinear shapes

c   use parallel lines, alternate angles and corresponding angles; understand the
properties of parallelograms and a proof that the angle sum of a triangle is
180 degrees; understand a proof that the exterior angle of a triangle is equal
to the sum of the interior angles at the other two vertices

d   use angle properties of equilateral, isosceles and right-angled triangles;
understand congruence; explain why the angle sum of any quadrilateral
is 360 degrees

e use their knowledge of rectangles, parallelograms and triangles to deduce formulae for the area of a parallelogram, and a triangle, from the formula for the area of a rectangle

f recall the essential properties of special types of quadrilateral, including square, rectangle, parallelogram, trapezium and rhombus; classify quadrilaterals by their geometric properties

g calculate and use the sums of the interior and exterior angles of quadrilaterals, pentagons and hexagons; calculate and use the angles of regular polygons

h understand, recall and use Pythagoras' theorem

Properties of circles

i recall the definition of a circle and the meaning of related terms, including centre, radius, chord, diameter, circumference, tangent, arc, sector and segment; understand that inscribed regular polygons can be constructed by equal division of a circle

3-D shapes

j explore the geometry of cuboids (including cubes), and shapes made from cuboids

k use 2-D representations of 3-D shapes and analyse 3-D shapes through 2-D projections and cross-sections, including plan and elevation.

Transformations and coordinates

3 Pupils should be taught to:

Specifying transformations

a understand that rotations are specified by a centre and an (anticlockwise) angle; rotate a shape about the origin, or any other point; measure the angle of rotation using right angles, simple fractions of a turn or degrees; understand that reflections are specified by a mirror line, at first using a line parallel to an axis, then a mirror line such as $y = x$ or $y = -x$; understand that translations are specified by a distance and direction, and enlargements by a centre and positive scale factor

Properties of transformations

b recognise and visualise rotations, reflections and translations, including reflection symmetry of 2-D and 3-D shapes, and rotation symmetry of 2-D shapes; transform triangles and other 2-D shapes by translation, rotation and reflection, recognising that these transformations preserve length and angle, so that any figure is congruent to its image under any of these transformations

c recognise, visualise and construct enlargements of objects using positive scale factors greater than one, then positive scale factors less than one; understand from this that any two circles and any two squares are mathematically similar, while, in general, two rectangles are not

d   recognise that enlargements preserve angle but not length; identify the scale factor of an enlargement as the ratio of the lengths of any two corresponding line segments and apply this to triangles; understand the implications of enlargement for perimeter; use and interpret maps and scale drawings; understand the implications of enlargement for area and for volume; distinguish between formulae for perimeter, area and volume by considering dimensions; understand and use simple examples of the relationship between enlargement and areas and volumes of shapes and solids

Coordinates

e   understand that one coordinate identifies a point on a number line, two coordinates identify a point in a plane and three coordinates identify a point in space, using the terms '1-D', '2-D' and '3-D'; use axes and coordinates to specify points in all four quadrants; locate points with given coordinates; find the coordinates of points identified by geometrical information [for example, find the coordinates of the fourth vertex of a parallelogram with vertices at $(2, 1)$ $(-7, 3)$ and $(5, 6)$]; find the coordinates of the midpoint of the line segment AB, given points A and B, then calculate the length AB.

Measures and construction

4   Pupils should be taught to:

Measures

a   interpret scales on a range of measuring instruments, including those for time and mass; know that measurements using real numbers depend on the choice of unit; recognise that measurements given to the nearest whole unit may be inaccurate by up to one half in either direction; convert measurements from one unit to another; know rough metric equivalents of pounds, feet, miles, pints and gallons; make sensible estimates of a range of measures in everyday settings

b   understand angle measure using the associated language [for example, use bearings to specify direction]

c   understand and use compound measures, including speed

Construction

d   measure and draw lines to the nearest millimetre, and angles to the nearest degree; draw triangles and other 2-D shapes using a ruler and protractor, given information about their side lengths and angles; understand, from their experience of constructing them, that triangles satisfying SSS, SAS, ASA and RHS are unique, but SSA triangles are not; construct cubes, regular tetrahedra, square-based pyramids and other 3-D shapes from given information e   use straight edge and compasses to do standard constructions, including an equilateral triangle with a given side, the midpoint and perpendicular bisector of a line segment, the perpendicular from a point to a line, the perpendicular from a point on a line, and the bisector of an angle

Mensuration

f   find areas of rectangles, recalling the formula, understanding the connection to counting squares and how it extends this approach; recall and use the formulae for the area of a parallelogram and a triangle; find the surface area of simple shapes using the area formulae for triangles and rectangles; calculate perimeters and areas of shapes made from triangles and rectangles

g   find volumes of cuboids, recalling the formula and understanding the connection to counting cubes and how it extends this approach; calculate volumes of right prisms and of shapes made from cubes and cuboids

h   find circumferences of circles and areas enclosed by circles, recalling relevant formulae

i   convert between area measures, including cm^2 and m^2, and volume measures, including cm^3 and m^3

Loci

j   find loci, both by reasoning and by using ICT to produce shapes and paths [for example, equilateral triangles].

1e → links to other subjects
This requirement builds on En1/3b and En2/1a.

1f → links to other subjects
This requirement builds on En1/1d and En3/1f.

1g → links to other subjects
This requirement builds on En1/1e, 3b and En3/1i, 1n.

Ma4 Handling data

Using and applying handling data

1   Pupils should be taught to:

Problem solving

a   carry out each of the four aspects of the handling data cycle to solve problems:

i   specify the problem and plan: formulate questions in terms of the data needed, and consider what inferences can be drawn from the data; decide what data to collect (including sample size and data format) and what statistical analysis is needed

ii   collect data from a variety of suitable sources, including experiments and surveys, and primary and secondary sources

iii   process and represent the data: turn the raw data into usable information that gives insight into the problem

iv   interpret and discuss: answer the initial question by drawing conclusions from the data

b   identify what further information is needed to pursue a particular line of enquiry

c   select and organise the appropriate mathematics and resources to use for a task

d   review progress while working; check and evaluate solutions

Communicating

e   interpret, discuss and synthesise information presented in a variety of forms

f   communicate mathematically, including using ICT, making use of diagrams and related explanatory text

g   examine critically, and justify, their choices of mathematical presentation of problems involving data

Reasoning

h   apply mathematical reasoning, explaining and justifying inferences and deductions

i   explore connections in mathematics and look for cause and effect when analysing data

j   recognise the limitations of any assumptions and the effects that varying the assumptions could have on conclusions drawn from the data analysis.

Specifying the problem and planning

2   Pupils should be taught to:

   a   see that random processes are unpredictable

   b   identify questions that can be addressed by statistical methods

   c   discuss how data relate to a problem; identify possible sources of bias
       and plan to minimise it

   d   identify which primary data they need to collect and in what format,
       including grouped data, considering appropriate equal class intervals

   e   design an experiment or survey; decide what secondary data to use.

Collecting data

3   Pupils should be taught to:

   a   design and use data-collection sheets for grouped discrete and continuous
       data; collect data using various methods, including observation, controlled
       experiment, data logging, questionnaires and surveys

   b   gather data from secondary sources, including printed tables and lists from
       ICT-based sources

   c   design and use two-way tables for discrete and grouped data.

Processing and representing data

4   Pupils should be taught to:

   a   draw and produce, using paper and ICT, pie charts for categorical data,
       and diagrams for continuous data, including line graphs for time series,
       scatter graphs, frequency diagrams and stem-and-leaf diagrams

   b   calculate mean, range and median of small data sets with discrete then
       continuous data; identify the modal class for grouped data

   c   understand and use the probability scale

   d   understand and use estimates or measures of probability from theoretical
       models (including equally likely outcomes), or from relative frequency

   e   list all outcomes for single events, and for two successive events, in a
       systematic way

   f   identify different mutually exclusive outcomes and know that the sum
       of the probabilities of all these outcomes is 1

   g   find the median for large data sets and calculate an estimate of the mean
       for large data sets with grouped data

   h   draw lines of best fit by eye, understanding what these represent.

5c → ICT opportunity
Pupils could use databases to present
their findings.

Interpreting and discussing results

5   Pupils should be taught to:

a   relate summarised data to the initial questions

b   interpret a wide range of graphs and diagrams and draw conclusions

c   look at data to find patterns and exceptions

d   compare distributions and make inferences, using the shapes of distributions and measures of average and range

e   consider and check results and modify their approach if necessary

f   have a basic understanding of correlation as a measure of the strength of the association between two variables; identify correlation or no correlation using lines of best fit

g   use the vocabulary of probability to interpret results involving uncertainty and prediction

h   compare experimental data and theoretical probabilities

i   understand that if they repeat an experiment, they may – and usually will – get different outcomes, and that increasing sample size generally leads to better estimates of probability and population characteristics

j   discuss implications of findings in the context of the problem

k   interpret social statistics including index numbers [for example, the General Index of Retail Prices]; **time series** [for example, population growth]; **and survey data** [for example, the National Census].

Breadth of study

1 During the key stage, pupils should be taught the **Knowledge, skills and understanding** through:

a extending mental and written calculation strategies and using efficient procedures confidently to calculate with integers, fractions, decimals, percentages, ratio and proportion

b solving a range of familiar and unfamiliar problems, including those drawn from real-life contexts and other areas of the curriculum

c activities that provide frequent opportunities to discuss their work, to develop reasoning and understanding and to explain their reasoning and strategies

d activities focused on developing short chains of deductive reasoning and correct use of the '=' sign

e activities in which they do practical work with geometrical objects, visualise them and work with them mentally

f practical work in which they draw inferences from data, consider how statistics are used in real life to make informed decisions, and recognise the difference between meaningful and misleading representations of data

g activities focused on the major ideas of statistics, including using appropriate populations and representative samples, using different measurement scales, using probability as a measure of uncertainty, using randomness and variability, reducing bias in sampling and measuring, and using inference to make decisions

h substantial use of tasks focused on using appropriate ICT [for example, spreadsheets, databases, geometry or graphic packages], using calculators correctly and efficiently, and knowing when not to use a calculator.

During **key stage 4 (higher)** pupils take increasing responsibility for planning and executing their work. They refine their calculating skills to include powers, roots and numbers expressed in standard form. They learn the importance of precision and rigour in mathematics. They use proportional reasoning with fluency and develop skills of algebraic manipulation and simplification. They extend their knowledge of functions and related graphs and solve a range of equations, including those with non-integer coefficients. They use short chains of deductive reasoning, develop their own proofs, and begin to understand the importance of proof in mathematics. Pupils use definitions and formal reasoning to describe and understand geometrical figures and the logical relationships between them. They learn to handle data through practical activities, using a broader range of skills and techniques, including sampling. Pupils develop the confidence and flexibility to solve unfamiliar problems and to use ICT appropriately. By seeing the importance of mathematics as an analytical tool for solving problems, they learn to appreciate its unique power.

Note

This programme of study is intended for pupils who have attained a secure level 5 at the end of key stage 3. Teachers are expected to plan work drawing on all the numbered sub-sections of the programme of study.

For some groups of pupils, all or part of particular lettered paragraphs may not be appropriate.

Note about sections

There is no separate section of the programme of study numbered Ma1 that corresponds to the first attainment target, **using and applying mathematics**. Teaching requirements relating to this attainment target are included within the other sections of the programme of study.

Programme of study: mathematics higher

Key stage 4

Knowledge, skills and understanding

Teaching should ensure that appropriate connections are made between the sections on **number and algebra, shape, space and measures**, and **handling data**.

Ma2 Number and algebra

Using and applying number and algebra

1 Pupils should be taught to:

Problem solving

a select and use appropriate and efficient techniques and strategies to solve problems of increasing complexity, involving numerical and algebraic manipulation

b identify what further information may be required in order to pursue a particular line of enquiry and give reasons for following or rejecting particular approaches

c break down a complex calculation into simpler steps before attempting a solution and justify their choice of methods

d make mental estimates of the answers to calculations; present answers to sensible levels of accuracy; understand how errors are compounded in certain calculations

Communicating

e discuss their work and explain their reasoning using an increasing range of mathematical language and notation

f use a variety of strategies and diagrams for establishing algebraic or graphical representations of a problem and its solution; move from one form of representation to another to get different perspectives on the problem

g present and interpret solutions in the context of the original problem

h use notation and symbols correctly and consistently within a given problem

i examine critically, improve, then justify their choice of mathematical presentation; present a concise, reasoned argument

Reasoning

j explore, identify, and use pattern and symmetry in algebraic contexts, investigating whether a particular case may be generalised further and understand the importance of a counter-example; identify exceptional cases when solving problems

k understand the difference between a practical demonstration and a proof

l show step-by-step deduction in solving a problem; derive proofs using short chains of deductive reasoning m recognise the significance of stating constraints and assumptions when deducing results; recognise the limitations of any assumptions that are made and the effect that varying the assumptions may have on the solution to a problem.

Numbers and the number system

2 Pupils should be taught to:

Integers

a use their previous understanding of integers and place value to deal with arbitrarily large positive numbers and round them to a given power of 10; understand and use negative integers both as positions and translations on a number line; order integers; use the concepts and vocabulary of factor (divisor), multiple, common factor, highest common factor, least common multiple, prime number and prime factor decomposition

Powers and roots

b use the terms square, positive square root, negative square root, cube and cube root; use index notation [for example, 8^2, $8^{\frac{1}{3}}$] and index laws for multiplication and division of integer powers; use standard index form, expressed in conventional notation and on a calculator display

Fractions

c understand equivalent fractions, simplifying a fraction by cancelling all common factors; order fractions by rewriting them with a common denominator

Decimals

d recognise that each terminating decimal is a fraction [for example, $0.137 = \frac{137}{1000}$]; recognise that recurring decimals are exact fractions, and that some exact fractions are recurring decimals [for example, $\frac{1}{7} = 0.142857142857\ldots$]; order decimals

Percentages

e understand that 'percentage' means 'number of parts per 100', and interpret percentage as the operator 'so many hundredths of' [for example, 10% means 10 parts per 100 and 15% of Y means $\frac{15}{100} \times Y$]

Ratio

f use ratio notation, including reduction to its simplest form and its various links to fraction notation.

1e → links to other subjects
This requirement builds on En1/1d, 1e.

1f → links to other subjects
This requirement builds on En1/1d.

1g → links to other subjects
This requirement builds on En3/1f, 1n.

1i → links to other subjects
This requirement builds on En1/1e, 3b and En2/1a and En3/1f, 1i.

Calculations

3   Pupils should be taught to:

Number operations and the relationships between them

a   multiply or divide any number by powers of 10, and any positive number by a number between 0 and 1; find the prime factor decomposition of positive integers; understand 'reciprocal' as multiplicative inverse, knowing that any non-zero number multiplied by its reciprocal is 1 (and that zero has no reciprocal, because division by zero is not defined); multiply and divide by a negative number; use index laws to simplify and calculate the value of numerical expressions involving multiplication and division of integer, fractional and negative powers; use inverse operations, understanding that the inverse operation of raising a positive number to power n is raising the result of this operation to power $\frac{1}{n}$

b   use brackets and the hierarchy of operations

c   calculate a given fraction of a given quantity, expressing the answer as a fraction; express a given number as a fraction of another; add and subtract fractions by writing them with a common denominator; perform short division to convert a simple fraction to a decimal; distinguish between fractions with denominators that have only prime factors of 2 and 5 (which are represented by terminating decimals), and other fractions (which are represented by recurring decimals); convert a recurring decimal to a fraction [for example, $0.142857142857\ldots = \frac{1}{7}$]

d   understand and use unit fractions as multiplicative inverses [for example, by thinking of multiplication by $\frac{1}{5}$ as division by 5, or multiplication by $\frac{6}{7}$ as multiplication by 6 followed by division by 7 (or vice versa)]; multiply and divide a given fraction by an integer, by a unit fraction and by a general fraction

e   convert simple fractions of a whole to percentages of the whole and vice versa; then understand the multiplicative nature of percentages as operators [for example, a 15% increase in value Y, followed by a 15% decrease is calculated as $1.15 \times 0.85 \times Y$]; calculate an original amount when given the transformed amount after a percentage change; reverse percentage problems [for example, given that a meal in a restaurant costs £36 with VAT at 17.5%, its price before VAT is calculated as $£\frac{36}{1.175}$]

f   divide a quantity in a given ratio

Mental methods

g recall integer squares from 2 × 2 to 15 × 15 and the corresponding square roots, the cubes of 2, 3, 4, 5 and 10, the fact that $n^0 = 1$ and $n^{-1} = \frac{1}{n}$ for positive integers n [for example, $10^0 = 1$; $9^{-1} = \frac{1}{9}$], the corresponding rule for negative numbers [for example, $5^{-2} = \frac{1}{5^2} = \frac{1}{25}$], $n^{\frac{1}{2}} = \sqrt{n}$ and $n^{\frac{1}{3}} = \sqrt[3]{n}$ for any positive number n [for example, $25^{\frac{1}{2}} = 5$ and $64^{\frac{1}{3}} = 4$]

h round to a given number of significant figures; develop a range of strategies for mental calculation; derive unknown facts from those they know; convert between ordinary and standard index form representations [for example, $0.1234 = 1.234 \times 10^{-1}$], converting to standard index form to make sensible estimates for calculations involving multiplication and/or division

Written methods

i use efficient methods to calculate with fractions, including cancelling common factors before carrying out the calculation, recognising that in many cases only a fraction can express the exact answer

j solve percentage problems, including percentage increase and decrease [for example, simple interest, VAT, annual rate of inflation]; and reverse percentages

k represent repeated proportional change using a multiplier raised to a power [for example, compound interest]

l calculate an unknown quantity from quantities that vary in direct or inverse proportion

m calculate with standard index form [for example, $2.4 \times 10^7 \times 5 \times 10^3 = 12 \times 10^{10} = 1.2 \times 10^{11}$, $(2.4 \times 10^7) \div (5 \times 10^3) = 4.8 \times 10^3$]

n use surds and π in exact calculations, without a calculator; rationalise a denominator such as $\frac{1}{\sqrt{3}} = \frac{\sqrt{3}}{3}$

Calculator methods

o use calculators effectively and efficiently, knowing how to enter complex calculations; use an extended range of function keys, including trigonometrical and statistical functions relevant across this programme of study

p understand the calculator display, knowing when to interpret the display, when the display has been rounded by the calculator, and not to round during the intermediate steps of a calculation

q use calculators, or written methods, to calculate the upper and lower bounds of calculations, particularly when working with measurements

r use standard index form display and how to enter numbers in standard index form

s use calculators for reverse percentage calculations by doing an appropriate division

t use calculators to explore exponential growth and decay [for example, in science or geography], using a multiplier and the power key.

Note for 3n

Numbers that can be written as the ratio of two integers are known as rational numbers. Surds and π are examples of irrational numbers, which cannot be written as the ratio of two integers.

Solving numerical problems

4   Pupils should be taught to:

a   draw on their knowledge of operations and inverse operations (including powers and roots), and of methods of simplification (including factorisation and the use of the commutative, associative and distributive laws of addition, multiplication and factorisation) in order to select and use suitable strategies and techniques to solve problems and word problems, including those involving ratio and proportion, repeated proportional change, fractions, percentages and reverse percentages, inverse proportion, surds, measures and conversion between measures, and compound measures defined within a particular situation

b   check and estimate answers to problems; select and justify appropriate degrees of accuracy for answers to problems; recognise limitations on the accuracy of data and measurements.

Equations, formulae and identities

5   Pupils should be taught to:

Use of symbols

a   distinguish the different roles played by letter symbols in algebra, using the correct notational conventions for multiplying or dividing by a given number, and knowing that letter symbols represent definite unknown numbers in equations [for example, $x^2 + 1 = 82$], defined quantities or variables in formula [for example, $V = IR$], general, unspecified and independent numbers in identities [for example, $(x + 1)^2 = x^2 + 2x + 1$ for all x], and in functions they define new expressions or quantities by referring to known quantities [for example, $y = 2 - 7x$; $f(x) = x^3$; $y = \frac{1}{x}$ with $x \neq 0$]

b   understand that the transformation of algebraic entities obeys and generalises the well-defined rules of generalised arithmetic [for example, $a(b + c) = ab + ac$]; expand the product of two linear expressions [for example, $(x + 1)(x + 2) = x^2 + 3x + 2$]; manipulate algebraic expressions by collecting like terms, multiplying a single term over a bracket, taking out common factors [for example, $9x - 3 = 3(3x - 1)$], factorising quadratic expressions including the difference of two squares [for example, $x^2 - 9 = (x + 3)(x - 3)$] and cancelling common factors in rational expressions [for example, $2(x + 1)^2/(x + 1) = 2(x + 1)$]

c   know the meaning of and use the words 'equation', 'formula', 'identity' and 'expression'

Index notation

d   use index notation for simple integer powers, and simple instances of index laws [for example, $x^3 \times x^2 = x^5$; $\frac{x^2}{x^3} = x^{-1}$; $(x^2)^3 = x^6$]; substitute positive and negative numbers into expressions such as $3x^2 + 4$ and $2x^3$

Equations

e   set up simple equations [for example, find the angle a in a triangle with angles a, $a + 10$, $a + 20$]; solve simple equations [for example, $5x = 7$; $11 - 4x = 2$; $3(2x + 1) = 8$; $2(1 - x) = 6(2 + x)$; $4x^2 = 49$; $3 = \frac{12}{x}$] by using inverse operations or by transforming both sides in the same way

Linear equations

f   solve linear equations in one unknown, with integer or fractional coefficients, in which the unknown appears on either side or on both sides of the equation; solve linear equations that require prior simplification of brackets, including those that have negative signs occurring anywhere in the equation, and those with a negative solution

Formulae

g   use formulae from mathematics and other subjects [for example, for area of a triangle or a parallelogram, area enclosed by a circle, volume of a prism, volume of a cone]; substitute numbers into a formula; change the subject of a formula, including cases where the subject occurs twice, or where a power of the subject appears [for example, find r given that $A = \pi r^2$, find x given $y = mx + c$]; generate a formula [for example, find the perimeter of a rectangle given its area A and the length l of one side]

Direct and inverse proportion

h   set up and use equations to solve word and other problems involving direct proportion or inverse proportion [for example, $y \propto x$, $y \propto x^2$, $y \propto \frac{1}{x}$, $y \propto \frac{1}{x^2}$] and relate algebraic solutions to graphical representation of the equations

Simultaneous linear equations

i   find the exact solution of two simultaneous equations in two unknowns by eliminating a variable, and interpret the equations as lines and their common solution as the point of intersection

j   solve simple linear inequalities in one variable, and represent the solution set on a number line; solve several linear inequalities in two variables and find the solution set

Quadratic equations

k   solve quadratic equations by factorisation, completing the square and using the quadratic formula

Simultaneous linear and quadratic equations

l   solve exactly, by elimination of an unknown, two simultaneous equations in two unknowns, one of which is linear in each unknown, and the other is linear in one unknown and quadratic in the other [for example, solve the simultaneous equations $y = 11x - 2$ and $y = 5x^2$], or where the second is of the form $x^2 + y^2 = r^2$

5g → ICT opportunity
Pupils could use a spreadsheet or graphic calculator to construct and use formulae.

6b–6f → ICT opportunity
Pupils could generate functions from plots of data, for example, from a science experiment, using simple curve fitting techniques on graphic calculators, or with graphics software.

Numerical methods

m use systematic trial and improvement to find approximate solutions of equations where there is no simple analytical method of solving them [for example, $x^3 - x = 900$].

Sequences, functions and graphs

6 Pupils should be taught to:

Sequences

a generate common integer sequences (including sequences of odd or even integers, squared integers, powers of 2, powers of 10, triangular numbers); generate terms of a sequence using term-to-term and position-to-term definitions of the sequence; use linear expressions to describe the nth term of an arithmetic sequence, justifying its form by reference to the activity or context from which it was generated

Graphs of linear functions

b use conventions for coordinates in the plane; plot points in all four quadrants; recognise (when values are given for m and c) that equations of the form $y = mx + c$ correspond to straight-line graphs in the coordinate plane; plot graphs of functions in which y is given explicitly in terms of x (as in $y = 2x + 3$), or implicitly (as in $x + y = 7$)

c find the gradient of lines given by equations of the form $y = mx + c$ (when values are given for m and c); understand that the form $y = mx + c$ represents a straight line and that m is the gradient of the line, and c is the value of the y-intercept; explore the gradients of parallel lines and lines perpendicular to these lines [for example, know that the lines represented by the equations $y = -5x$ and $y = 3 - 5x$ are parallel, each having gradient (-5) and that the line with equation $y = \frac{x}{5}$ is perpendicular to these lines and has gradient $\frac{1}{5}$]

Interpreting graphical information

d construct linear functions and plot the corresponding graphs arising from real-life problems; discuss and interpret graphs modelling real situations [for example, distance–time graph for a particle moving with constant speed, the depth of water in a container as it empties, the velocity–time graph for a particle moving with constant acceleration]

Quadratic functions

e generate points and plot graphs of simple quadratic functions [for example, $y = x^2$; $y = 3x^2 + 4$], then more general quadratic functions [for example, $y = x^2 - 2x + 1$]; find approximate solutions of a quadratic equation from the graph of the corresponding quadratic function; find the intersection points of the graphs of a linear and quadratic function, knowing that these are the approximate solutions of the corresponding simultaneous equations representing the linear and quadratic functions

Other functions

f   plot graphs of: simple cubic functions [for example, $y = x^3$], the reciprocal function $y = \frac{1}{x}$ with $x \neq 0$, the exponential function $y = k^x$ for integer values of x and simple positive values of k [for example, $y = 2^x$; $y = (\frac{1}{2})^x$], the circular functions $y = \sin x$ and $y = \cos x$, using a spreadsheet or graph plotter as well as pencil and paper; recognise the characteristic shapes of all these functions

Transformation of functions

g   apply to the graph of $y = f(x)$ the transformations $y = f(x) + a$, $y = f(ax)$, $y = f(x + a)$, $y = af(x)$ for linear, quadratic, sine and cosine functions $f(x)$

Loci

h   construct the graphs of simple loci, including the circle $x^2 + y^2 = r^2$ for a circle of radius r centred at the origin of coordinates; find graphically the intersection points of a given straight line with this circle and know that this corresponds to solving the two simultaneous equations representing the line and the circle.

6g → ICT opportunity
Pupils could use software to explore transformations of graphs.

Note for 6h
The derivation of the circle equation is an application of Pythagoras' theorem. Loci can be considered from an algebraic point of view as here or from a geometric point of view as in Ma3/3e.

1d, 1e → links to other subjects
These requirements build on En1/1d,
1e and En3/1f, 1i, 1n.

Ma3 Shape, space and measures

Using and applying shape, space and measures

1 Pupils should be taught to:

Problem solving

a select the problem-solving strategies to use in geometrical work, and consider and explain the extent to which the selections they made were appropriate

b select and combine known facts and problem-solving strategies to solve more complex geometrical problems

c develop and follow alternative lines of enquiry, justifying their decisions to follow or reject particular approaches

Communicating

d communicate mathematically, with emphasis on a critical examination of the presentation and organisation of results, and on effective use of symbols and geometrical diagrams

e use precise formal language and exact methods for analysing geometrical configurations

Reasoning

f apply mathematical reasoning, progressing from brief mathematical explanations towards full justifications in more complex contexts

g explore connections in geometry; pose conditional constraints of the type 'If … then …'; and ask questions 'What if …?' or 'Why?'

h show step-by-step deduction in solving a geometrical problem

i state constraints and give starting points when making deductions

j understand the necessary and sufficient conditions under which generalisations, inferences and solutions to geometrical problems remain valid.

Geometrical reasoning

2 Pupils should be taught to:

Properties of triangles and other rectilinear shapes

a distinguish between lines and line segments; use parallel lines, alternate angles and corresponding angles; understand the consequent properties of parallelograms and a proof that the angle sum of a triangle is 180 degrees; understand a proof that the exterior angle of a triangle is equal to the sum of the interior angles at the other two vertices

b use angle properties of equilateral, isosceles and right-angled triangles; explain why the angle sum of a quadrilateral is 360 degrees c recall the definitions of special types of quadrilateral, including square, rectangle, parallelogram, trapezium and rhombus; classify quadrilaterals by their geometric properties

d calculate and use the sums of the interior and exterior angles of quadrilaterals, pentagons, hexagons; calculate and use the angles of regular polygons

e understand and use SSS, SAS, ASA and RHS conditions to prove the congruence of triangles using formal arguments, and to verify standard ruler and compass constructions

f understand, recall and use Pythagoras' theorem in 2-D, then 3-D problems; investigate the geometry of cuboids including cubes, and shapes made from cuboids, including the use of Pythagoras' theorem to calculate lengths in three dimensions

g understand similarity of triangles and of other plane figures, and use this to make geometric inferences; understand, recall and use trigonometrical relationships in right-angled triangles, and use these to solve problems, including those involving bearings, then use these relationships in 3-D contexts, including finding the angles between a line and a plane (but not the angle between two planes or between two skew lines); calculate the area of a triangle using $\frac{1}{2}ab \sin C$; draw, sketch and describe the graphs of trigonometric functions for angles of any size, including transformations involving scalings in either or both the x and y directions; use the sine and cosine rules to solve 2-D and 3-D problems

Properties of circles

h recall the definition of a circle and the meaning of related terms, including centre, radius, chord, diameter, circumference, tangent, arc, sector and segment; understand that the tangent at any point on a circle is perpendicular to the radius at that point; understand and use the fact that tangents from an external point are equal in length; explain why the perpendicular from the centre to a chord bisects the chord; understand that inscribed regular polygons can be constructed by equal division of a circle; prove and use the facts that the angle subtended by an arc at the centre of a circle is twice the angle subtended at any point on the circumference, the angle subtended at the circumference by a semicircle is a right angle, that angles in the same segment are equal, and that opposite angles of a cyclic quadrilateral sum to 180 degrees; prove and use the alternate segment theorem

i use 2-D representations of 3-D shapes and analyse 3-D shapes through 2-D projections and cross-sections, including plan and elevation; solve problems involving surface areas and volumes of prisms, pyramids, cylinders, cones and spheres; solve problems involving more complex shapes and solids, including segments of circles and frustums of cones.

3b–3f → ICT opportunity
Pupils could use software to explore transformations and their effects on properties of shapes.

Transformations and coordinates

3 Pupils should be taught to:

Specifying transformations

a understand that rotations are specified by a centre and an (anticlockwise) angle; use any point as the centre of rotation; measure the angle of rotation, using right angles, fractions of a turn or degrees; understand that reflections are specified by a (mirror) line; understand that translations are specified by giving a distance and direction (or a vector), and enlargements by a centre and a positive scale factor

Properties of transformations

b recognise and visualise rotations, reflections and translations including reflection symmetry of 2-D and 3-D shapes, and rotation symmetry of 2-D shapes; transform triangles and other 2-D shapes by translation, rotation and reflection and combinations of these transformations; use congruence to show that translations, rotations and reflections preserve length and angle, so that any figure is congruent to its image under any of these transformations; distinguish properties that are preserved under particular transformations

c recognise, visualise and construct enlargements of objects; understand from this that any two circles and any two squares are mathematically similar, while, in general, two rectangles are not, then use positive fractional and negative scale factors

d recognise that enlargements preserve angle but not length; identify the scale factor of an enlargement as the ratio of the lengths of any two corresponding line segments; understand the implications of enlargement for perimeter; use and interpret maps and scale drawings; understand the difference between formulae for perimeter, area and volume by considering dimensions; understand and use the effect of enlargement on areas and volumes of shapes and solids

Coordinates

e understand that one coordinate identifies a point on a number line, that two coordinates identify a point in a plane and three coordinates identify a point in space, using the terms '1-D', '2-D' and '3-D'; use axes and coordinates to specify points in all four quadrants; locate points with given coordinates; find the coordinates of points identified by geometrical information; find the coordinates of the midpoint of the line segment AB, given the points A and B, then calculate the length AB

Vectors

f understand and use vector notation; calculate, and represent graphically
the sum of two vectors, the difference of two vectors and a scalar multiple
of a vector; calculate the resultant of two vectors; understand and use the
commutative and associative properties of vector addition; solve simple
geometrical problems in 2-D using vector methods.

Measures and construction

4 Pupils should be taught to:

Measures

a use angle measure [for example, use bearings to specify direction]; know
that measurements using real numbers depend on the choice of unit;
recognise that measurements given to the nearest whole unit may be
inaccurate by up to one half in either direction; convert measurements
from one unit to another; understand and use compound measures,
including speed and density

Construction

b draw approximate constructions of triangles and other 2-D shapes, using
a ruler and protractor, given information about side lengths and angles;
construct specified cubes, regular tetrahedra, square-based pyramids and
other 3-D shapes

c use straight edge and compasses to do standard constructions including
an equilateral triangle with a given side, the midpoint and perpendicular
bisector of a line segment, the perpendicular from a point to a line, the
perpendicular from a point on a line, and the bisector of an angle

Mensuration

d find the surface area of simple shapes by using the formulae for the areas of
triangles and rectangles; find volumes of cuboids, recalling the formula and
understanding the connection to counting cubes and how it extends this
approach; calculate volumes of right prisms and of shapes made from cubes
and cuboids; convert between volume measures including cm^3 and m^3; find
circumferences of circles and areas enclosed by circles, recalling relevant
formulae; calculate the lengths of arcs and the areas of sectors of circles

Loci

e find loci, both by reasoning and by using ICT to produce shapes and paths
[for example, a region bounded by a circle and an intersecting line].

1c → links to other subjects
This requirement builds on En1/1d, 1e and
En3/1f, 1i, 1n.

1c → ICT opportunity
Pupils could use databases or spreadsheets to
present their findings and display their data.

Ma4 Handling data

Using and applying handling data

1   Pupils should be taught to:

Problem solving

a   carry out each of the four aspects of the handling data cycle to solve problems:

i   specify the problem and plan: formulate questions in terms of the data needed, and consider what inferences can be drawn from the data; decide what data to collect (including sample size and data format) and what statistical analysis is needed)

ii   collect data from a variety of suitable sources, including experiments and surveys, and primary and secondary sources

iii   process and represent the data: turn the raw data into usable information that gives insight into the problem

iv   interpret and discuss the data: answer the initial question by drawing conclusions from the data

b   select the problem-solving strategies to use in statistical work, and monitor their effectiveness (these strategies should address the scale and manageability of the tasks, and should consider whether the mathematics and approach used are delivering the most appropriate solutions)

Communicating

c   communicate mathematically, with emphasis on the use of an increasing range of diagrams and related explanatory text, on the selection of their mathematical presentation, explaining its purpose and approach, and on the use of symbols to convey statistical meaning

Reasoning

d   apply mathematical reasoning, explaining and justifying inferences and deductions, justifying arguments and solutions

e   identify exceptional or unexpected cases when solving statistical problems

f   explore connections in mathematics and look for relationships between variables when analysing data

g   recognise the limitations of any assumptions and the effects that varying the assumptions could have on the conclusions drawn from data analysis.

Specifying the problem and planning

2   Pupils should be taught to:

a   see that random processes are unpredictable

b   identify key questions that can be addressed by statistical methods

c   discuss how data relate to a problem; identify possible sources of bias and plan to minimise it d   identify which primary data they need to collect and in what format, including grouped data, considering appropriate equal class intervals; select and justify a sampling scheme and a method to investigate a population, including random and stratified sampling

e   design an experiment or survey; decide what primary and secondary data to use.

Collecting data

3   Pupils should be taught to:

a   collect data using various methods, including observation, controlled experiment, data logging, questionnaires and surveys

b   gather data from secondary sources, including printed tables and lists from ICT-based sources

c   design and use two-way tables for discrete and grouped data

d   deal with practical problems such as non-response or missing data.

Processing and representing data

4   Pupils should be taught to:

a   draw and produce, using paper and ICT, pie charts for categorical data, and diagrams for continuous data, including line graphs (time series), scatter graphs, frequency diagrams, stem-and-leaf diagrams, cumulative frequency tables and diagrams, box plots and histograms for grouped continuous data

b   understand and use estimates or measures of probability from theoretical models, or from relative frequency

c   list all outcomes for single events, and for two successive events, in a systematic way

d   identify different mutually exclusive outcomes and know that the sum of the probabilities of all these outcomes is 1

e   find the median, quartiles and interquartile range for large data sets and calculate the mean for large data sets with grouped data

f   calculate an appropriate moving average

g   know when to add or multiply two probabilities: if A and B are mutually exclusive, then the probability of A or B occurring is $P(A) + P(B)$, whereas if A and B are independent events, the probability of A and B occurring is $P(A) \times P(B)$

h   use tree diagrams to represent outcomes of compound events, recognising when events are independent

i   draw lines of best fit by eye, understanding what these represent

j   use relevant statistical functions on a calculator or spreadsheet.

5c → ICT opportunity
Pupils could use databases to present
their findings.

Interpreting and discussing results

5   Pupils should be taught to:

a   relate summarised data to the initial questions

b   interpret a wide range of graphs and diagrams and draw conclusions; identify seasonality and trends in time series

c   look at data to find patterns and exceptions

d   compare distributions and make inferences, using shapes of distributions and measures of average and spread, including median and quartiles; understand frequency density

e   consider and check results, and modify their approaches if necessary

f   appreciate that correlation is a measure of the strength of the association between two variables; distinguish between positive, negative and zero correlation using lines of best fit; appreciate that zero correlation does not necessarily imply 'no relationship' but merely 'no linear relationship'

g   use the vocabulary of probability to interpret results involving uncertainty and prediction [for example, 'there is some evidence from this sample that …']

h   compare experimental data and theoretical probabilities

i   understand that if they repeat an experiment, they may – and usually will – get different outcomes, and that increasing sample size generally leads to better estimates of probability and population parameters.

Breadth of study

1   During the key stage, pupils should be taught the **Knowledge, skills and understanding** through:

a   activities that ensure they become familiar with and confident using standard procedures for the range of calculations appropriate to this level of study

b   solving familiar and unfamiliar problems in a range of numerical, algebraic and graphical contexts and in open-ended and closed form

c   using standard notations for decimals, fractions, percentages, ratio and indices

d   activities that show how algebra, as an extension of number using symbols, gives precise form to mathematical relationships and calculations

e   activities in which they progress from using definitions and short chains of reasoning to understanding and formulating proofs in algebra and geometry

f   a sequence of practical activities that address increasingly demanding statistical problems in which they draw inferences from data and consider the uses of statistics in society

g   choosing appropriate ICT tools and using these to solve numerical and graphical problems, to represent and manipulate geometrical configurations and to present and analyse data.

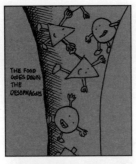

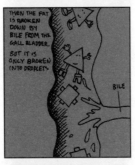

Science does not tell us everything that we want to know about life, or all we need to know. But it does provide us with the most robust information about the way the universe works that has so far become available to us.
Colin Tudge, Science Writer

Science is valuable because it meshes with all our lives and allows us to channel and use our spontaneous curiosity.
Professor Susan Greenfield, Director, Royal Institution

Studying science teaches us to be good at analysis and helps us to make complex things simple. It trains minds in a way that industry prizes.
Brendan O'Neill, Chief Executive, Imperial Chemical Industries PLC

Science is an integral part of modern culture. It stretches the imagination and creativity of young people. Its challenges are quite enormous.
Professor Malcolm Longair, Institute of Physics Fellow in Public Understanding of Physics, Head of Cavendish Laboratory, University of Cambridge

Science

The importance of science

Science stimulates and excites pupils' curiosity about phenomena and events in the world around them. It also satisfies this curiosity with knowledge. Because science links direct practical experience with ideas, it can engage learners at many levels. Scientific method is about developing and evaluating explanations through experimental evidence and modelling. This is a spur to critical and creative thought. Through science, pupils understand how major scientific ideas contribute to technological change – impacting on industry, business and medicine and improving quality of life. Pupils recognise the cultural significance of science and trace its worldwide development. They learn to question and discuss science-based issues that may affect their own lives, the direction of society and the future of the world.

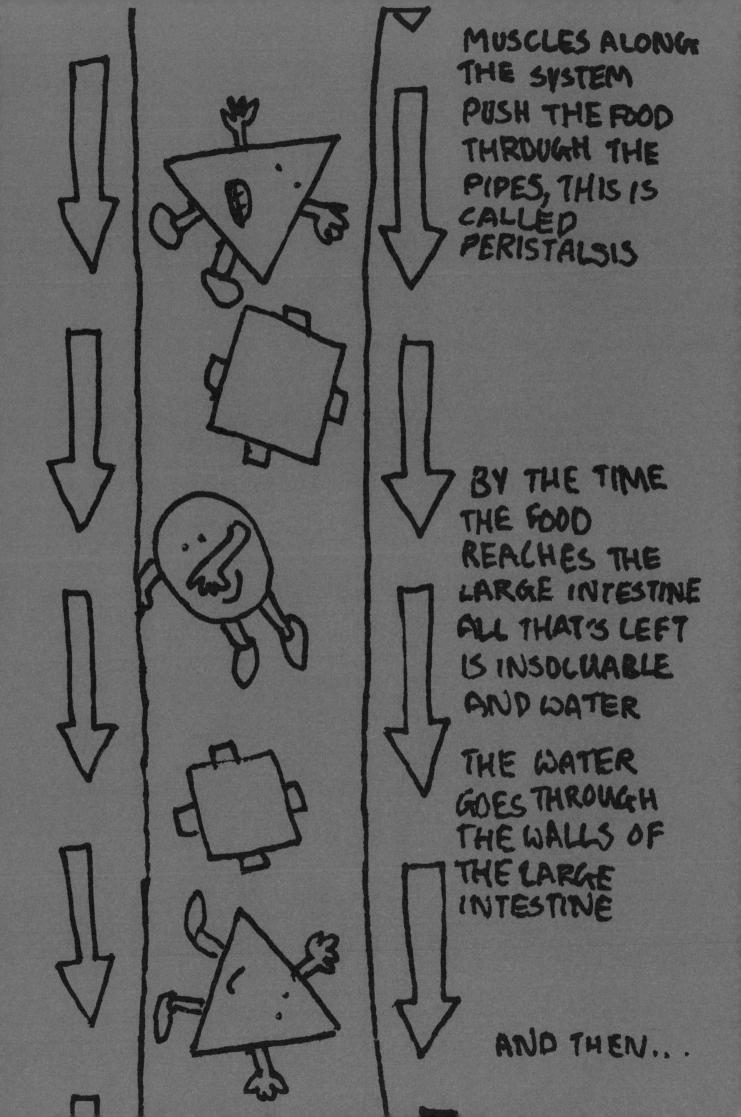

MUSCLES ALONG THE SYSTEM PUSH THE FOOD THROUGH THE PIPES, THIS IS CALLED PERISTALSIS

BY THE TIME THE FOOD REACHES THE LARGE INTESTINE ALL THAT'S LEFT IS INSOLUABLE AND WATER

THE WATER GOES THROUGH THE WALLS OF THE LARGE INTESTINE

AND THEN...

Programme of study: science

Key stage 3

Knowledge, skills and understanding

Teaching should ensure that **scientific enquiry** is taught through contexts taken from the sections on **life processes and living things**, **materials and their properties** and **physical processes**.

Sc1 Scientific enquiry

Ideas and evidence in science

1   Pupils should be taught:

a   about the interplay between empirical questions, evidence and scientific explanations using historical and contemporary examples [for example, Lavoisier's work on burning, the possible causes of global warming]

b   that it is important to test explanations by using them to make predictions and by seeing if evidence matches the predictions

c   about the ways in which scientists work today and how they worked in the past, including the roles of experimentation, evidence and creative thought in the development of scientific ideas.

Investigative skills

2   Pupils should be taught to:

   Planning

a   use scientific knowledge and understanding to turn ideas into a form that can be investigated, and to decide on an appropriate approach

b   decide whether to use evidence from first-hand experience or secondary sources

c   carry out preliminary work and to make predictions, where appropriate

d   consider key factors that need to be taken into account when collecting evidence, and how evidence may be collected in contexts [for example, fieldwork, surveys] in which the variables cannot readily be controlled

e   decide the extent and range of data to be collected and the techniques, equipment and materials to use [for example, appropriate sample size for biological work]

   Obtaining and presenting evidence

f   use a range of equipment and materials appropriately and take action to control risks to themselves and to others

g   make observations and measurements, including the use of ICT for datalogging [for example, variables changing over time] to an appropriate degree of precision

h   make sufficient relevant observations and measurements to reduce error and obtain reliable evidence

i   use a wide range of methods, including diagrams, tables, charts, graphs and ICT, to represent and communicate qualitative and quantitative data

---

During key stage 3 pupils build on their scientific knowledge and understanding and make connections between different areas of science. They use scientific ideas and models to explain phenomena and events, and to understand a range of familiar applications of science. They think about the positive and negative effects of scientific and technological developments on the environment and in other contexts. They take account of others' views and understand why opinions may differ. They do more quantitative work, carrying out investigations on their own and with others. They evaluate their work, in particular the strength of the evidence they and others have collected. They select and use a wide range of reference sources. They communicate clearly what they did and its significance. They learn how scientists work together on present-day scientific developments and about the importance of experimental evidence in supporting scientific ideas.

Note
The general teaching requirement for health and safety applies in this subject.

2 → links to other subjects
These requirements build on En1/10a.

2b → links to other subjects
This requirement builds on En2/4a–4c.

2d → ICT opportunity
Pupils could use data-handling software with fieldwork data.

2e → links to other subjects
This requirement builds on Ma4/1a, 2c.

2g → links to other subjects
This requirement builds on Ma3/4a and Ma4/3a, 3b and ICT/2b.

2i → links to other subjects
This requirement builds on Ma4/4a, 4b, 4h.

Considering evidence

j   use diagrams, tables, charts and graphs, including lines of best fit, to identify and describe patterns or relationships in data

k   use observations, measurements and other data to draw conclusions

l   decide to what extent these conclusions support a prediction or enable further predictions to be made

m use their scientific knowledge and understanding to explain and interpret observations, measurements or other data, and conclusions

Evaluating

n   consider anomalies in observations or measurements and try to explain them

o   consider whether the evidence is sufficient to support any conclusions or interpretations made

p   suggest improvements to the methods used, where appropriate.

2j–2o → links to other subjects
These requirements build on Ma4/5a–5g, 5j.

2j → ICT opportunity
Pupils could use data-handling software to create, analyse and evaluate charts and graphs.

2a → ICT opportunity
Pupils could use databases or spreadsheets to record, analyse and evaluate information about diets.

Sc2 Life processes and living things

Cells and cell functions

1   Pupils should be taught:

a   that animal and plant cells can form tissues, and tissues can form organs

b   the functions of chloroplasts and cell walls in plant cells and the functions of the cell membrane, cytoplasm and nucleus in both plant and animal cells

c   ways in which some cells, including ciliated epithelial cells, sperm, ova, and root hair cells, are adapted to their functions

d   that fertilisation in humans and flowering plants is the fusion of a male and a female cell

e   to relate cells and cell functions to life processes in a variety of organisms.

Humans as organisms

2   Pupils should be taught:

Nutrition

a   about the need for a balanced diet containing carbohydrates, proteins, fats, minerals, vitamins, fibre and water, and about foods that are sources of these

b   the principles of digestion, including the role of enzymes in breaking down large molecules into smaller ones

c   that the products of digestion are absorbed into the bloodstream and transported throughout the body, and that waste material is egested

d   that food is used as a fuel during respiration to maintain the body's activity and as a raw material for growth and repair

Movement

e   the role of the skeleton and joints and the principle of antagonistic muscle pairs [for example, biceps and triceps] in movement

Reproduction

f   about the physical and emotional changes that take place during adolescence

g   about the human reproductive system, including the menstrual cycle and fertilisation

h   how the fetus develops in the uterus, including the role of the placenta

Breathing

i   the role of lung structure in gas exchange, including the effect of smoking

Respiration

j   that aerobic respiration involves a reaction in cells between oxygen and food, in which glucose is broken down into carbon dioxide and water

k   to summarise aerobic respiration in a word equation

l   that the reactants and products of respiration are transported throughout the body in the bloodstream

Health

m   that the abuse of alcohol, solvents, and other drugs affects health

n   how the growth and reproduction of bacteria and the replication of viruses can affect health, and how the body's natural defences may be enhanced by immunisation and medicines.

Green plants as organisms

3   Pupils should be taught:

Nutrition and growth

a   that plants need carbon dioxide, water and light for photosynthesis, and produce biomass and oxygen

b   to summarise photosynthesis in a word equation

c   that nitrogen and other elements, in addition to carbon, oxygen and hydrogen, are required for plant growth

d   the role of root hairs in absorbing water and minerals from the soil

Respiration

e   that plants carry out aerobic respiration.

Variation, classification and inheritance

4   Pupils should be taught:

Variation

a   about environmental and inherited causes of variation within a species

Classification

b   to classify living things into the major taxonomic groups

Inheritance

c   that selective breeding can lead to new varieties.

Living things in their environment

5   Pupils should be taught:

Adaptation and competition

a   about ways in which living things and the environment can be protected, and the importance of sustainable development

b   that habitats support a diversity of plants and animals that are interdependent

c   how some organisms are adapted to survive daily and seasonal changes in their habitats

d   how predation and competition for resources affect the size of populations [for example, bacteria, growth of vegetation]

Feeding relationships

e   about food webs composed of several food chains, and how food chains can be quantified using pyramids of numbers

f   how toxic materials can accumulate in food chains.

2n → ICT opportunity
Pupils could use simulation software to model changes in populations of bacteria in different conditions.

3a → ICT opportunity
Pupils could use sensors to record or use simulation software to model factors that affect photosynthesis.

5f → ICT opportunity
Pupils could use simulation software to explore toxic materials in food chains.

1a → ICT opportunity
Pupils could search a database for information about properties of materials.

2a → ICT opportunity
Pupils could use dataloggers to collect, analyse and evaluate changes of temperature and mass.

Sc3 Materials and their properties

Classifying materials

1 Pupils should be taught:

Solids, liquids and gases

a how materials can be characterised by melting point, boiling point and density

b how the particle theory of matter can be used to explain the properties of solids, liquids and gases, including changes of state, gas pressure and diffusion

Elements, compounds and mixtures

c that the elements are shown in the periodic table and consist of atoms, which can be represented by symbols

d how elements vary widely in their physical properties, including appearance, state at room temperature, magnetic properties and thermal and electrical conductivity, and how these properties can be used to classify elements as metals or non-metals

e how elements combine through chemical reactions to form compounds [for example, water, carbon dioxide, magnesium oxide, sodium chloride, most minerals] with a definite composition

f to represent compounds by formulae and to summarise reactions by word equations

g that mixtures [for example, air, sea water and most rocks] are composed of constituents that are not combined

h how to separate mixtures into their constituents using distillation, chromatography and other appropriate methods.

Changing materials

2 Pupils should be taught:

Physical changes

a that when physical changes [for example, changes of state, formation of solutions] take place, mass is conserved

b about the variation of solubility with temperature, the formation of saturated solutions, and the differences in solubility of solutes in different solvents

c to relate changes of state to energy transfers

Geological changes

d how forces generated by expansion, contraction and the freezing of water can lead to the physical weathering of rocks

e about the formation of rocks by processes that take place over different timescales, and that the mode of formation determines their texture and the minerals they contain

f   how igneous rocks are formed by the cooling of magma, sedimentary rocks by processes including the deposition of rock fragments or organic material, or as a result of evaporation, and metamorphic rocks by the action of heat and pressure on existing rocks

Chemical reactions

g   how mass is conserved when chemical reactions take place because the same atoms are present, although combined in different ways

h   that virtually all materials, including those in living systems, are made through chemical reactions, and to recognise the importance of chemical change in everyday situations [for example, ripening fruit, setting superglue, cooking food]

i   about possible effects of burning fossil fuels on the environment [for example, production of acid rain, carbon dioxide and solid particles] and how these effects can be minimised.

Patterns of behaviour

3   Pupils should be taught:

Metals

a   how metals react with oxygen, water, acids and oxides of other metals, and what the products of these reactions are

b   about the displacement reactions that take place between metals and solutions of salts of other metals

c   how a reactivity series of metals can be determined by considering these reactions, and used to make predictions about other reactions

Acids and bases

d   to use indicators to classify solutions as acidic, neutral or alkaline, and to use the pH scale as a measure of the acidity of a solution

e   how metals and bases, including carbonates, react with acids, and what the products of these reactions are

f   about some everyday applications of neutralisation [for example, the treatment of indigestion, the treatment of acid soil, the manufacture of fertilizer]

g   how acids in the environment can lead to corrosion of some metals and chemical weathering of rock [for example, limestone]

h   to identify patterns in chemical reactions.

2i → ICT opportunity
Pupils could use the internet to find up-to-date information about environmental issues.

3a → ICT opportunity
Pupils could use video or CD-ROM to see reactions that are dangerous.

1a → ICT opportunity
Pupils could use simulation software
to investigate and model circuits.

2a, 2f, 2g → links to other subjects
These requirements build on Ma2/5f.

Sc4 Physical processes

Electricity and magnetism

1   Pupils should be taught:

Circuits

a   how to design and construct series and parallel circuits, and how to measure current and voltage

b   that the current in a series circuit depends on the number of cells and the number and nature of other components and that current is not 'used up' by components

c   that energy is transferred from batteries and other sources to other components in electrical circuits

Magnetic fields

d   about magnetic fields as regions of space where magnetic materials experience forces, and that like magnetic poles repel and unlike poles attract

Electromagnets

e   that a current in a coil produces a magnetic field pattern similar to that of a bar magnet

f   how electromagnets are constructed and used in devices [for example, relays, lifting magnets].

Forces and motion

2   Pupils should be taught:

Force and linear motion

a   how to determine the speed of a moving object and to use the quantitative relationship between speed, distance and time

b   that the weight of an object on Earth is the result of the gravitational attraction between its mass and that of the Earth

c   that unbalanced forces change the speed or direction of movement of objects and that balanced forces produce no change in the movement of an object

d   ways in which frictional forces, including air resistance, affect motion [for example, streamlining cars, friction between tyre and road]

Force and rotation

e   that forces can cause objects to turn about a pivot

f   the principle of moments and its application to situations involving one pivot

Force and pressure

g   the quantitative relationship between force, area and pressure and its application [for example, the use of skis and snowboards, the effect of sharp blades, hydraulic brakes].

Light and sound

3   Pupils should be taught:

The behaviour of light

a   that light travels in a straight line at a finite speed in a uniform medium

b   that non-luminous objects are seen because light scattered from them enters the eye

c   how light is reflected at plane surfaces

d   how light is refracted at the boundary between two different materials

e   that white light can be dispersed to give a range of colours

f   the effect of colour filters on white light and how coloured objects appear in white light and in other colours of light

Hearing

g   that sound causes the eardrum to vibrate and that different people have different audible ranges

h   some effects of loud sounds on the ear [for example, temporary deafness]

Vibration and sound

i   that light can travel through a vacuum but sound cannot, and that light travels much faster than sound

j   the relationship between the loudness of a sound and the amplitude of the vibration causing it

k   the relationship between the pitch of a sound and the frequency of the vibration causing it.

The Earth and beyond

4   Pupils should be taught:

The solar system

a   how the movement of the Earth causes the apparent daily and annual movement of the Sun and other stars

b   the relative positions of the Earth, Sun and planets in the solar system

c   about the movements of planets around the Sun and to relate these to gravitational forces

d   that the Sun and other stars are light sources and that the planets and other bodies are seen by reflected light

e   about the use of artificial satellites and probes to observe the Earth and to explore the solar system.

Energy resources and energy transfer

5   Pupils should be taught:

Energy resources

a   about the variety of energy resources, including oil, gas, coal, biomass, food, wind, waves and batteries, and the distinction between renewable and non-renewable resources

4a, 4c, 4e → ICT opportunity
Pupils could use video or CD-ROM to study the solar system.

5a, 5c → ICT opportunity
Pupils could use the internet to find up-to-date information about energy resources.

2a → links to other subjects

This requirement builds on En1/1e and En3/9b–9d and Ma2/1g.

b   about the Sun as the ultimate source of most of the Earth's energy resources and to relate this to how coal, oil and gas are formed

c   that electricity is generated by means of a variety of energy resources

Conservation of energy

d   the distinction between temperature and heat, and that differences in temperature can lead to transfer of energy

e   ways in which energy can be usefully transferred and stored

f   how energy is transferred by the movement of particles in conduction, convection and evaporation, and that energy is transferred directly by radiation

g   that although energy is always conserved, it may be dissipated, reducing its availability as a resource.

Breadth of study

1   During the key stage, pupils should be taught the **Knowledge, skills and understanding** through:

a   a range of domestic, industrial and environmental contexts

b   considering ways in which science is applied in technological developments

c   considering the benefits and drawbacks of scientific and technological developments, including those related to the environment, health and quality of life

d   using a range of sources of information, including ICT-based sources

e   using first-hand and secondary data to carry out a range of scientific investigations, including complete investigations

f   using quantitative approaches where appropriate, including calculations based on simple relationships between physical quantities.

2   During the key stage, pupils should be taught to:

Communication

a   use scientific language, conventions and symbols, including SI units, word equations and chemical symbols, formulae and equations, where appropriate, to communicate scientific ideas and to provide scientific explanations based on evidence

Health and safety

b   recognise that there are hazards in living things, materials and physical processes, and assess risks and take action to reduce risks to themselves and others.

Programme of study: single science

Key stage 4

Knowledge, skills and understanding

Teaching should ensure that **scientific enquiry** is taught through contexts taken from the sections on **life processes and living things**, **materials and their properties** and **physical processes**.

Sc1 Scientific enquiry

Ideas and evidence in science

1 Pupils should be taught:

a   how scientific ideas are presented, evaluated and disseminated [for example, by publication, review by other scientists]

b   how scientific controversies can arise from different ways of interpreting empirical evidence [for example, Darwin's theory of evolution]

c   ways in which scientific work may be affected by the contexts in which it takes place [for example, social, historical, moral, spiritual], and how these contexts may affect whether or not ideas are accepted

d   to consider the power and limitations of science in addressing industrial, social and environmental questions, including the kinds of questions science can and cannot answer, uncertainties in scientific knowledge, and the ethical issues involved.

Investigative skills

2 Pupils should be taught to:

Planning

a   use scientific knowledge and understanding to turn ideas into a form that can be investigated, and to plan an appropriate strategy

b   decide whether to use evidence from first-hand experience or secondary sources

c   carry out preliminary work and make predictions, where appropriate

d   consider key factors that need to be taken into account when collecting evidence, and how evidence can be collected in contexts [for example, fieldwork, surveys] in which the variables cannot readily be controlled

e   decide the extent and range of data to be collected [for example, appropriate sample size for biological work] and the techniques, equipment and materials to use

Obtaining and presenting evidence

f   use a wide range of equipment and materials appropriately, and manage their working environment to ensure the safety of themselves and others

g   make observations and measurements, including the use of ICT for datalogging [for example, to monitor several variables at the same time] to a degree of precision appropriate to the context

h   make sufficient observations and measurements to reduce error and obtain reliable evidence

During key stage 4 pupils learn about a wider range of scientific ideas and consider them in greater depth, laying the foundations for further study. They explore how technological advances relate to the scientific ideas underpinning them. They consider the power and limitations of science in addressing industrial, ethical and environmental issues, and how different groups have different views about the role of science. When they carry out investigations they use a range of approaches and select appropriate reference sources, working on their own and with others. They do more quantitative work and evaluate critically the evidence collected and conclusions drawn. They communicate their ideas clearly and precisely in a variety of ways. They see how scientists work together to develop new ideas, how new theories may, at first, give rise to controversy and how social and cultural contexts may affect the extent to which theories are accepted.

Note
The general teaching requirement for health and safety applies in this subject.

1a → links to other subjects
This requirement builds on En2/1a, 1c, 1d.

2 → links to other subjects
These requirements build on En1/10a.

2d → ICT opportunity
Pupils could use data-handling software to analyse data from fieldwork.

2e → links to other subjects
This requirement builds on Ma4/2c−2e (foundation and higher).

2g, 2h → links to other subjects
These requirements build on Ma3/4a and Ma4/3a, 3b (foundation and higher).

2g → links to other subjects
This requirement builds on ICT/1.

2j → links to other subjects
This requirement builds on Ma4/4a, 4b, 4h (foundation) and Ma4/4a, 4i (higher) and ICT/3.

2k → links to other subjects
This requirement builds on Ma4/5b, 5c (foundation and higher).

2l → links to other subjects
This requirement builds on Ma2/4c (foundation) and Ma2/4b (higher).

2m–2q → links to other subjects
These requirements build on Ma4/5a–5f, 5i (foundation and higher).

i   judge the level of uncertainty in observations and measurements
    [for example, by using the variation in repeat measurements to judge the likely accuracy of the average measured value]

j   represent and communicate qualitative and quantitative data using diagrams, tables, charts, graphs and ICT

Considering evidence

k   use diagrams, tables, charts and graphs, and identify and explain patterns or relationships in data

l   present the results of calculations to an appropriate degree of accuracy

m   use observations, measurements or other data to draw conclusions

n   explain to what extent these conclusions support any prediction made, and enable further predictions to be made

o   use scientific knowledge and understanding to explain and interpret observations, measurements or other data, and conclusions

Evaluating

p   consider anomalous data giving reasons for rejecting or accepting them, and consider the reliability of data in terms of the uncertainty of measurements and observations

q   consider whether the evidence collected is sufficient to support any conclusions or interpretations made

r   suggest improvements to the methods used

s   suggest further investigations.

Sc2 Life processes and living things

Cell activity

1   Pupils should be taught:

   a   that the nucleus contains chromosomes that carry the genes

   b   how cells divide by mitosis during growth, and by meiosis to produce gametes

   c   to relate ways in which animals function as organisms to cell structure and activity.

Humans as organisms

2   Pupils should be taught:

   Nutrition

   a   the processes of digestion, including the function of organs and the role of enzymes, stomach acid and bile

   Circulation

   b   the composition and functions of blood

   Nervous system

   c   the pathway taken by impulses in response to a variety of stimuli

   d   how the reflex arc makes rapid response to a stimulus possible

   e   how the eye functions in response to light

   Hormones

   f   the way in which hormonal control occurs, including the effects of sex hormones

   g   some medical uses of hormones, including the control and promotion of fertility

   Homeostasis

   h   the importance of maintaining a constant internal environment

   i   how waste products of body functions are removed by the kidneys

   j   how the kidneys regulate the water content of the body

   k   how humans maintain a constant body temperature

   Health

   l   the defence mechanisms of the body, including the role of the skin and blood

   m   the effects of solvents, alcohol, tobacco and other drugs on body functions.

2d → ICT opportunity
Pupils could use multimedia simulation of nerve impulse.

3g → ICT opportunity
Pupils could use the internet to find out
about current developments and issues.

4a → ICT opportunity
Pupils could use spreadsheets to model
the effects of competition and predation.

Variation, inheritance and evolution

3   Pupils should be taught:

Variation

a   how variation arises from genetic causes, environmental causes, and
a combination of both

b   that sexual reproduction is a source of genetic variation, while asexual
reproduction produces clones

c   that mutation is a source of genetic variation and has a number of causes

Inheritance

d   how sex is determined in humans

e   the mechanism of monohybrid inheritance where there are dominant
and recessive alleles

f   that some diseases are inherited

g   the basic principles of cloning, selective breeding and genetic engineering

Evolution

h   that the fossil record is evidence for evolution

i   how variation and selection may lead to evolution or to extinction.

Living things in their environment

4   Pupils should be taught:

Adaptation and competition

a   how the distribution and relative abundance of organisms in habitats
can be explained using ideas of interdependence, adaptation, competition
and predation

b   how the impact of humans on the environment depends on social and
economic factors, including population size, industrial processes and levels
of consumption and waste

c   about the importance of sustainable development.

Sc3 Materials and their properties

Classifying materials

1   Pupils should be taught:

Atomic structure

a   that atoms consist of nuclei and electrons

b   about a model of the way electrons are arranged in atoms

c   how the reactions of elements depend on the arrangement of electrons
in their atoms.

Changing materials

2   Pupils should be taught:

Useful products from organic sources

a   how the mixture of substances in crude oil, most of which are
hydrocarbons, can be separated by fractional distillation

b   the use of some of the products from crude oil distillation as fuels

c   the products of burning hydrocarbons

d   how addition polymers can be formed from the products of crude
oil by cracking and polymerisation

e   some uses of addition polymers.

Patterns of behaviour

3   Pupils should be taught:

The periodic table

a   that there are approximately 100 elements and that all materials are
composed of one or more of these

b   that the periodic table shows all the elements, arranged in order
of ascending atomic number

c   the connection between the arrangement of outer electrons and the
position of an element in the periodic table

d   that elements in the same group of the periodic table have similar properties

e   how the properties of elements change gradually from the top to the
bottom of a group, illustrated by the study of at least one group

Chemical reactions

f   about different types of chemical reaction, including neutralisation,
oxidation, reduction and thermal decomposition, and examples of how
these are used to make new materials

g   to recognise patterns in chemical reactions

1b, 1c → ICT opportunity
Pupils could use software simulations to
explore models of the atom and reactions.

2b, 2c, 2e → ICT opportunity
Pupils could use the internet to find out
about products and processes.

3c–3e → ICT opportunity
Pupils could use a database of the elements
to explore patterns.

3h, 3i → ICT opportunity
Pupils could use dataloggers to analyse and evaluate reaction data.

3i → links to other subjects
This requirement builds on Ma4/5c (foundation and higher).

Rates of reaction

h   about the great variation in the rates at which different reactions take place

i   how the rates of reactions can be altered by varying temperature or concentration, or by changing the surface area of a solid reactant, or by adding a catalyst

j   how the rates of many reactions depend on the frequency and energy of collisions between particles

Reactions involving enzymes

k   how enzymes may be used in biotechnology.

Sc4 Physical processes

Electricity

1 Pupils should be taught:

Circuits

a that resistors are heated when a charge flows through them

b the qualitative effect of changing resistance on the current in a circuit

c the quantitative relationship between resistance, voltage and current

d how current varies with voltage in a range of devices [for example, resistors, filament bulbs, diodes, light dependent resistors (LDRs) and thermistors]

Mains electricity

e the difference between direct current (dc) and alternating current (ac)

f the functions of the live, neutral and earth wires in the domestic mains supply, and the use of insulation, earthing, fuses and circuit breakers to protect users of electrical equipment

g how electrical heating is used in a variety of ways in domestic contexts

h how measurements of energy transferred are used to calculate the costs of using common domestic appliances.

Waves

2 Pupils should be taught:

Characteristics of waves

a about the reflection and refraction of waves, including light and sound as examples of transverse and longitudinal waves

b the meaning of frequency, wavelength and amplitude of a wave

The electromagnetic spectrum

c that the electromagnetic spectrum includes radio waves, microwaves, infrared, visible light, ultraviolet waves, X-rays and gamma rays

d some ways in which microwaves, infrared and ultraviolet waves are used and the potential dangers of these

e some uses of X-rays and gamma rays in medicine

f that radio waves, microwaves, infrared and visible light carry information over large and small distances, including global transmission via satellites

g the difference between analogue and digital signals

Sound and ultrasound

h about sound and ultrasound waves, and some medical and other uses of ultrasound.

1c → links to other subjects
This requirement builds on Ma2/5f (foundation) and Ma2/5g (higher).

1d → links to other subjects
This requirement builds on Ma4/5c (foundation and higher).

1c, 1d → ICT opportunity
Pupils could use dataloggers to investigate relationships.

2a, 2b → ICT opportunity
Pupils could use CD-ROM software to explore wave models.

3a, 3b → ICT opportunity
Pupils could use video or CD-ROM software to simulate movements in the solar system and universe.

4b → ICT opportunity
Pupils could use a spreadsheet to model energy loss in a house.

The Earth and beyond

3   Pupils should be taught:

The solar system and the wider universe

a   the relative positions and sizes of planets, stars and other bodies in the universe [for example, comets, meteors, galaxies, black holes]

b   how gravity acts as a force throughout the universe

c   how stars evolve over a long timescale

d   about some ideas used to explain the origin and evolution of the universe

e   about the search for evidence of life elsewhere in the universe.

Energy resources and energy transfer

4   Pupils should be taught:

Energy transfer

a   how insulation is used to reduce transfer of energy from hotter to colder objects

b   about the efficient use of energy, the need for economical use of energy resources, and the environmental implications of generating energy

Electromagnetic effects

c   how simple ac generators work

d   how energy is transferred from power stations to consumers.

Radioactivity

5   Pupils should be taught:

a   that radioactivity arises from the breakdown of an unstable nucleus

b   about some sources of the ionising radiation found in all environments

c   the characteristics of alpha and beta particles and of gamma radiation

d   the beneficial and harmful effects of radiation on matter and living organisms.

Breadth of study

1   During the key stage, pupils should be taught the **Knowledge, skills and understanding** through:

a   a range of domestic, industrial and environmental contexts

b   considering ways in which science is applied in technological developments

c   considering and evaluating the benefits and drawbacks of scientific and technological developments, including those related to the environment, personal health and quality of life, and those raising ethical issues

d   using a range of sources of information, including ICT-based sources

e   using first-hand and secondary data to carry out a range of scientific investigations, including complete investigations

f   using quantitative approaches, where appropriate, including calculations based on relationships between physical quantities.

2   During the key stage, pupils should be taught to:

Communication

a   use a wide range of scientific, technical and mathematical language, symbols and conventions, including SI units, balanced chemical equations and standard form to communicate ideas and develop an argument

Health and safety

b   recognise that there are hazards in living things, materials and physical processes, and assess risks and take action to reduce risks to themselves and others.

2a → links to other subjects
This requirement builds on En1/1e and En3/9b–9d and Ma2/1f (foundation) and Ma2/1h (higher).

Programme of study: double science

Key stage 4

During key stage 4 pupils learn about a wider range of scientific ideas and consider them in greater depth, laying the foundations for further study. They explore how technological advances relate to the scientific ideas underpinning them. They consider the power and limitations of science in addressing industrial, ethical and environmental issues, and how different groups have different views about the role of science. When they carry out investigations they use a range of approaches and select appropriate reference sources, working on their own and with others. They do more quantitative work and evaluate critically the evidence collected and conclusions drawn. They communicate their ideas clearly and precisely in a variety of ways. They see how scientists work together to develop new ideas, how new theories may, at first, give rise to controversy and how social and cultural contexts may affect the extent to which theories are accepted.

Note
The general teaching requirement for health and safety applies in this subject.

1a → links to other subjects
This requirement builds on En2/1a, 1c, 1d.

2 → links to other subjects
These requirements build on En1/10a.

2d → ICT opportunity
Pupils could use data-handling software to analyse data from fieldwork.

2e → links to other subjects
This requirement builds on Ma4/2c–2e (foundation and higher).

2g, 2h → links to other subjects
These requirements build on Ma3/4a and Ma4/3a, 3b (foundation and higher).

2g → links to other subjects
This requirement builds on ICT/1.

Knowledge, skills and understanding

Teaching should ensure that **scientific enquiry** is taught through contexts taken from the sections on **life processes and living things, materials and their properties** and **physical processes.**

Sc1 Scientific enquiry

Ideas and evidence in science

1 Pupils should be taught:

a how scientific ideas are presented, evaluated and disseminated [for example, by publication, review by other scientists]

b how scientific controversies can arise from different ways of interpreting empirical evidence [for example, Darwin's theory of evolution]

c ways in which scientific work may be affected by the contexts in which it takes place [for example, social, historical, moral and spiritual], and how these contexts may affect whether or not ideas are accepted

d to consider the power and limitations of science in addressing industrial, social and environmental questions, including the kinds of questions science can and cannot answer, uncertainties in scientific knowledge, and the ethical issues involved.

Investigative skills

2 Pupils should be taught to:

Planning

a use scientific knowledge and understanding to turn ideas into a form that can be investigated, and to plan an appropriate strategy

b decide whether to use evidence from first-hand experience or secondary sources

c carry out preliminary work and make predictions, where appropriate

d consider key factors that need to be taken into account when collecting evidence, and how evidence can be collected in contexts [for example, fieldwork, surveys] in which the variables cannot readily be controlled

e decide the extent and range of data to be collected [for example, appropriate sample size for biological work], and the techniques, equipment and materials to use

Obtaining and presenting evidence

f use a wide range of equipment and materials appropriately, and manage their working environment to ensure the safety of themselves and others

g make observations and measurements, including the use of ICT for datalogging [for example, to monitor several variables at the same time] to a degree of precision appropriate to the context

h make sufficient observations and measurements to reduce error and obtain reliable evidence

i   judge the level of uncertainty in observations and measurements
[for example, by using the variation in repeat measurements to judge
the likely accuracy of the average measured value]

j   represent and communicate qualitative and quantitative data using
diagrams, tables, charts, graphs and ICT

Considering evidence

k   use diagrams, tables, charts and graphs, and identify and explain patterns
or relationships in data

l   present the results of calculations to an appropriate degree of accuracy

m use observations, measurements or other data to draw conclusions

n   explain to what extent these conclusions support any predictions made,
and enable further predictions to be made

o   use scientific knowledge and understanding to explain and interpret
observations, measurements or other data, and conclusions

Evaluating

p   consider anomalous data giving reasons for rejecting or accepting them,
and consider the reliability of data in terms of the uncertainty of
measurements and observations

q   consider whether the evidence collected is sufficient to support any
conclusions or interpretations made

r   suggest improvements to the methods used

s   suggest further investigations.

2j → links to other subjects
This requirement builds on Ma4/4a, 4b, 4h
(foundation) and Ma4/4a, 4i (higher) and ICT/3.

2k → links to other subjects
This requirement builds on Ma4/5b, 5c
(foundation and higher).

2k → ICT opportunity
Pupils could use data-handling software
to create, analyse and evaluate charts
and graphs of data.

2l → links to other subjects
This requirement builds on Ma2/4c
(foundation) and Ma2/4b (higher).

2m–2q → links to other subjects
These requirements build on Ma4/5a–5f,
5i (foundation and higher).

2d, 2h → ICT opportunity
Pupils could use multimedia sources to see
things that cannot readily be observed.

Sc2 Life processes and living things

Cell activity

1   Pupils should be taught:

    a   about similarities and differences in structure between plant and animal cells

    b   how substances enter and leave cells through the cell membrane by diffusion, osmosis and active transport

    c   that the nucleus contains chromosomes that carry the genes

    d   how cells divide by mitosis during growth, and by meiosis to produce gametes

    e   to relate ways in which animals and plants function as organisms to cell structure and activity.

Humans as organisms

2   Pupils should be taught:

    Nutrition

    a   the processes of digestion, including the function of organs and the role of enzymes, stomach acid and biles

    Circulation

    b   the structure of the human circulatory system, including the composition and functions of blood

    c   that there is an exchange of substances between capillaries and tissues

    Breathing

    d   how the structure of the thorax enables ventilation of the lungs

    Respiration

    e   that respiration may be either aerobic or anaerobic, depending on the availability of oxygen

    f   that an 'oxygen debt' may occur in muscle during vigorous exercise

    Nervous system

    g   the pathway taken by impulses in response to a variety of stimuli

    h   how the reflex arc makes rapid response to a stimulus possible

    i   how the eye functions in response to light

    Hormones

    j   the way in which hormonal control occurs, including the effects of insulin and sex hormones

    k   some medical uses of hormones, including the control and promotion of fertility and the treatment of diabetes

Homeostasis

l   the importance of maintaining a constant internal environment

m   how waste products of body functions are removed by the lungs and kidneys

n   how the kidneys regulate the water content of the body

o   how humans maintain a constant body temperature

Health

p   the defence mechanisms of the body, including the role of the skin, blood and mucous membranes of the respiratory tract

q   the effects of solvents, alcohol, tobacco and other drugs on body functions.

Green plants as organisms

3   Pupils should be taught:

Nutrition

a   the reactants in, and products of, photosynthesis

b   that the rate of photosynthesis may be limited by light intensity, carbon dioxide concentration or temperature

c   how the products of photosynthesis are utilised by the plant

d   the importance to healthy plant growth of the uptake and utilisation of mineral salts

Hormones

e   the hormonal control of plant growth and development, including commercial applications

Transport and water relations

f   how plants take up water and transpire

g   the importance of water in the support of plant tissues

h   that substances required for growth and reproduction are transported within plants.

Variation, inheritance and evolution

4   Pupils should be taught:

Variation

a   how variation arises from genetic causes, environmental causes, and a combination of both

b   that sexual reproduction is a source of genetic variation, while asexual reproduction produces clones

c   that mutation is a source of genetic variation and has a number of causes

3b → links to other subjects

This requirement builds on Ma4/5c (foundation and higher).

3b → ICT opportunity

Pupils could use dataloggers in investigations of photosynthesis.

3e → ICT opportunity

Pupils could use the internet to find information about commercial applications.

4h → ICT opportunity
Pupils could use the internet to find out about current developments and issues.

5a → ICT opportunity
Pupils could use spreadsheets to model the effects of competition and predation.

Inheritance

d how sex is determined in humans

e the mechanism of monohybrid inheritance where there are dominant and recessive alleles

f about mechanisms by which some diseases are inherited

g that the gene is a section of DNA

h the basic principles of cloning, selective breeding and genetic engineering

Evolution

i that the fossil record is evidence for evolution

j how variation and selection may lead to evolution or to extinction.

Living things in their environment

5 Pupils should be taught:

Adaptation and competition

a how the distribution and relative abundance of organisms in habitats can be explained using ideas of interdependence, adaptation, competition and predation

b how the impact of humans on the environment depends on social and economic factors, including population size, industrial processes and levels of consumption and waste

c about the importance of sustainable development

Energy and nutrient transfer

d how to describe food chains quantitatively using pyramids of biomass

e how energy is transferred through an ecosystem

f the role of microbes and other organisms in the decomposition of organic materials and in the cycling of carbon and nitrogen

g how food production and distribution systems can be managed to improve the efficiency of energy transfers.

Sc3 Materials and their properties

Classifying materials

1   Pupils should be taught:

Atomic structure

a   that atoms consist of nuclei and electrons

b   the charges and relative masses of protons, neutrons and electrons

c   about mass number, atomic number and isotopes

d   about a model of the way electrons are arranged in atoms

e   how the reactions of elements depend on the arrangement of electrons in their atoms

Bonding

f   that new substances are formed when atoms combine

g   that chemical bonding can be explained in terms of the transfer or sharing of electrons

h   how ions are formed when atoms gain or lose electrons and how giant ionic lattices are held together by the attraction between oppositely charged ions

i   how covalent bonds are formed when atoms share electrons

j   that substances with covalent bonds may form simple molecular structures or giant structures

k   ways in which the physical properties of some substances with giant structures differ from those with simple molecular structures.

Changing materials

2   Pupils should be taught:

Useful products from organic sources

a   how the mixture of substances in crude oil, most of which are hydrocarbons, can be separated by fractional distillation

b   the use of some of the products from crude oil distillation as fuels

c   the products of burning hydrocarbons

d   that alkanes are saturated hydrocarbons, and alkenes are unsaturated hydrocarbons

e   how addition polymers can be formed from the products of crude oil by cracking and polymerisation

f   some uses of addition polymers

1d, 1e → **ICT opportunity**
Pupils could use software simulations to explore models of the atom and reactions.

2b, 2c, 2f, 2g → **ICT opportunity**
Pupils could use the internet to find out about products from oil, rocks and minerals and current processes.

2n, 2o → links to other subjects
These requirements build on Ma2/3n, 4a
(foundation) and Ma2/4a (higher).

3 → ICT opportunity
Pupils could use a database of the elements
to explore patterns.

Useful products from metal ores and rocks

g   about the variety of useful substances [for example, chlorine, sodium hydroxide, glass, cement] that can be made from rocks and minerals

h   how the reactivity of a metal affects how it is extracted from its naturally occurring ores

i   an example of how a less reactive metal can be extracted by reduction with carbon or carbon monoxide

j   an example of how a metal can be purified or recycled by electrolysis

k   an example of how a reactive metal can be extracted by electrolysis

Useful products from air

l   the importance for agriculture of converting nitrogen to ammonia

m   how nitrogenous fertilisers are manufactured, their effect on plant growth, and the environmental consequences of over-use

Quantitative chemistry

n   to represent chemical reactions by balanced symbol equations and to use these to predict reacting quantities

o   to determine the formulae of simple compounds from reacting masses

Changes to the Earth and atmosphere

p   how the Earth's atmosphere and oceans have changed over time

q   how the carbon cycle helps to maintain atmospheric composition

r   how the sequence of, and evidence for, rock formation and deformation is obtained from the rock record.

Patterns of behaviour

3   Pupils should be taught:

The periodic table

a   that there are approximately 100 elements and that all materials are composed of one or more of these

b   that the periodic table shows all the elements, arranged in order of ascending atomic number

c   the connection between the arrangement of outer electrons and the position of an element in the periodic table

d   that elements in the same group of the periodic table have similar properties

e   how the properties of elements change gradually from the top to the bottom of a group

f   the properties and uses of the noble gases

g   the properties and reactions of the alkali metals

h   the properties, reactions and uses of the halogens

i   about similarities between transition metals and about the characteristic properties of their compounds

j   some uses of transition metals

Chemical reactions

k   about different types of chemical reaction, including neutralisation, oxidation, reduction and thermal decomposition, and examples of how these are used to make new materials

l   to recognise patterns in chemical reactions and use these to make predictions

m   about ways in which knowledge about chemical reactions is applied when new substances are made

Rates of reaction

n   about the great variation in the rates at which different reactions take place

o   how the rates of reactions can be altered by varying temperature or concentration, or by changing the surface area of a solid reactant, or by adding a catalyst

p   how the rates of many reactions depend on the frequency and energy of collisions between particles

Reactions involving enzymes

q   about the effect of temperature on the rates of enzyme-catalysed reactions and their dependence on pH

r   how enzymes may be used in biotechnology

Reversible reactions

s   about manufacturing processes based on reversible reactions, and how the yield of these depends on the conditions

Energy transfer in reactions

t   that changes of temperature often accompany reactions

u   that reactions can be exothermic or endothermic

v   how making and breaking chemical bonds in chemical reactions involves energy transfers.

3n, 3o → ICT opportunity
Pupils could use datalogging to analyse and evaluate reaction data.

3o → links to other subjects
This requirement builds on Ma4/5c (foundation and higher).

3r, 3s → ICT opportunity
Pupils could use the internet to find out about the use of enzymes in biotechnology and other manufacturing processes.

3s → ICT opportunity
Pupils could use simulation software to explore the effects of changing conditions.

1c, 1d, 1e → ICT opportunity
Pupils could use dataloggers to
investigate relationships.

**1c, 1e, 1f, 1j, 1o, 2a, 2b, 2d, 2f →
links to other subjects**
These requirements build on Ma2/5f
(foundation) and Ma2/5g (higher).

1d → links to other subjects
This requirement builds on Ma4/5c
(foundation and higher).

2b → ICT opportunity
Pupils could use a spreadsheet
to analyse data.

Sc4 Physical processes

Electricity

1 Pupils should be taught:

Circuits

a that resistors are heated when charge flows through them

b the qualitative effect of changing resistance on the current in a circuit

c the quantitative relationship between resistance, voltage and current

d how current varies with voltage in a range of devices [for example, resistors, filament bulbs, diodes, light dependent resistors (LDRs) and thermistors]

e that voltage is the energy transferred per unit charge

f the quantitative relationship between power, voltage and current

Mains electricity

g the difference between direct current (dc) and alternating current (ac)

h the functions of the live, neutral and earth wires in the domestic mains supply, and the use of insulation, earthing, fuses and circuit breakers to protect users of electrical equipment

i how electrical heating is used in a variety of ways in domestic contexts

j how measurements of energy transferred are used to calculate the costs of using common domestic appliances

Electric charge

k how an insulating material can be charged by friction

l about forces of attraction between positive and negative charges, and forces of repulsion between like charges

m about common electrostatic phenomena, in terms of the movement of electrons

n the uses and potential dangers of electrostatic charges generated in everyday situations [for example, in photocopiers and inkjet printers]

o the quantitative relationship between steady current, charge and time

p about electric current as the flow of charge carried by free electrons in metals or ions during electrolysis.

Forces and motion

2 Pupils should be taught:

Force and acceleration

a how distance, time and speed can be determined and represented graphically

b about factors affecting vehicle stopping distances

c the difference between speed and velocity

d that acceleration is change in velocity per unit time

e that balanced forces do not alter the velocity of a moving object

f the quantitative relationship between force, mass and acceleration

g that when two bodies interact, the forces they exert on each other are equal and opposite

Force and non-uniform motion

h   how the forces acting on falling objects change with velocity

i   why falling objects may reach a terminal velocity.

Waves

3   Pupils should be taught:

Characteristics of waves

a   about the reflection, refraction and diffraction of waves, including light and sound as examples of transverse and longitudinal waves

b   the meaning of frequency, wavelength and amplitude of a wave

c   the quantitative relationship between the speed, frequency and wavelength of a wave

d   that waves transfer energy without transferring matter

The electromagnetic spectrum

e   that the electromagnetic spectrum includes radio waves, microwaves, infrared, visible light, ultraviolet waves, X-rays and gamma rays

f   some ways in which microwaves, infrared and ultraviolet waves are used and the potential dangers of these

g   some uses of X-rays and gamma rays in medicine

h   how information can be transmitted along optical fibres

i   that radio waves, microwaves, infrared and visible light carry information over large and small distances, including global transmission via satellites

j   about ways in which reflection, refraction and diffraction affect communication

k   the difference between analogue and digital signals and how more information can be transmitted

Sound and ultrasound

l   about sound and ultrasound waves, and some medical and other uses of ultrasound

Seismic waves

m   that longitudinal and transverse earthquake waves are transmitted through the Earth, and how their travel times and paths provide evidence for the Earth's layered structure

n   that the Earth's outermost layer, the lithosphere, is composed of plates in relative motion, and that plate tectonic processes result in the formation, deformation and recycling of rocks.

2i → ICT opportunity
Pupils could use simulations to investigate falling objects.

3a–3c → ICT opportunity
Pupils could use CD-ROM software to explore wave models.

3c → links to other subjects
This requirement builds on Ma2/5f (foundation) and Ma2/5g (higher).

3n → ICT opportunity
Pupils could use simulation software to model plate tectonic processes.

4a, 4b → ICT opportunity
Pupils could use CD-ROM software to simulate movements in the solar system and the universe.

5b → ICT opportunity
Pupils could use the internet to find out about current issues relating to the use of energy sources in Britain and worldwide.

5c–5e, 5i → links to other subjects
These requirements build on Ma2/5f (foundation) and Ma2/5g (higher).

6d → ICT opportunity
Pupils could use simulations to explore half-life.

The Earth and beyond

4   Pupils should be taught:

The solar system and the wider universe

a   the relative positions and sizes of planets, stars and other bodies in the universe [for example, comets, meteors, galaxies, black holes]

b   that gravity acts as a force throughout the universe

c   how stars evolve over a long timescale

d   about some ideas used to explain the origin and evolution of the universe

e   about the search for evidence of life elsewhere in the universe.

Energy resources and energy transfer

5   Pupils should be taught:

Energy transfer

a   how insulation is used to reduce transfer of energy from hotter to colder objects

b   about the efficient use of energy, the need for economical use of energy resources, and the environmental implications of generating energy

Work, power and energy

c   the quantitative relationship between force and work

d   to calculate power in terms of the rate of working or of transferring energy

e   to calculate kinetic energy and potential energy

Electromagnetic effects

f   that a force is exerted on a current-carrying wire in a magnetic field and the application of this effect in simple electric motors

g   that a voltage is induced when a conductor cuts magnetic field lines and when the magnetic field through a coil changes

h   how simple ac generators and transformers work

i   the quantitative relationship between the voltages across the coils in a transformer and the numbers of turns in them

j   how energy is transferred from power stations to consumers.

Radioactivity

6   Pupils should be taught:

a   that radioactivity arises from the breakdown of an unstable nucleus

b   about some sources of the ionising radiation found in all environments

c   the characteristics of alpha and beta particles and of gamma radiation

d   the meaning of the term 'half-life'

e   the beneficial and harmful effects of ionising radiation on matter and living organisms

f   some uses of radioactivity, including radioactive dating of rocks.

Breadth of study

1   During the key stage, pupils should be taught the **Knowledge, skills and understanding** through:

   a   a range of domestic, industrial and environmental contexts

   b   considering ways in which science is applied in technological developments

   c   considering and evaluating the benefits and drawbacks of scientific and technological developments, including those related to the environment, personal health and quality of life, and those raising ethical issues

   d   using a range of sources of information, including ICT-based sources

   e   using first-hand and secondary data to carry out a range of scientific investigations, including complete investigations

   f   using quantitative approaches, where appropriate, including calculations based on relationships between physical quantities.

2   During the key stage, pupils should be taught to:

   Communication

   a   use a wide range of scientific, technical and mathematical language, symbols and conventions, including SI units, balanced chemical equations and standard form to communicate ideas and develop an argument

   Health and safety

   b   recognise that there are hazards in living things, materials and physical processes, and assess risks and take action to reduce risks to themselves and others.

2a → **links to other subjects**
This requirement builds on En1/1e and En3/9b–9d and Ma2/1f (foundation) and Ma2/1h (higher).

The importance of design and technology

Design and technology prepares pupils to participate in tomorrow's rapidly changing technologies. They learn to think and intervene creatively to improve quality of life. The subject calls for pupils to become autonomous and creative problem solvers, as individuals and members of a team. They must look for needs, wants and opportunities and respond to them by developing a range of ideas and making products and systems. They combine practical skills with an understanding of aesthetics, social and environmental issues, function and industrial practices. As they do so, they reflect on and evaluate present and past design and technology, its uses and effects. Through design and technology, all pupils can become discriminating and informed users of products, and become innovators.

Design

Dowel rods

Cams

Axle

Handle

and
technology

The design of an object defines its meaning and ultimately its utility. The nature of the connection between technology and people is determined by the designer.

Jonathan Ive, Apple Computer

An understanding of the technical possibilities available, together with an interest in and sensitivity to use of language, gives you the confidence to express your design ideas.

Freda Sack, Type Designer and Typographer, The Foundry

'Tell me and I forget – show me and I may remember – let me do it, and I learn.' Learning through making works!

Prue Leith, Leith's School of Food and Wine

Design and technology is about making things that people want and that work well. Creating these things is hugely exciting: it is an inventive, fun activity.

James Dyson, Chairman, Dyson Ltd

EXTENSION WORK – FURNITURE BASED ON CHOSEN INSECT

MANTIS RECLINER

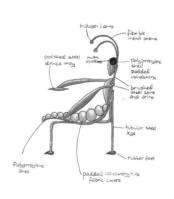

During **key stage 3** pupils use a wide range of materials to design and make products. They work out their ideas with some precision, taking into account how products will be used, who will use them, how much they cost and their appearance. They develop their understanding of designing and making by investigating products and finding out about the work of professional designers and manufacturing industry. They use computers, including computer-aided design and manufacture (CAD/CAM) and control software, as an integral part of designing and making. They draw on knowledge and understanding from other areas of the curriculum.

Note
The general teaching requirement for health and safety applies in this subject.

1a → links to other subjects
This requirement builds on En2/4a–4c and ICT/1b.

1f → links to other subjects
This requirement builds on En3/10.

1g → ICT opportunity
Pupils could use spreadsheets to model time and costs.

1h → links to other subjects
This requirement builds on ICT/3a.

2b → links to other subjects
This requirement builds on A&D/2a.

Programme of study: design and technology

Key stage 3

Knowledge, skills and understanding
Teaching should ensure that **knowledge and understanding** are applied when **developing ideas**, **planning**, **producing products** and **evaluating** them.

Developing, planning and communicating ideas
1   Pupils should be taught to:
   a   identify relevant sources of information, using a range of resources including ICT
   b   respond to design briefs and produce their own design specifications for products
   c   develop criteria for their designs to guide their thinking and to form a basis for evaluation
   d   generate design proposals that match the criteria
   e   consider aesthetics and other issues that influence their planning [for example, the needs and values of intended users, function, hygiene, safety, reliability, cost]
   f   suggest outline plans for designing and making, and change them if necessary
   g   prioritise actions and reconcile decisions as a project develops, taking into account the use of time and costs when selecting materials, components, tools, equipment and production methods
   h   use graphic techniques and ICT, including computer-aided design (CAD), to explore, develop, model and communicate design proposals [for example, using CAD software or clip-art libraries, CD-ROM and internet-based resources, or scanners and digital cameras].

Working with tools, equipment, materials and components to produce quality products
2   Pupils should be taught:
   a   to select and use tools, equipment and processes, including computer-aided design and manufacture (CAD/CAM), to shape and form materials safely and accurately and finish them appropriately [for example, using CAM software linked to a cutter/plotter, lathe, milling machine or sewing machine]
   b   to take account of the working characteristics and properties of materials and components when deciding how and when to use them
   c   to join and combine materials and ready-made components accurately to achieve functional results
   d   to make single products and products in quantity, using a range of techniques, including CAD/CAM to ensure consistency and accuracy
   e   about the working characteristics and applications of a range of modern materials, including smart materials.

Evaluating processes and products

3   Pupils should be taught to:

  a   evaluate their design ideas as these develop, and modify their proposals to ensure that their product meets the design specification

  b   test how well their products work, then evaluate them

  c   identify and use criteria to judge the quality of other people's products, including the extent to which they meet a clear need, their fitness for purpose, whether resources have been used appropriately, and their impact beyond the purpose for which they were designed [for example, the global, environmental impact of products and assessment for sustainability].

Knowledge and understanding of materials and components

4   Pupils should be taught:

  a   to consider physical and chemical properties and working characteristics of a range of common and modern materials

  b   that materials and components can be classified according to their properties and working characteristics

  c   that materials and components can be combined, processed and finished to create more useful properties and particular aesthetic effects [for example, combining different ingredients to create products with different sensory characteristics]

  d   how multiple copies can be made of the same product.

Knowledge and understanding of systems and control

5   Pupils should be taught:

  a   to recognise inputs, processes and outputs in their own and existing products

  b   that complex systems can be broken down into sub-systems to make it easier to analyse them, and that each sub-system also has inputs, processes and outputs

  c   the importance of feedback in control systems

  d   about mechanical, electrical, electronic and pneumatic control systems, including the use of switches in electrical systems, sensors in electronic switching circuits, and how mechanical systems can be joined together to create different kinds of movement

  e   how different types of systems and sub-systems can be interconnected to achieve a particular function

  f   how to use electronics, microprocessors and computers to control systems, including the use of feedback

  g   how to use ICT to design sub-systems and systems.

Note for 2e

Modern materials are those that are continually being developed through the invention of new or improved processes (for example, Teflon, optical fibres, neoprene, modified enzymes, antioxidants, genetically engineered foods, synthetic flavours, synthetic microfibres, Lycra blends, polartec, composite materials, cellular materials, carbon or Kevlar fibre).

Smart materials respond to differences in temperature or light and change in some way. They are called 'smart' because they sense conditions in their environment and respond to them. Some examples are:

- shape memory alloy (such as nitinol), which can be used to give mechanical movement when a set temperature is reached (such as to trigger a sprinkler system)

- liquid crystals in coated fabrics or thermochromic dyes, used to produce clothing that changes colour with light or temperature (such as colour change to warn of hypothermia possibility or excessive UV exposure)

- modified starches, such as starches that are chemically modified to set at high temperature and then become fluid again at low temperatures.

4a → links to other subjects

This requirement builds on Sc3/1a, 1d, 1g.

4b → ICT opportunity

Pupils could analyse materials and their properties using data-handling software.

6b → links to other subjects
This requirement builds on Ma2/1b–1d.

Note for 7c
'Compliant materials' is a broad term used to describe plastics and the full range of textiles, including some composites.

Knowledge and understanding of structures

6   Pupils should be taught:

   a   to recognise and use structures and how to support and reinforce them

   b   simple tests and appropriate calculations to work out the effect of loads

   c   that forces of compression, tension, torsion and shear produce different effects.

Breadth of study

7   During the key stage, pupils should be taught the **Knowledge, skills and understanding** through:

   a   product analysis

   b   focused practical tasks that develop a range of techniques, skills, processes and knowledge

   c   design and make assignments in different contexts. The assignments should include control systems, and work using a range of contrasting materials, including resistant materials, *compliant materials and/or food* .

Programme of study: design and technology

Key stage 4

Knowledge, skills and understanding

Teaching should ensure that **knowledge and understanding** are applied when **developing ideas**, **planning**, **producing products** and **evaluating** them.

Developing, planning and communicating ideas

1 Pupils should be taught to:

a develop and use design briefs, detailed specifications and criteria

b consider issues that affect their planning [for example, the needs and values of a range of users; moral, economic, social, cultural and environmental considerations; product maintenance; safety; the degree of accuracy needed in production]

c design for manufacturing in quantity

d produce and use detailed working schedules, setting realistic deadlines and identifying critical points

e match materials and components with tools, equipment and processes, taking account of critical dimensions and tolerances when deciding how to manufacture the product

f be flexible and adaptable in responding to changing circumstances and new opportunities

g use graphic techniques and ICT, including computer-aided design (CAD), to generate, develop, model and communicate design proposals [for example, using CAD software to generate accurate drawings and part drawings to help with manufacturing].

Working with tools, equipment, materials and components to produce quality products

2 Pupils should be taught to:

a select and use tools, equipment and processes effectively and safely to make products that match a specification

b use a range of industrial applications when working with familiar materials and processes

c manufacture single products and products in quantity, applying quality assurance techniques

d use computer-aided manufacture (CAM) in single item production and in batch or volume production [for example, using vinyl cutters, embroiderers, knitting machines, engravers, milling machines, lathes]

e simulate production and assembly lines, including the use of ICT.

During key stage 4 pupils take part in design and make projects that are linked to their own interests, industrial practice and the community. Projects may involve an enterprise activity, where pupils identify an opportunity, design to meet a need, manufacture products and evaluate the whole design and make process. Pupils use ICT to help with their work, including computer-aided design and manufacture (CAD/CAM) software, control programs and ICT-based sources for research. They consider how technology affects society and their own lives, and learn that new technologies have both advantages and disadvantages.

Note
The general teaching requirement for health and safety applies in this subject.

1d → ICT opportunity
Pupils could use spreadsheets to model schedules.

4b → ICT opportunity
Pupils could research industrial
applications on the internet.

Evaluating processes and products

3 Pupils should be taught to:

a check design proposals against design criteria, and review and modify them if necessary as they develop their product

b devise and apply tests to check the quality of their work at critical points during development

c ensure that their products are of a suitable quality for intended users [for example, how well products meet a range of considerations such as moral, cultural and environmental] and suggest modifications that would improve their performance if necessary

d recognise the difference between quality of design and quality of manufacture, and use essential criteria to judge the quality of other people's products.

Knowledge and understanding of materials and components

4 Pupils should be taught:

a how materials are cut, shaped and formed to specified tolerances

b how materials can be combined and processed to create more useful properties, and how these changed materials are used in industry

c how materials are prepared for manufacture and how pre-manufactured standard components are used

d about a variety of finishing processes, and why they are important for aesthetic and functional reasons

e that to achieve the optimum use of materials and components, they need to take into account the relationships between material, form and intended manufacturing processes.

Knowledge and understanding of systems and control

5 Pupils should be taught:

a the concepts of input, process and output, and the importance of feedback in controlling systems, including:

  i how control systems and sub-systems can be designed, used and connected to achieve different purposes

  ii how feedback is incorporated into systems

  iii how to analyse the performance of systems.

Breadth of study

6   During the key stage, pupils should be taught the **Knowledge, skills and understanding** through:

   a   product analysis

   b   focused practical tasks that develop a range of techniques, skills, processes and knowledge

   c   design and make assignments, which include activities related to industrial practices and the application of systems and control.

Robot Arm

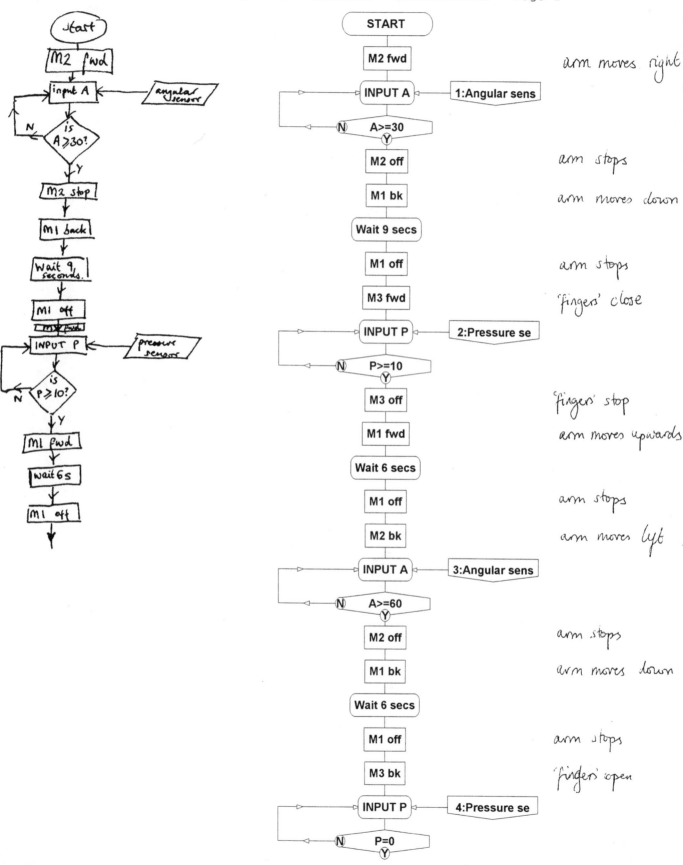

Start
- M2 fwd
- input A ← angular sensor
- is A≥30? N
- Y → M2 stop
- M1 back
- Wait 9 seconds.
- M1 off
- INPUT P ← pressure sensor
- is P≥10? N
- Y → M1 fwd
- Wait 6s
- M1 off

START
- M2 fwd — arm moves right
- INPUT A ← 1:Angular sens
- A>=30 N / Y
- M2 off — arm stops
- M1 bk — arm moves down
- Wait 9 secs
- M1 off — arm stops
- M3 fwd — 'fingers' close
- INPUT P ← 2:Pressure se
- P>=10 N / Y
- M3 off — 'fingers' stop
- M1 fwd — arm moves upwards
- Wait 6 secs
- M1 off — arm stops
- M2 bk — arm moves lyft
- INPUT A ← 3:Angular sens
- A>=60 N / Y
- M2 off — arm stops
- M1 bk — arm moves down
- Wait 6 secs
- M1 off — arm stops
- M3 bk — 'fingers' open
- INPUT P ← 4:Pressure se
- P=0 N / Y

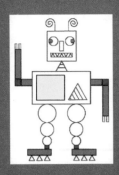

The importance of information and communication technology

Information and communication technology (ICT) prepares pupils to participate in a rapidly changing world in which work and other activities are increasingly transformed by access to varied and developing technology. Pupils use ICT tools to find, explore, analyse, exchange and present information responsibly, creatively and with discrimination.

They learn how to employ ICT to enable rapid access to ideas and experiences from a wide range of people, communities and cultures. Increased capability in the use of ICT promotes initiative and independent learning, with pupils being able to make informed judgements about when and where to use ICT to best effect, and to consider its implications for home and work both now and in the future.

Information and communication technology

ICT has enormous potential not just for a National Curriculum. It will change the way we learn as well as the way we work.

Chris Yapp, ICL Fellow for Lifelong Learning

The modern world requires new skills. Understanding ICT and, more importantly, being able to apply it to the problems we face is one of the most important. Increasingly ICT will be vital for our individual prospects and for our economy's future.

Lord Dennis Stevenson, Prime Minister's Adviser on ICT and Education

ICT expands horizons by shrinking worlds.

David Brown, Chairman, Motorola Ltd

With scientific method, we took things apart to see how they work. Now with computers we can put things back together to see how they work, by modelling complex, interrelated processes, even life itself. This is a new age of discovery, and ICT is the gateway.

Douglas Adams, Author

Programme of study: information and communication technology

Key stage 3

During key stage 3 pupils become increasingly independent users of ICT tools and information sources. They have a better understanding of how ICT can help their work in other subjects and develop their ability to judge when and how to use ICT and where it has limitations. They think about the quality and reliability of information, and access and combine increasing amounts of information. They become more focused, efficient and rigorous in their use of ICT, and carry out a range of increasingly complex tasks.

Note
The general teaching requirement for health and safety applies in this subject.

1b → links to other subjects
This requirement builds on En2/1a, 1b.

3a → links to other subjects
This requirement builds on En2/4.

Knowledge, skills and understanding

Finding things out

1 Pupils should be taught:

a   to be systematic in considering the information they need and to discuss how it will be used

b   how to obtain information well matched to purpose by selecting appropriate sources, using and refining search methods and questioning the plausibility and value of the information found

c   how to collect, enter, analyse and evaluate quantitative and qualitative information, checking its accuracy [for example, carrying out a survey of local traffic, analysing data gathered in fieldwork].

Developing ideas and making things happen

2 Pupils should be taught:

a   to develop and explore information, solve problems and derive new information for particular purposes [for example, deriving totals from raw data, reaching conclusions by exploring information]

b   how to use ICT to measure, record, respond to and control events by planning, testing and modifying sequences of instructions [for example, using automatic weather stations, datalogging in fieldwork and experiments, using feedback to control devices]

c   how to use ICT to test predictions and discover patterns and relationships, by exploring, evaluating and developing models and changing their rules and values

d   to recognise where groups of instructions need repeating and to automate frequently used processes by constructing efficient procedures that are fit for purpose [for example, templates and macros, control procedures, formulae and calculations in spreadsheets].

Exchanging and sharing information

3 Pupils should be taught:

a   how to interpret information and to reorganise and present it in a variety of forms that are fit for purpose [for example, information about a charitable cause presented in a leaflet for a school fundraising event]

b   to use a range of ICT tools efficiently to draft, bring together and refine information and create good-quality presentations in a form that is sensitive to the needs of particular audiences and suits the information content

c   how to use ICT, including e-mail, to share and exchange information effectively [for example, web publishing, video conferencing].

Reviewing, modifying and evaluating work as it progresses

4   Pupils should be taught to:

a   reflect critically on their own and others' uses of ICT to help them develop and improve their ideas and the quality of their work

b   share their views and experiences of ICT, considering the range of its uses and talking about its significance to individuals, communities and society

c   discuss how they might use ICT in future work and how they would judge its effectiveness, using relevant technical terms

d   be independent and discriminating when using ICT.

Breadth of study

5   During the key stage, pupils should be taught the **Knowledge, skills and understanding** through:

a   working with a range of information to consider its characteristics, structure, organisation and purposes [for example, using database, spreadsheet and presentation software to manage membership and finances of a club and present the annual report]

b   working with others to explore a variety of information sources and ICT tools in a variety of contexts

c   designing information systems and evaluating and suggesting improvements to existing systems [for example, evaluating a web site or researching, designing and producing a multimedia presentation for a science topic]

d   comparing their use of ICT with its use in the wider world.

Programme of study: information and communication technology

Key stage 4

During key stage 4 pupils become more responsible for choosing and using ICT tools and information sources. They use a wide range of ICT applications confidently and effectively, and are able to work independently much of the time. They choose and design ICT systems to suit particular needs and may design and implement systems for other people to use. They work with others to carry out and evaluate their work.

Notes
The general teaching requirement for health and safety applies in this subject. This programme of study aligns with the key skills unit for IT.

Knowledge, skills and understanding

Finding things out
1 Pupils should be taught:
  a how to analyse the requirements of tasks, taking into account the information they need and the ways they will use it
  b to be discriminating in their use of information sources and ICT tools.

Developing ideas and making things happen
2 Pupils should be taught to:
  a use ICT to enhance their learning and the quality of their work
  b use ICT effectively to explore, develop and interpret information and solve problems in a variety of subjects and contexts
  c apply, as appropriate, the concepts and techniques of using ICT to measure, record, respond to, control and automate events
  d apply, as appropriate, the concepts and techniques of ICT-based modelling, considering their advantages and limitations against other methods.

Exchanging and sharing information
3 Pupils should be taught to:
  a use information sources and ICT tools effectively to share, exchange and present information in a variety of subjects and contexts
  b consider how the information found and developed using ICT should be interpreted and presented in forms that are sensitive to the needs of particular audiences, fit for purpose and suit the information content.

Reviewing, modifying and evaluating work as it progresses
4 Pupils should be taught to:
  a evaluate the effectiveness of their own and others' uses of information sources and ICT tools, using the results to improve the quality of their work and to inform future judgements
  b reflect critically on the impact of ICT on their own and others' lives, considering the social, economic, political, legal, ethical and moral issues [for example, changes to working practices, the economic impact of e-commerce, the implications of personal information gathered, held and exchanged using ICT]
  c use their initiative to find out about and exploit the potential of more advanced or new ICT tools and information sources [for example, new sites on the internet, new or upgraded application software].

Breadth of study

5   During the key stage, pupils should be taught the **Knowledge, skills and understanding** through:

   a   tackling demanding problems in a wide variety of contexts, including work in other subjects

   b   using a range of information sources and ICT tools to improve efficiency and extend capability

   c   working with others to explore, develop and pass on information

   d   designing information systems and evaluating and suggesting improvements to existing systems, with use by others in mind [for example, designing an integrated system for running a school production or a small company]

   e   comparing their use of ICT with its use in the wider world.

6   Pupils should be taught to be independent, responsible, effective and reflective in their selection, development and use of information sources and ICT tools to support their work, including application in other areas of their study and in other contexts [for example, work experience, community activity].

7   Pupils should be taught to integrate the four aspects of the **Knowledge, skills and understanding** in their work with ICT.

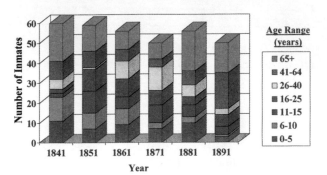

A Graph Showing the Ages of Inmates at the Workhouse From Census Data (1841-1891)

History

History is made by people. When you understand people, you can live a full life.

Charles Miller Smith, Chairman, Imperial Chemical Industries PLC

History adds colour to the curriculum. It tells you about how the princes and the people fit together – or fight. That's life itself. If you miss out on that, you miss out on some of the most exotic, colourful characters you'll have the chance to learn about at school.

Brian Walden, Author and Television Presenter

History is an unusual discipline. Its core is hard fact that you cannot get away from and have to learn to master. At the same time you have to be deductive, perceptive and imaginative in the use of that fact.

Dr Christine Carpenter, University of Cambridge

How do you know who you are unless you know where you've come from? How can you tell what's going to happen, unless you know what's happened before? History isn't just about the past. It's about why we are who we are – and about what's next.

Tony Robinson, Actor and Television Presenter

The importance of history

History fires pupils' curiosity about the past in Britain and the wider world. Pupils consider how the past influences the present, what past societies were like, how these societies organised their politics, and what beliefs and cultures influenced people's actions. As they do this, pupils develop a chronological framework for their knowledge of significant events and people. They see the diversity of human experience, and understand more about themselves as individuals and members of society. What they learn can influence their decisions about personal choices, attitudes and values. In history, pupils find evidence, weigh it up and reach their own conclusions. To do this they need to be able to research, sift through evidence, and argue for their point of view – skills that are prized in adult life.

The graph shows us that in 1841 just over one third of the population of Ringwood Workhouse were children aged between 0 and 15 years of age.

This figure slowly declines to about a third in 1881 and then drops significantly to about one sixth of the total population of the workhouse.

This could just be a one off, however, as there is no data from any further censuses to show that the trend continued to be so low.

During key stage 3 pupils learn about significant individuals and events in the history of Britain from the Middle Ages to the twentieth century. They also learn about key aspects of European and world history. They show their understanding by making connections between events and changes in the different periods and areas studied, and by comparing the structure of societies and economic, cultural and political developments. They evaluate and use sources of information, using their historical knowledge to analyse the past and explain how it can be represented and interpreted in different ways.

Note for 3
People represent and interpret the past in many different ways, including: in pictures, plays, films, reconstructions, museum displays, and fictional and non-fiction accounts. Interpretations reflect the circumstances in which they are made, the available evidence, and the intentions of those who make them (for example, writers, archaeologists, historians, film-makers).

4a → links to other subjects
This requirement builds on En1/2 and En2/1a–1f, 4, 5 and ICT/1a–1c.

4b → ICT opportunity
Pupils could use a spreadsheet or a data file of information about an historical event to search and analyse patterns, for example, mortality rates.

5c → links to other subjects
This requirement builds on En1/1, 3 and En3/1e–1o.

Programme of study: history
Key stage 3

Knowledge, skills and understanding

Chronological understanding
1   Pupils should be taught to recognise and make appropriate use of dates, vocabulary and conventions that describe historical periods and the passing of time.

Knowledge and understanding of events, people and changes in the past
2   Pupils should be taught:
   a   to describe and analyse the relationships between the characteristic features of the periods and societies studied including the experiences and range of ideas, beliefs and attitudes of men, women and children in the past
   b   about the social, cultural, religious and ethnic diversity of the societies studied, both in Britain and the wider world
   c   to analyse and explain the reasons for, and results of, the historical events, situations and changes in the periods studied
   d   to identify trends, both within and across different periods, and links between local, British, European and world history
   e   to consider the significance of the main events, people and changes studied.

Historical interpretation
3   Pupils should be taught:
   a   how and why historical events, people, situations and changes have been interpreted in different ways
   b   to evaluate interpretations.

Historical enquiry
4   Pupils should be taught to:
   a   identify, select and use a range of appropriate sources of information including oral accounts, documents, printed sources, the media, artefacts, pictures, photographs, music, museums, buildings and sites, and ICT-based sources as a basis for independent historical enquiries
   b   evaluate the sources used, select and record information relevant to the enquiry and reach conclusions.

Organisation and communication
5   Pupils should be taught to:
   a   recall, prioritise and select historical information
   b   accurately select and use chronological conventions and historical vocabulary appropriate to the periods studied to organise historical information
   c   communicate their knowledge and understanding of history, using a range of techniques, including spoken language, structured narratives, substantiated explanations and the use of ICT.

Breadth of study

6   During the key stage, pupils should be taught the **Knowledge, skills and understanding** through three British studies, a European study and two world studies.

7   In their study of local, British, European and world history, pupils should be taught about:

  a   significant events, people and changes from the recent and more distant past

  b   history from a variety of perspectives including political, religious, social, cultural, aesthetic, economic, technological and scientific

  c   aspects of the histories of England, Ireland, Scotland and Wales where appropriate

  d   the history of Britain in its European and wider world context

  e   some aspects in overview and others in depth.

Britain 1066–1500

8   A study of major features of Britain's medieval past: the development of the monarchy, and significant events and characteristic features of the lives of people living throughout the British Isles, including the local area if appropriate.

Britain 1500–1750

9   A study of crowns, parliaments and people: the major political, religious and social changes affecting people throughout the British Isles, including the local area if appropriate.

Examples for 8: Britain 1066–1500

The development of the monarchy and significant events: the Norman Conquest including the Battle of Hastings; the Domesday survey; Matilda and Stephen; Henry II and Thomas Becket; Richard I, Salah ad-Din and the Crusades; John and the Magna Carta; John in Ireland; Edward I in Wales and Edward III in Scotland; the Black Death; the Peasants' Revolt; Henry V, Henry VI, Joan of Arc and the Hundred Years' War; the Wars of the Roses.

Characteristic features of life: the structure of medieval society; the influence of communities of monks and nuns; towns, guilds and charters; the Jews, Hansards and Staplers and overseas trade; religious and secular art and architecture; the impact of the written and printed word including monastic writings; life as reflected in the work of Geoffrey Chaucer and the Paston letters.

Examples for 9: Britain 1500–1750

Political and religious changes: reformation and religious settlement; relations with other European countries in the sixteenth century; the Plantations in Ireland; religious persecution and the voyage of the Pilgrim Fathers; Charles I and the Civil Wars; Oliver Cromwell and the Commonwealth including relations with Scotland and Ireland; Charles II and the Restoration; Mary, William III and the Glorious Revolution; Queen Anne, Marlborough and Blenheim; the effects of the Acts of Union on Wales; relations between England and Scotland, the impact of the Treaty of Union and the Jacobite rebellions.

Social changes: the Elizabethan poor laws; the foundation and fortunes of the East India Company; the changing role of women; the rebuilding of London; life in restoration London; law and order; advances in medicine and surgery including the work of William Harvey; the founding of the Royal Society and the scientific discoveries of Isaac Newton, Robert Boyle and Edmund Halley; developments in the arts and architecture.

Note for Breadth of study

Not all of the aspects of the **Knowledge, skills and understanding** need be developed in each study.

Note for 7e

An overview study could consider the main issues within a period or across periods and identify and analyse links and trends.

An in-depth study could consider events, people or changes in detail, for example, analysing the reasons for an event, its consequences, different interpretations of its significance, and links with other events or changes.

Britain 1750–1900

10 A study of how expansion of trade and colonisation, industrialisation and political changes affected the United Kingdom, including the local area.

A European study before 1914

11 A study of a significant period *or* event in the pre-history or history of Europe.

A world study before 1900

12 A study of the cultures, beliefs and achievements of an African, American, Asian *or* Australasian society in the past (other than those included in the programme of study for key stage 2).

A world study after 1900

13 A study of some of the significant individuals, events and developments from across the twentieth century, including the two World Wars, the Holocaust, the Cold War, and their impact on Britain, Europe and the wider world.

Examples for 10: Britain 1750–1900

Expansion of trade and colonisation: the American Revolution; the Napoleonic Wars and the role of Nelson and Wellington; the development of Empire and colonial rule in India, South-East Asia or Africa; the Opium Wars in China.

Industrialisation: industrialisation in the local area; changes in agriculture and rural life; the development of legislation to improve working and living conditions; the role of scientists and inventors such as Edward Jenner, Humphry Davy, James Watt, Michael Faraday, Mary Somerville, Charles Darwin; the impact of industrialisation on cultural developments such as the works of William Hogarth, J M W Turner, Jane Austen, Charles Dickens, George Eliot; Gustav Holst, Henry Wood, William Gilbert and Arthur Sullivan.

Political changes: the abolition of slavery and the slave trade in the British Empire, and the work of reformers such as William Wilberforce and Olaudah Equiano; Chartism; the extension of the franchise; the development of political parties; relations between Ireland and Britain; the role of political leaders such as: Queen Victoria, Robert Peel, William Gladstone, Benjamin Disraeli; the role of reformers such as John Howard and Elizabeth Garret.

Examples for 11: European study before 1914

Periods: the Neolithic Revolution; the Roman Empire; Europe in the time of Charlemagne; astronomy, navigation, exploration and trade in the early modern period; Spain under Philip II; the Dutch Republic in the seventeenth century; the Ottoman Empire in the sixteenth and seventeenth centuries; France at the time of the Sun King; the reign of Peter the Great.

Events: the Crusades against Islam; the Italian Renaissance; Reformation and Counter-Reformation in the sixteenth century; the Thirty Years War; the French Revolution and the Napoleonic era; the revolutions of 1848; German and Italian Unification; European imperialism in the nineteenth century.

Examples for 12: a world study before 1900

Societies in the past: Islamic civilisations (seventh to sixteenth centuries); the Qin Dynasty in China; Imperial China from the First Emperor to Kublai Khan; the Manchu invasion and the fall of the Ming dynasty; India from the Mughal Empire to the coming of the British; the civilisations of Peru; indigenous peoples of North America; black peoples of the Americas; the West African empires; Japan under the Shoguns; Tokugawa Japan; the Phoenicians; the Maoris; Muhammad and Makkah; the empires of Islam in Africa; the Sikhs and the Mahrattas; the Zulu kingdoms.

Examples for 13: a world study after 1900

Individuals: Winston Churchill; Adolf Hitler; Joseph Stalin; Benito Mussolini; Franklin Roosevelt; Mahatma Gandhi; Mao Zedong; Martin Luther King.

Events: the Western Front in the First World War; the Russian Revolution; the Depression and the New Deal in the USA; the rise of National Socialism in Germany; the emergence of Japan as a major world power; the partition of Ireland and its impact; the rise of modern China; the Vietnam War; the fall of the Berlin Wall.

Developments: the changing role and status of women; the extension of the franchise in Britain and the work of reformers such as Christabel and Emmeline Pankhurst; the Welfare State; the origins and role of the United Nations, including the UN Charter and Universal Declaration of Human Rights; the break up of the overseas empires of European countries; the origins and development of the Commonwealth and its impact; the development of the European Union; the impact on the lives of people in different parts of the world of changes in the arts, communications, science and technology, such as the work of Marie Curie, Albert Einstein, and of James Watson, Francis Crick, Rosalind Franklin and Maurice Wilkins on the structure of DNA.

Geography brings theory down to earth. And in a world where 80 per cent of information is referenced to locations, it develops spatial awareness.

Dr Rita Gardner, Director and Secretary, Royal Geographical Society
(with the Institute of British Geographers)

What is our knowledge worth if we know nothing about the world that sustains us, nothing about natural systems and climate, nothing about other countries and cultures?

Jonathon Porritt, Forum for the Future

What other subject tells us so much about the great issues of the age – global change, natural and human?

Professor Andrew Goudie, University of Oxford

Geography makes us aware that we must think globally.

Bill Giles OBE, Head, BBC Weather

Geography

The importance of geography

Geography provokes and answers questions about the natural and human worlds, using different scales of enquiry to view them from different perspectives. It develops knowledge of places and environments throughout the world, an understanding of maps, and a range of investigative and problem-solving skills both inside and outside the classroom. As such, it prepares pupils for adult life and employment. Geography is a focus within the curriculum for understanding and resolving issues about the environment and sustainable development. It is also an important link between the natural and social sciences. As pupils study geography, they encounter different societies and cultures. This helps them realise how nations rely on each other. It can inspire them to think about their own place in the world, their values, and their rights and responsibilities to other people and the environment.

THE STEAMING RAIN,
THE HOT BLINDING SUN,
HE RICH GREEN TREES, THE BEAUTIFUL
ADLY CREATURES, THE CIRCLING BIRDS IN
THE RICH COLOURED EXOTIC PLANTS, BEAUTIFUL ORCHIDS,
PLANT, EVERY PLANT HAS A USE, THE NIGHT HUNTER
REY, THE EXOTIC FISH SWIM IN THE WARM WATER,
ING FROM TREES, SOME PEOPLE DESTROY THE RAINFOREST,
PROTECT THE RAINFOREST, TRY TO SAVE THE RAINFOREST,
THE RAINFOREST, TRY TO SAVE THE RAINFOREST,
IVILIZATIONS ARE DISAPPEARING, NUTRIENTS
ROYED BY FIRE, THE TREES GIVE OXYGEN
RLD TO BREATHE, THE RAIN COMES DOWN
TREES HELP SHELTER THE PEOPLE
EATURES. PEOPLE STEAL IRON AND
T AWAY BY TRAIN, THE MOUNTAINS
GROW INCREASINGLY SMALLER,
THE FOREST BURNS IN PLACES,
THERE COULD BE PRECIOUS
GOLD HIDDEN, MENDEZ
WAS MURDERED FOR
TRYING TO PROTECT
THE RAINFOREST, HE
IS NOW A SYMBOL,
TRY TO SAVE THE
RAINFOREST, TRY
TO SAVE THE
RAINFOREST, TRY
TO SAVE THE
RAINFOREST

THE AMAZON

Programme of study: geography

Key stage 3

During key stage 3 pupils investigate a wide range of people, places and environments at different scales around the world. They learn about geographical patterns and processes and how political, economic, social and environmental factors affect contemporary geographical issues. They also learn about how places and environments are interdependent. They carry out geographical enquiry inside and outside the classroom. In doing this they identify geographical questions, collect and analyse written and statistical evidence, and develop their own opinions. They use a wide range of geographical skills and resources such as maps, satellite images and ICT.

1c → links to other subjects
This requirement builds on Ma4/1a, 3a, 3b.

1c → ICT opportunity
Pupils could use a digital camera to record appropriate images to support fieldwork.

1d → links to other subjects
This requirement builds on Ma4/1a, 4a, 5a–5c, 5f and ICT/1c.

1f → links to other subjects
This requirement builds on En1/1a–1e and En3/1.

Note for 2
Geographical skills are developed in the context of geographical enquiry.

Note for 2b
Fieldwork techniques are developed during fieldwork investigations outside the classroom.

2c, 2e → links to other subjects
These requirements build on Ma3/3d, 3e.

2d → links to other subjects
This requirement builds on En2/1a–1e, 4a–4c.

Knowledge, skills and understanding

Teaching should ensure that **geographical enquiry and skills** are used when developing **knowledge and understanding of places, patterns and processes**, and **environmental change and sustainable development**.

Geographical enquiry and skills

1   In undertaking geographical enquiry, pupils should be taught to:

a   ask geographical questions [for example, 'How and why is this landscape changing?', 'What is the impact of the changes?', 'What do I think about them?'] and to identify issues

b   suggest appropriate sequences of investigation [for example, gathering views and factual evidence about a local issue and using them to reach a conclusion]

c   collect, record and present evidence [for example, statistical information about countries, data about river channel characteristics]

d   analyse and evaluate evidence and draw and justify conclusions [for example, analysing statistical data, maps and graphs, evaluating publicity leaflets that give different views about a planning issue]

e   appreciate how people's values and attitudes [for example, about overseas aid], including their own, affect contemporary social, environmental, economic and political issues, and to clarify and develop their own values and attitudes about such issues

f   communicate in ways appropriate to the task and audience [for example, by using desktop publishing to produce a leaflet, drawing an annotated sketch map, producing persuasive or discursive writing about a place].

2   In developing geographical skills, pupils should be taught:

a   to use an extended geographical vocabulary [for example, drainage basin, urban regeneration]

b   to select and use appropriate fieldwork techniques [for example, land-use survey, datalogging] and instruments [for example, cameras]

c   to use atlases and globes, and maps and plans at a range of scales, including Ordnance Survey 1:25,000 and 1:50,000 maps

d   to select and use secondary sources of evidence, including photographs (including vertical and oblique aerial photographs), satellite images and evidence from ICT-based sources [for example, from the internet]

e   to draw maps and plans at a range of scales, using symbols, keys and scales [for example, annotated sketch maps] and to select and use appropriate graphical techniques to present evidence on maps and diagrams [for example, pie charts, choropleth maps], including using ICT [for example, using mapping software to plot the distribution of shops and services in a town centre] f   to communicate in different ways, including using ICT [for example, by writing a report about an environmental issue, exchanging fieldwork data using e-mail]

g   decision-making skills, including using ICT [for example, by using a spreadsheet to help find the best location for a superstore].

Knowledge and understanding of places

3   Pupils should be taught:

a   the location of places and environments studied, places and environments in the news and other significant places and environments [for example, those listed on pages 160 and 161]

b   to describe the national, international and global contexts of places studied [for example, on the Pacific Rim, a member of the European Union]

c   to describe and explain the physical and human features that give rise to the distinctive character of places

d   to explain how and why changes happen in places, and the issues that arise from these changes

e   to explain how places are interdependent [for example, through trade, aid, international tourism, acid rain], and to explore the idea of global citizenship.

Knowledge and understanding of patterns and processes

4   Pupils should be taught to:

a   describe and explain patterns of physical and human features and relate these to the character of places and environments

b   identify, describe and explain physical and human processes, and their impact on places and environments.

Knowledge and understanding of environmental change and sustainable development

5   Pupils should be taught to:

a   describe and explain environmental change [for example, deforestation, soil erosion] and recognise different ways of managing it

b   explore the idea of sustainable development and recognise its implications for people, places and environments and for their own lives.

2f → links to other subjects
This requirement builds on ICT/3b.

Note for 3a
This develops pupils' framework of locational knowledge. Places they study could include those studied in other subjects (for example, Germany or France in modern foreign languages).

Note for 3b, 3e
These develop pupils' understanding of global citizenship, which includes awareness of what it means to be a citizen in the local community and of the United Kingdom, Europe and the wider world.

5a → ICT opportunity
Pupils could use the internet to obtain Earth observation, satellite and other information about rainforest depletion and sustainable use.

Note for 6a

If the United Kingdom is one of the countries selected for study, the contexts chosen for the studies of themes should ensure an appropriate range of study.

Note for 6b–6k

The 10 geographical themes may be taught separately, in combination with other themes, or as parts of studies of places. However they are combined, the study of themes should always be set within the context of real places.

6b → ICT opportunity

Pupils could use the internet to access resources that explain and explore tectonic processes.

6c → links to other subjects

This requirement builds on Sc3/2d, 2f.

6d → ICT opportunity

Pupils could use an automatic weather station for datalogging weather information for comparison with similar data from other places.

Note for 6e

A biome is a global-scale community of plants and animals that exists in relative equilibrium with its environment.

6g → ICT opportunity

Pupils could collect information from ICT-based sources about different settlements and select and revise some of this for a report, using presentation software.

Breadth of study

6 During the key stage, pupils should be taught the **Knowledge, skills and understanding** through the study of two countries and 10 themes:

Countries

a two countries in significantly different states of economic development, including:

　i　the regional differences that exist in each country and their causes and consequences

　ii　how and why each country may be judged to be more or less developed

Themes

b tectonic processes and their effects on landscapes and people, including:

　i　the global distribution of tectonic activity and its relationship with the boundaries of plates

　ii　the nature, causes and effects of earthquakes *or* volcanic eruptions

　iii　human responses to the hazards associated with them

c geomorphological processes and their effects on landscapes and people, including:

　i　the processes responsible for the development of selected landforms and the role of rock type and weathering

　ii　the causes and effects of a hazard [for example, flooding, landslides], and human responses to it

d how and why weather and climate vary, including:

　i　the differences between 'weather' and 'climate'

　ii　the components and links in the water cycle

　iii　how and why aspects of weather and climate vary from place to place

e ecosystems – how physical and human processes influence vegetation, including:

　i　the characteristics and distribution of one major biome [for example, savannah grassland, tropical rainforest, temperate forest]

　ii　how the ecosystems of this biome are related to climate, soil and human activity

f population distribution and change, including:

　i　the global distribution of population

　ii　the causes and effects of changes in the population of regions and countries, including migration

　iii　the interrelationship between population and resources

g the changing characteristics of settlements, including:

　i　the reasons for the location, growth and nature of individual settlements

　ii　how and why the provision of goods and services in settlements varies

　iii　how and why changes in the functions of settlements occur and how these changes affect groups of people in different ways

　iv　patterns and changes in urban land use

h changing distribution of economic activity and its impact, including:

   i types and classifications of economic activity

   ii the geographical distribution of one or more economic activities [for example, farming, tourism]

   iii how and why the distribution has changed and is changing [for example, the impact of new technologies], and the effects of such changes

i development, including:

   i ways of identifying differences in development within and between countries

   ii effects of differences in development on the quality of life of different groups of people

   iii factors, including the interdependence of countries, that influence development

j environmental issues, including:

   i how conflicting demands on an environment arise

   ii how and why attempts are made to plan and manage environments

   iii effects of environmental planning and management on people, places and environments [for example, managing coastal retreat, building a reservoir]

k resource issues, including:

   i the sources and supply of a resource

   ii the effects on the environment of the use of a resource

   iii resource planning and management [for example, reducing energy use, developing alternative energy sources].

7 In their study of countries and themes, pupils should:

a study at a range of scales – local, regional, national, international and global

b study different parts of the world and different types of environments, including their local area, the United Kingdom, the European Union and parts of the world in different states of economic development

c carry out fieldwork investigations outside the classroom

d study issues of topical significance.

6h → ICT opportunity
Pupils could consider the increase in 'telecommuting' and its impact on the distribution of economic activities.

6j → ICT opportunity
Pupils could use a speadsheet to collate transport management information and graph the findings.

Note for 7b
The study of places and themes in the United Kingdom and European Union contributes towards pupils' broader knowledge and understanding of the geography of the United Kingdom and of the European Union.

Exemplar maps showing this information can be found on the National Curriculum web site (www.nc.uk.net) and in the schemes of work for geography.

Locational knowledge – examples of significant places and environments

British Isles	Significant places and environments
The two largest islands of the British Isles	Great Britain, Ireland
The two countries of the British Isles	The United Kingdom, the Republic of Ireland
Parts of the United Kingdom	England, Scotland, Wales, Northern Ireland
Capital cities	London, Dublin, Edinburgh, Cardiff, Belfast
The six largest cities (apart from the capital cities)	Birmingham, Glasgow, Leeds, Liverpool, Manchester, Newcastle
Four other important regional cities selected on the basis of population and regional spread	Bristol, Norwich, Nottingham, Sheffield
The six largest mountain areas in the United Kingdom	The Cambrian Mountains, the Grampian Mountains, the Lake District, the North West Highlands, the Pennines, the Southern Uplands
The three longest rivers in the United Kingdom	River Severn, River Thames, River Trent
The seas around the United Kingdom	The English Channel, the Irish Sea, the North Sea

Europe	Significant places and environments
The two countries of the British Isles	The United Kingdom, the Republic of Ireland
The six countries in Europe with the highest populations and their capital cities	France, Germany, Italy, Poland, Spain, Ukraine; Paris, Berlin, Rome, Warsaw, Madrid, Kiev
The six countries in Europe with the largest areas and their capital cities	France, Germany, Norway, Spain, Sweden, Ukraine; Paris, Berlin, Oslo, Madrid, Stockholm, Kiev
The six countries in Europe with the highest population density (excluding very small countries) and their capital cities	Belgium, Germany, Italy, Luxembourg, Netherlands, Switzerland; Brussels, Berlin, Rome, Luxembourg, Amsterdam*, Bern
Other European Union member countries not included above and their capital cities	Austria, Denmark, Finland, Greece, Portugal; Vienna, Copenhagen, Helsinki, Athens, Lisbon
The largest mountain range in Europe	The Alps
The two longest rivers in West and Central Europe	River Danube and River Rhine
The four largest seas around Europe	The Baltic Sea, the Black Sea, the Mediterranean Sea, the North Sea

* Amsterdam is the capital of the Netherlands; The Hague is the seat of government.

The world	Significant places and environments
The continents	Africa, Asia, Europe, North America, Oceania, South America, Antarctica
Two countries from each continent on the basis of population, area, gross national product (GNP), population density	Nigeria, South Africa, China, India, France, Germany, Canada, USA, Australia, New Zealand, Argentina, Brazil
Five other countries on the basis of population, area and population density	Bangladesh, Indonesia, Japan, Pakistan, Russia
Areas of family origin of the main minority ethnic groups in the United Kingdom	Bangladesh, the Caribbean, India, Pakistan, the Republic of Ireland
Cities with the highest population in each continent	Lagos, Tokyo, Paris, New York, Sydney, Sao Paulo
The nine largest world cities (apart from those identified above)	Beijing, Bombay (Mumbai), Buenos Aires, Calcutta (Kolkata), Jakarta, Los Angeles, Mexico City, Seoul, Shanghai
The three largest mountain ranges in the world (on the basis of height and geographical extent)	The Andes, the Himalayas, the Rocky Mountains
The four longest rivers in the world	River Amazon, River Mississippi, River Nile, River Yangtse
The largest desert in the world	The Sahara
The oceans Two canals linking seas and/or oceans	The Arctic, Atlantic, Indian and Pacific Oceans The Panama Canal, the Suez Canal
Main lines of latitude and meridian of longitude	The Poles, the Equator, the Tropics, the Antarctic and Arctic Circles, the Prime Meridian, the International Date Line

The importance of modern foreign languages
Through the study of a foreign language, pupils understand and appreciate different countries, cultures, people and communities – and as they do so, begin to think of themselves as citizens of the world as well as of the United Kingdom. Pupils also learn about the basic structures of language. They explore the similarities and differences between the foreign language they are learning and English or another language, and learn how language can be manipulated and applied in different ways. Their listening, reading and memory skills improve, and their speaking and writing become more accurate. The development of these skills, together with pupils' knowledge and understanding of the structure of language, lay the foundations for future study of other languages.

Modern foreign languages

Ma Jolie Tartine

Ô ma jolie tartine
Comme je t'adore!
Tu es une tranche de pain
Au beurre et à la confiture.

Je vais garder ma tartine pour l'éternité
Tous les jours, tous les soirs
Je ne peux pas manger, je ne peux pas toucher,
Une vision de beauté et de gloire.

My wife and I learnt Spanish and Japanese when I played at Barcelona and Nagoya. We spent hours and hours in tuition – yet we could have learnt either language years earlier at school. Modern languages prepare you for modern life.

Gary Lineker, Footballer and Television Presenter

Learning a language makes our minds stronger and more flexible. Actually using it gives us an entirely new experience of the world.

John Cleese, Actor

Learning another language is part of making the civilised world go around, so start early.

Sir Peter Parker, Chair, DTI National Languages for Export Campaign

It is arrogant to assume that we can get by in English or that everyone else will speak our language. Learning a foreign language is polite, demonstrates commitment – and in today's world is absolutely necessary.

Sir Trevor McDonald, Chair, Nuffield Languages Inquiry

Ich bin umweltfreundlich und ich verwende umweltfreundliche Produkte. Ich finde Umweltschutz sehr wichtig also kaufe ich keine Spraydosen. Jede Woche bringe ich meine Glasflaschen zu dem Altglascontainer am Supermarkt und ich recycle mein Papier und Plastik.

Die Umwelt

Es muy importante aprender porque al colegio venimos a ser inteligentes, listos e ingeniosos, así que nosotros no somos tontos.

A mon avis c'est très important d'étudier les langues et je pense que tout le monde devrait le faire.

Les langues permettent de voyager à l'étranger sans avoir de difficultés de communication. Si on sait parler la langue du pays, les vacances sont plus amusantes. On peut faire de nouvelles connaissances, rencontrer des amis et généralement c'est plus facile d'obtenir des informations. C'est essentiel pour encourager de bonnes relations internationales, surtout de nos jours quand il y a beaucoup de conflits.

Programme of study: modern foreign languages

Key stages 3 & 4

During key stage 3 pupils begin to understand, speak, read and write at least one modern foreign language. They become familiar with the sounds, written form and grammar of the language, and use this knowledge with increasing confidence and competence to express themselves in role plays, conversations and writing. They improve their understanding of the language by listening to people talking about different subjects and by reading a range of texts. They also increase their cultural awareness by communicating with people who speak the language and by using materials from countries and communities where the language is spoken.

During key stage 4 pupils begin to use a modern foreign language more independently, drawing on a firmer grasp of grammar and a wider and more complex range of expression. They adapt their use of the language according to context, purpose and audience. They learn to understand a more extensive range of unfamiliar language by reading and listening to a variety of materials from countries and communities where the language is spoken. They also increase their cultural awareness through more direct contact with people who live in those countries and communities.

Note about using the target language
The target language is the modern foreign language that pupils are learning. Pupils are expected to use and respond to the target language, and to use English only when necessary (for example, when discussing a grammar point or when comparing English and the target language).

Knowledge, skills and understanding

Acquiring knowledge and understanding of the target language

1   Pupils should be taught:
    a   the principles and interrelationship of sounds and writing in the target language
    b   the grammar of the target language and how to apply it
    c   how to express themselves using a range of vocabulary and structures.

Developing language skills

2   Pupils should be taught:
    a   how to listen carefully for gist and detail
    b   correct pronunciation and intonation
    c   how to ask and answer questions
    d   how to initiate and develop conversations
    e   how to vary the target language to suit context, audience and purpose
    f   how to adapt language they already know for different contexts
    g   strategies for dealing with the unpredictable [for example, unfamiliar language, unexpected responses]
    h   techniques for skimming and for scanning written texts for information, including those from ICT-based sources
    i   how to summarise and report the main points of spoken or written texts, using notes where appropriate
    j   how to redraft their writing to improve its accuracy and presentation, including the use of ICT.

Developing language-learning skills

3   Pupils should be taught:
    a   techniques for memorising words, phrases and short extracts
    b   how to use context and other clues to interpret meaning [for example, by identifying the grammatical function of unfamiliar words or similarities with words they know]
    c   to use their knowledge of English or another language when learning the target language
    d   how to use dictionaries and other reference materials appropriately and effectively
    e   how to develop their independence in learning and using the target language.

Developing cultural awareness

4   Pupils should be taught about different countries and cultures by:

a   working with authentic materials in the target language, including some from ICT-based sources [for example, handwritten texts, newspapers, magazines, books, video, satellite television, texts from the internet]

b   communicating with native speakers [for example, in person, by correspondence]

c   considering their own culture and comparing it with the cultures of the countries and communities where the target language is spoken

d   considering the experiences and perspectives of people in these countries and communities.

Breadth of study

5   During key stages 3 and 4, pupils should be taught the **Knowledge, skills and understanding** through:

a   communicating in the target language in pairs and groups, and with their teacher

b   using everyday classroom events as an opportunity for spontaneous speech

c   expressing and discussing personal feelings and opinions

d   producing and responding to different types of spoken and written language, including texts produced using ICT

e   using a range of resources, including ICT, for accessing and communicating information

f   using the target language creatively and imaginatively

g   listening, reading or viewing for personal interest and enjoyment, as well as for information

h   using the target language for real purposes [for example, by sending and receiving messages by telephone, letter, fax or e-mail]

i   working in a variety of contexts, including everyday activities, personal and social life, the world around us, the world of work and the international world.

Note for eligible languages

6   Schools must offer, in key stages 3 and 4, one or more of the official working languages of the European Union (Danish, Dutch, Finnish, French, German, Modern Greek, Italian, Portuguese, Spanish, Swedish). Schools may, in addition, offer any other modern foreign language. Non-EU languages count as a foundation subject only when offered to pupils alongside the possibility of studying an official working language of the EU. A pupil may, therefore, study any modern foreign language that the school offers, but the offer must include an EU language.

1b, 3c → links to other subjects
These requirements build on En1/5 and En2/6 and En3/7.

2j → links to other subjects
This requirement builds on En3/2 and ICT/3b.

4b → ICT opportunity
Pupils could communicate by e-mail with speakers of the target language, including those in more distant countries.

5d → links to other subjects
This requirement builds on ICT/3b.

5e → links to other subjects
This requirement builds on ICT/3c.

Art and design is the freedom of the individual, the freedom of expression and the freedom to fail without retort.

Simon Waterfall, Creative Director, Deepend

Art develops spiritual values and contributes a wider understanding to the experience of life, which helps to build a balanced personality.

Bridget Riley, Painter

Art and design is not just a subject to learn, but an activity that you can practise: with your hands, your eyes, your whole personality.

Quentin Blake, Children's Laureate

Awareness and interaction with design is part of the contemporary professional environment. Design issues enter our life every day.

Peter Saville, Art Director and Designer

Art and design

The importance of art and design*
Art and design stimulates creativity and imagination. It provides visual, tactile and sensory experiences and a unique way of understanding and responding to the world. Pupils use colour, form, texture, pattern and different materials and processes to communicate what they see, feel and think. Through art and design activities, they learn to make informed value judgements and aesthetic and practical decisions, becoming actively involved in shaping environments.

They explore ideas and meanings in the work of artists, craftspeople and designers. They learn about the diverse roles and functions of art, craft and design in contemporary life, and in different times and cultures. Understanding, appreciation and enjoyment of the visual arts have the power to enrich our personal and public lives.
* Art and design includes craft.

Programme of study: art and design

Key stage 3

During key stage 3 pupils develop their creativity and imagination through more sustained activities. These help them to build on and improve their practical and critical skills and to extend their knowledge and experience of materials, processes and practices. They engage confidently with art, craft and design in the contemporary world and from different times and cultures. They become more independent in using the visual language to communicate their own ideas, feelings and meanings.

Note
The general teaching requirement for health and safety applies in this subject.

1b → links to other subjects
This requirement builds on En1/2f, 3b.

1c → ICT opportunity
Pupils could use electronic sketchbooks to record their observations and ideas.

2a → ICT opportunity
Pupils could manipulate and interpret digital images to create 2-D and 3-D work.

2b → links to other subjects
This requirement builds on D&T/2c.

3a → links to other subjects
This requirement builds on En1/3e.

3a → ICT opportunity
Pupils could recreate works of art in a contemporary context and share their work with others via e-mail.

Knowledge, skills and understanding

Teaching should ensure that **investigating and making** includes **exploring and developing ideas** and **evaluating and developing work. Knowledge and understanding** should inform this process.

Exploring and developing ideas
1   Pupils should be taught to:
    a   record and analyse first-hand observations, to select from experience and imagination and to explore ideas for different purposes and audiences
    b   discuss and question critically, and select from a range of visual and other information [for example, exhibitions, interviews with practitioners, CD-ROMs] to help them develop ideas for independent work
    c   organise and present this information in different ways, including using a sketchbook.

Investigating and making art, craft and design
2   Pupils should be taught to:
    a   investigate, combine and manipulate materials and images, taking account of purpose and audience
    b   apply and extend their experience of a range of materials and processes, including drawing, refining their control of tools and techniques
    c   experiment with and select methods and approaches, synthesise observations, ideas and feelings, and design and make images and artefacts.

Evaluating and developing work
3   Pupils should be taught to:
    a   analyse and evaluate their own and others' work, express opinions and make reasoned judgements
    b   adapt and refine their work and plan and develop this further, in the light of their own and others' evaluations.

Knowledge and understanding
4   Pupils should be taught about:
    a   the visual and tactile qualities of materials and processes and how these can be manipulated and matched to ideas, purposes and audiences
    b   codes and conventions and how these are used to represent ideas, beliefs, and values in works of art, craft and design
    c   continuity and change in the purposes and audiences of artists, craftspeople and designers from Western Europe and the wider world [for example, differences in the roles and functions of art in contemporary life, medieval, Renaissance and post-Renaissance periods in Western Europe, and in different cultures such as Aboriginal, African, Islamic and Native American].

Breadth of study

5   During the key stage, pupils should be taught the **Knowledge, skills and understanding** through:

a   exploring a range of starting points for practical work including themselves, their experiences and natural and made objects and environments

b   working on their own, and collaborating with others, on projects in two and three dimensions and on different scales

c   using a range of materials and processes, including ICT [for example, painting, collage, print making, digital media, textiles, sculpture]

d   investigating art, craft and design in the locality, in a variety of genres, styles and traditions, and from a range of historical, social and cultural contexts [for example, in original and reproduction form, during visits to museums, galleries and sites, on the internet].

Music

Music makes a kind of liquid link between the study of languages, literature and the other arts, history, and the sciences – joining them together in the outer world of feelings and relationships and the inner world of the imagination.

Dr Robin Holloway, Composer

Music is the most universal of all the arts. Ask any person in any city in any country what their favourite music is, and they'll always have an answer. So treasure music and keep it with you always.

John Suchet, Newscaster

Music is our daily medicine which aids far better communication with others and ourselves.

Evelyn Glennie OBE, Percussionist

The importance of music

Music is a powerful, unique form of communication that can change the way pupils feel, think and act. It brings together intellect and feeling and enables personal expression, reflection and emotional development. As an integral part of culture, past and present, it helps pupils understand themselves and relate to others, forging important links between the home, school and the wider world. The teaching of music develops pupils' ability to listen and appreciate a wide variety of music and to make judgements about musical quality. It encourages active involvement in different forms of amateur music making, both individual and communal, developing a sense of group identity and togetherness. It also increases self-discipline and creativity, aesthetic sensitivity and fulfilment.

Programme of study: music

Key stage 3

During key stage 3 pupils deepen and extend their own musical interests and skills. They perform and compose music in different styles with increasing understanding of musical devices, processes and contextual influences. They work individually and in groups of different sizes and become increasingly aware of different roles and contributions of each member of the group. They actively explore specific genres, styles and traditions from different times and cultures with increasing ability to discriminate, think critically and make connections between different areas of knowledge.

1a → links to other subjects
This requirement builds on En1/1c.

1c → links to other subjects
This requirement builds on En1/4.

Note for 4
Listening is integral to the development of all aspects of pupils' knowledge and understanding of music.

Knowledge, skills and understanding

Teaching should ensure that **listening, and applying knowledge and understanding,** are developed through the interrelated skills of **performing, composing** and **appraising.**

Controlling sounds through singing and playing – performing skills

1 Pupils should be taught how to:

  a sing unison and part songs developing vocal techniques and musical expression

  b perform with increasing control of instrument-specific techniques

  c practise, rehearse and perform with awareness of different parts, the roles and contribution of the different members of the group, and the audience and venue.

Creating and developing musical ideas – composing skills

2 Pupils should be taught how to:

  a improvise, exploring and developing musical ideas when performing

  b produce, develop and extend musical ideas, selecting and combining resources within musical structures and given genres, styles and traditions.

Responding and reviewing – appraising skills

3 Pupils should be taught how to:

  a analyse, evaluate and compare pieces of music

  b communicate ideas and feelings about music using expressive language and musical vocabulary to justify their own opinions

  c adapt their own musical ideas and refine and improve their own and others' work.

Listening, and applying knowledge and understanding

4 Pupils should be taught to:

  a listen with discrimination and to internalise and recall sounds

  b identify the expressive use of musical elements, devices, tonalities and structures

  c identify the resources, conventions, processes and procedures, including use of ICT, staff notation and other relevant notations, used in selected musical genres, styles and traditions

  d identify the contextual influences that affect the way music is created, performed and heard [for example, intention, use, venue, occasion, development of resources, impact of ICT, the cultural environment and the contribution of individuals].

Breadth of study

5   During the key stage, pupils should be taught the **Knowledge, skills and understanding** through:

    a   a range of musical activities that integrate performing, composing and appraising

    b   responding to a range of musical and non-musical starting points

    c   working on their own, in groups of different sizes and as a class

    d   using ICT to create, manipulate and refine sounds

    e   a range of live and recorded music from different times and cultures including music from the British Isles, the 'Western classical' tradition, folk, jazz and popular genres, and by well-known composers and performers.

5b → links to other subjects
This requirement builds on En1/1a–1c and En3/1a–1d and PE/6a.

To see young people growing in physical skills, self-confidence and self-worth is a truly enriching experience. Nowhere in school is it more visible than in PE.

Duncan Goodhew, Swimmer

Exercise activates your brain and gives you energy for everything else, the energy to be enthusiastic about your work. So all your school work will gain from physical education.

Darcey Bussell, Dancer, The Royal Ballet

Physical education is about pupils learning about themselves: their capabilities, their potential and their limitations. It is the foundation of all sports participation. But it goes beyond the individual and understanding themselves – it's learning how to work with and to respect others.

Lucy Pearson, England Cricketer and Teacher

Physical education

The importance of physical education

Physical education develops pupils' physical competence and confidence, and their ability to use these to perform in a range of activities. It promotes physical skilfulness, physical development and a knowledge of the body in action. Physical education provides opportunities for pupils to be creative, competitive and to face up to different challenges as individuals and in groups and teams. It promotes positive attitudes towards active and healthy lifestyles. Pupils learn how to think in different ways to suit a wide variety of creative, competitive and challenging activities. They learn how to plan, perform and evaluate actions, ideas and performances to improve their quality and effectiveness. Through this process pupils discover their aptitudes, abilities and preferences, and make choices about how to get involved in lifelong physical activity.

Programme of study: physical education

Key stage 3

During key stage 3 pupils become more expert in their skills and techniques, and how to apply them in different activities. They start to understand what makes a performance effective and how to apply these principles to their own and others' work. They learn to take the initiative and make decisions for themselves about what to do to improve performance. They start to identify the types of activity they prefer to be involved with, and to take a variety of roles such as leader and official.

Note
The general teaching requirement for health and safety applies in this subject.

3b → links to other subjects
This requirement builds on En1/3e.

4 → links to other subjects
These requirements build on Sc2/2e, 2i, 2j, 2l.

4 → ICT opportunity
Pupils could use heart and pulse rate monitors and a variety of other measuring and recording devices to collect, analyse and interpret data.

Knowledge, skills and understanding

Teaching should ensure that, when **evaluating and improving performance**, connections are made between **developing, selecting and applying skills, tactics and compositional ideas**, and **fitness and health**.

Acquiring and developing skills

1   Pupils should be taught to:
    a   refine and adapt existing skills
    b   develop them into specific techniques that suit different activities and perform these with consistent control.

Selecting and applying skills, tactics and compositional ideas

2   Pupils should be taught to:
    a   use principles to plan and implement strategies, compositional and organisational ideas in individual, pair, group and team activities
    b   modify and develop their plans
    c   apply rules and conventions for different activities.

Evaluating and improving performance

3   Pupils should be taught to:
    a   be clear about what they want to achieve in their own work, and what they have actually achieved
    b   take the initiative to analyse their own and others' work, using this information to improve its quality.

Knowledge and understanding of fitness and health

4   Pupils should be taught:
    a   how to prepare for and recover from specific activities
    b   how different types of activity affect specific aspects of their fitness
    c   the benefits of regular exercise and good hygiene
    d   how to go about getting involved in activities that are good for their personal and social health and well-being.

Breadth of study

5   During the key stage, pupils should be taught the **Knowledge, skills and understanding** through four areas of activity. These should include:

a   games activities

and three of the following, *at least one of which must be dance or gymnastic activities:*

b   dance activities

c   gymnastic activities

d   swimming activities and water safety

e   athletic activities

f   outdoor and adventurous activities.

Dance activities

6   Pupils should be taught to:

a   create and perform dances using a range of complex movement patterns and techniques

b   use a range of dance styles and forms

c   use compositional principles when composing their dances [for example, motif development, awareness of group relationships, spatial awareness]

d   apply performance skills in their dances.

Games activities

7   Pupils should be taught to:

a   play competitive invasion, net and striking/fielding games, using techniques that suit the games

b   use the principles of attack and defence when planning and implementing complex team strategies

c   respond to changing situations in the games.

Gymnastic activities

8   Pupils should be taught to:

a   create and perform complex sequences on the floor and using apparatus

b   use techniques and movement combinations in different gymnastic styles

c   use compositional principles when designing their sequences [for example, changes in level, speed, direction, and relationships with apparatus and partners].

Swimming activities and water safety

9   Pupils should be taught to:

a   set and meet personal and group targets in swimming events, water-based activities, personal survival challenges and competitions

b   use a range of recognised strokes, techniques and personal survival skills with technical proficiency.

6 → links to other subjects
These requirements build on Mu/2b.

7 → ICT opportunity
Pupils could use data-recording and analysis software to analyse patterns of play and individual contributions.

7, 9–11 → ICT opportunity
Pupils could use stop watches with lap recorders linked to data-collection devices to analyse and evaluate performance.

9, 10 → ICT opportunity
Pupils could use spreadsheets to record and track progress.

11b → links to other subjects
This requirement builds on Gg/2c.

Athletic activities

10 Pupils should be taught to:

a set and meet personal and group targets in a range of athletic events, challenges and competitions

b use a range of running, jumping and throwing techniques, singly and in combination, with precision, speed, power or stamina.

Outdoor and adventurous activities

11 Pupils should be taught to:

a meet challenges in outdoor activities and journeys

b use a range of orienteering and problem-solving skills and techniques in these challenges

c identify the roles and responsibilities of individuals within a group when planning strategies

d respond to changing conditions and situations.

Programme of study: physical education

Key stage 4

Knowledge, skills and understanding

Teaching should ensure that, when **evaluating and improving performance**, connections are made between **developing, selecting and applying skills, tactics and compositional ideas**, and **fitness and health**.

Acquiring and developing skills

1 Pupils should be taught to:
   a develop and apply advanced skills and techniques
   b apply them in increasingly demanding situations.

Selecting and applying skills, tactics and compositional ideas

2 Pupils should be taught to:
   a use advanced strategic and/or choreographic and organisational concepts and principles
   b apply these concepts and principles in increasingly demanding situations
   c apply rules and conventions for different activities.

Evaluating and improving performance

3 Pupils should be taught to:
   a make informed choices about what role they want to take in each activity
   b judge how good a performance is and decide how to improve it
   c prioritise and carry out these decisions to improve their own and others' performances
   d develop leadership skills.

Knowledge and understanding of fitness and health

4 Pupils should be taught:
   a how preparation, training and fitness relate to and affect performance
   b how to design and carry out activity and training programmes that have specific purposes
   c the importance of exercise and activity to personal, social and mental health and well-being
   d how to monitor and develop their own training, exercise and activity programmes in and out of school.

During key stage 4 pupils tackle complex and demanding activities applying their knowledge of skills, techniques and effective performance. They decide whether to get involved in physical activity that is mainly focused on competing or performing, promoting health and well-being, or developing personal fitness. They also decide on roles that suit them best including performer, coach, choreographer, leader and official. The view they have of their skilfulness and physical competence gives them the confidence to get involved in exercise and activity out of school and in later life.

Note
The general teaching requirement for health and safety applies in this subject.

3 → links to other subjects
These requirements build on En1/3a–3e.

4 → links to other subjects
These requirements build on Sc2/2e, 2f (double).

6 → ICT opportunity
Pupils could use multimedia devices to create sounds and music and provide lighting and other effects to enhance their dance.

6, 8, 10 → ICT opportunity
Pupils could use databases of movement ideas and techniques to analyse and evaluate performance.

6, 8–10 → ICT opportunity
Pupils could use digital cameras to help them to analyse actions and techniques.

7 → ICT opportunity
Pupils could use videos of games analysis to develop understanding of patterns of play and individual contributions.

9–11 → ICT opportunity
Pupils could use a variety of electronic and digital recording, measuring and timing devices to measure the effectiveness of performance.

9, 10 → ICT opportunity
Pupils could use spreadsheets to collect, analyse and interpret data.

Breadth of study

5   During the key stage, pupils should be taught the **Knowledge, skills and understanding** through *two of the six activity areas.*

Dance activities

6   Pupils should be taught to:
   a   choreograph and perform complex dances using advanced techniques and skills with accuracy and expression
   b   reflect different social and cultural contexts in their dances and communicate artistic intention
   c   use presentational skills in their dances.

Games activities

7   Pupils should be taught to:
   a   play competitive games
   b   use advanced techniques and skills specific to the games played with consistency and control
   c   respond effectively to changing situations within their games.

Gymnastic activities

8   Pupils should be taught to:
   a   compose and perform sequences, both on the floor and using apparatus, in specific gymnastic styles, applying set criteria
   b   use advanced techniques and skills with precision and accuracy
   c   use advanced compositional concepts and principles when composing their sequences.

Swimming activities and water safety

9   Pupils should be taught to:
   a   meet challenges in specific swimming events and water-based activities
   b   use advanced techniques and skills with control, power or stamina and technical proficiency.

Athletic activities

10 Pupils should be taught to:
   a   take part in specific athletic events
   b   use advanced techniques and skills with precision, speed, power or stamina and technical proficiency.

Outdoor and adventurous activities

11 Pupils should be taught to:

a   meet challenges in large-scale outdoor activities and journeys

b   use a range of complex outdoor activity skills and techniques [for example, canoeing, sailing, rock climbing, hillwalking]

c   solve problems and overcome challenges in unfamiliar environments

d   respond to changing conditions and environments.

There are two reasons why I initially joined the council. One, because I like to have a say in things that go on, and I wanted to see things happen. I wanted to see changes in the school and I suppose that's selfish but it's also I think that I don't want to see everyone getting a raw deal.

" Please we need help! Our village and many others are starving to death. We used to grow our own food and we did quite well, but the Government encouraged us to start growing coffee beans instead. We all thought that we would have more money with which we could buy food. We did for a while until the coffee beans gradually went down in price. Now we are suffering because people in your country are producing more coffee beans which means we have to bring down the price of ours to make sure we stay in business. We are a poor country and whenever we have money, no matter how much, or food no matter how little, it's so important. You take the food and clothes and the money you have forgranted. Please think of us while you're having your dinner because you can be sure we won't be having any tonight."

I feel it is a good book to study, as it is relevant to racism in our lives today and from the story we can see that racism goes a long way back and it's really about time that it was stopped for good. I personally think that racism is the cruellest form of prejudice, as making someone feel lower than yourself for something they are born into is futile, ignorant and low.

"The book is really telling people to be wary of dictatorship and showing how a dictatorship can reduce a country's wealth so all the people are poor while they are rich. Napoleon oppresses the other animals using his team of dogs, he keeps the people under control and stops them from realising they are no better than they were before. It is part of human nature to want power or to want others to look up to us but not everybody went to the extent that Napoleon did".

Listening to your conscience can be a good idea because it's normally what you really feel or think, even if you don't like it. Some people turn to God for guidance, often to back up their own ideas or opinions.

The importance of citizenship

Citizenship gives pupils the knowledge, skills and understanding to play an effective role in society at local, national and international levels. It helps them to become informed, thoughtful and responsible citizens who are aware of their duties and rights. It promotes their spiritual, moral, social and cultural development, making them more self-confident and responsible both in and beyond the classroom. It encourages pupils to play a helpful part in the life of their schools, neighbourhoods, communities and the wider world. It also teaches them about our economy and democratic institutions and values; encourages respect for different national, religious and ethnic identities; and develops pupils' ability to reflect on issues and take part in discussions.

Citizenship is complemented by the framework for personal, social and health education at key stages 3 and 4.

Citizenship

Citizenship is more than a statutory subject. If taught well and tailored to local needs, its skills and values will enhance democratic life for us all, both rights and responsibilities, beginning in school, and radiating out.

Professor Bernard Crick, Birkbeck College, London

We need to be aware of the racial diversity that exists in our society and value each individual.

Doreen Lawrence

It is only when you know how to be a citizen of your own country that you can learn how to be a citizen of the world.

Terry Waite, CBE

Citizenship education will enhance understanding of and participation in our democratic, legal and other civic processes.

Rt Hon Betty Boothroyd, Speaker of the House of Commons

Create a society where people matter more than things.

Archbishop Desmond Tutu

Programme of study: citizenship

Key stage 3

During key stage 3 pupils study, reflect upon and discuss topical political, spiritual, moral, social and cultural issues, problems and events. They learn to identify the role of the legal, political, religious, social and economic institutions and systems that influence their lives and communities. They continue to be actively involved in the life of their school, neighbourhood and wider communities and learn to become more effective in public life. They learn about fairness, social justice, respect for democracy and diversity at school, local, national and global level, and through taking part responsibly in community activities.

1a → links to other subjects
This requirement builds on Hi/10, 13.

1b → links to other subjects
This requirement builds on Hi/2b and Gg/6f and A&D/5d and Mu/5e.

1c–1e → links to other subjects
These requirements build on Hi/9, 10.

1h, 1i → ICT opportunity
Pupils could explore the growing importance of the internet, e-mail and e-commerce.

1i → links to other subjects
This requirement builds on Sc2/5a and Hi/13 and Gg/3b, 3e, 5a, 5b, 6f, 6h–6k and MFL/4c.

2a → links to other subjects
This requirement builds on En2/4a–4c.

2b → links to other subjects
This requirement builds on En1/1a–1e and En3/1i–1o.

2b → ICT opportunity
Pupils could use e-mail to exchange views.

2c → links to other subjects
This requirement builds on En1/3.

Knowledge, skills and understanding

Teaching should ensure that **knowledge and understanding about becoming informed citizens** are acquired and applied when **developing skills of enquiry and communication**, and **participation and responsible action**.

Knowledge and understanding about becoming informed citizens

1   Pupils should be taught about:
   a   the legal and human rights and responsibilities underpinning society, basic aspects of the criminal justice system, and how both relate to young people
   b   the diversity of national, regional, religious and ethnic identities in the United Kingdom and the need for mutual respect and understanding
   c   central and local government, the public services they offer and how they are financed, and the opportunities to contribute
   d   the key characteristics of parliamentary and other forms of government
   e   the electoral system and the importance of voting
   f   the work of community-based, national and international voluntary groups
   g   the importance of resolving conflict fairly
   h   the significance of the media in society
   i   the world as a global community, and the political, economic, environmental and social implications of this, and the role of the European Union, the Commonwealth and the United Nations.

Developing skills of enquiry and communication

2   Pupils should be taught to:
   a   think about topical political, spiritual, moral, social and cultural issues, problems and events by analysing information and its sources, including ICT-based sources
   b   justify orally and in writing a personal opinion about such issues, problems or events
   c   contribute to group and exploratory class discussions, and take part in debates.

Developing skills of participation and responsible action

3   Pupils should be taught to:
   a   use their imagination to consider other people's experiences and be able to think about, express and explain views that are not their own
   b   negotiate, decide and take part responsibly in both school and community-based activities
   c   reflect on the process of participating.

Programme of study: citizenship

Key stage 4

Knowledge, skills and understanding

Teaching should ensure that **knowledge and understanding about becoming informed citizens** are acquired and applied when **developing skills of enquiry and communication**, and **participation and responsible action.**

Knowledge and understanding about becoming informed citizens

1   Pupils should be taught about:

   a   the legal and human rights and responsibilities underpinning society and how they relate to citizens, including the role and operation of the criminal and civil justice systems

   b   the origins and implications of the diverse national, regional, religious and ethnic identities in the United Kingdom and the need for mutual respect and understanding

   c   the work of parliament, the government and the courts in making and shaping the law

   d   the importance of playing an active part in democratic and electoral processes

   e   how the economy functions, including the role of business and financial services

   f   the opportunities for individuals and voluntary groups to bring about social change locally, nationally, in Europe and internationally

   g   the importance of a free press, and the media's role in society, including the internet, in providing information and affecting opinion

   h   the rights and responsibilities of consumers, employers and employees

   i   the United Kingdom's relations in Europe, including the European Union, and relations with the Commonwealth and the United Nations

   j   the wider issues and challenges of global interdependence and responsibility, including sustainable development and Local Agenda 21.

Developing skills of enquiry and communication

2   Pupils should be taught to:

   a   research a topical political, spiritual, moral, social or cultural issue, problem or event by analysing information from different sources, including ICT-based sources, showing an awareness of the use and abuse of statistics

   b   express, justify and defend orally and in writing a personal opinion about such issues, problems or events

   c   contribute to group and exploratory class discussions, and take part in formal debates.

During key stage 4 pupils continue to study, think about and discuss topical political, spiritual, moral, social and cultural issues, problems and events. They study the legal, political, religious, social, constitutional and economic systems that influence their lives and communities, looking more closely at how they work and their effects. They continue to be actively involved in the life of their school, neighbourhood and wider communities, taking greater responsibility. They develop a range of skills to help them do this, with a growing emphasis on critical awareness and evaluation. They develop knowledge, skills and understanding in these areas through, for example, learning more about fairness, social justice, respect for democracy and diversity at school, local, national and global level, and through taking part in community activities.

1i → links to other subjects
This requirement builds on MFL/5i.

Note for 1j
Local Agenda 21 gives local authorities responsibility to improve sustainable development.

1j → links to other subjects
This requirement builds on Sc2/4b, 4c (single) and Sc2/5b, 5c (double).

2a → links to other subjects
This requirement builds on En2/4a–4c and Ma4/5k (foundation and higher).

2b → links to other subjects
This requirement builds on En1/1a–1e and En3/1i–1o.

2c → links to other subjects
This requirement builds on En1/3.

Developing skills of participation and responsible action

3   Pupils should be taught to:

  a   use their imagination to consider other people's experiences and be able to think about, express, explain and critically evaluate views that are not their own

  b   negotiate, decide and take part responsibly in school and community-based activities

  c   reflect on the process of participating.

Guidelines

Framework for personal, social and health education at key stages 3 & 4

The importance of personal, social and health education

Personal, social and health education (PSHE) at key stages 3 and 4 helps pupils to lead confident, healthy and responsible lives as individuals and members of society. Through work in lesson time and a wide range of activities across and beyond the curriculum, pupils gain practical knowledge and skills to help them live healthily and deal with the spiritual, moral, social and cultural issues they face as they approach adulthood. PSHE gives pupils opportunities to reflect on their experiences and how they are developing. It helps them to understand and manage responsibly a wider range of relationships as they mature, and to show respect for the diversity of, and differences between, people. It also develops pupils' well-being and self-esteem, encouraging belief in their ability to succeed and enabling them to take responsibility for their learning and future choice of courses and career. PSHE at key stages 3 and 4 builds on pupils' own experiences and on work at key stages 1 and 2 and complements citizenship in the curriculum, which covers public policy dilemmas related to health, law and family.

The following are non-statutory guidelines

Key stage 3

Knowledge, skills and understanding

Developing confidence and responsibility and making the most of their abilities

1 Pupils should be taught:

a to reflect on and assess their strengths in relation to personality, work and leisure

b to respect the differences between people as they develop their own sense of identity

c to recognise how others see them, and be able to give and receive constructive feedback and praise

d to recognise the stages of emotions associated with loss and change caused by death, divorce, separation and new family members, and how to deal positively with the strength of their feelings in different situations

e to relate job opportunities to their personal qualifications and skills, and understand how the choices they will make at key stage 4 should be based not only on knowledge of their personal strengths and aptitudes, but also on the changing world of work

f to plan realistic targets for key stage 4, seeking out information and asking for help with career plans

g what influences how we spend or save money and how to become competent at managing personal money.

Developing a healthy, safer lifestyle

2 Pupils should be taught:

a to recognise the physical and emotional changes that take place at puberty and how to manage these changes in a positive way

b how to keep healthy and what influences health, including the media

c that good relationships and an appropriate balance between work, leisure and exercise can promote physical and mental health

d basic facts and laws, including school rules, about alcohol and tobacco, illegal substances and the risks of misusing prescribed drugs

e in a context of the importance of relationships, about human reproduction, contraception, sexually transmitted infections, HIV and high-risk behaviours including early sexual activity

f to recognise and manage risk and make safer choices about healthy lifestyles, different environments and travel

g to recognise when pressure from others threatens their personal safety and well-being, and to develop effective ways of resisting pressures, including knowing when and where to get help

h basic emergency aid procedures and where to get help and support.

During key stage 3 pupils learn about themselves as growing and changing individuals and as members of their communities with more maturity, independence and power. They become more self-aware, and are capable of more sophisticated moral reasoning. They take more responsibility for themselves and become more aware of the views, needs and rights of people of all ages. They build on the experience, confidence and competence they developed in key stage 2, learning new skills to help them make decisions and play an active part in their personal and social life. They learn how to plan and manage choices for their courses and career. They continue to develop and maintain a healthy lifestyle, coping well with their changing bodies and feelings. They also learn to cope with changing relationships and understand how these can affect their health and well-being. They make the most of new opportunities to take part in the life of the school and its communities.

PSHE opportunity in science
2 → Sc2/2.

PSHE opportunity in physical education
2b, 2c → PE/4.

PSHE opportunity in design and technology
2f → D&T/2a.

PSHE opportunity in history
3d → Hi/2b.

Developing good relationships and respecting the differences between people

3   Pupils should be taught:

a   about the effects of all types of stereotyping, prejudice, bullying, racism and discrimination and how to challenge them assertively

b   how to empathise with people different from themselves

c   about the nature of friendship and how to make and keep friends

d   to recognise some of the cultural norms in society, including the range of lifestyles and relationships

e   the changing nature of, and pressure on, relationships with friends and family, and when and how to seek help

f   about the role and importance of marriage in family relationships

g   about the role and feelings of parents and carers and the value of family life

h   to recognise that goodwill is essential to positive and constructive relationships

i   to negotiate within relationships, recognising that actions have consequences, and when and how to make compromises

j   to resist pressure to do wrong, to recognise when others need help and how to support them

k   to communicate confidently with their peers and adults.

Breadth of opportunities

4   During the key stage, pupils should be taught the **Knowledge, skills and understanding** through opportunities to:

a   take responsibility [for example, for carrying out tasks and meeting deadlines such as taking assembly, running the school newspaper]

b   feel positive about themselves [for example, by taking part in a public performance]

c   participate [for example, in developing and putting into practice school policies about anti-bullying; in an action research project designed to reduce crime and improve personal safety in their neighbourhood]

d   make real choices and decisions [for example, about options for their future, based on their own research and career portfolios]

e   meet and work with people [for example, people who can give them reliable information about health and safety issues, such as school nurses, community drug awareness workers]

f   develop relationships [for example, by working together in a range of groups and social settings with their peers and others; by being responsible for a mini-enterprise scheme as part of a small group]

g   consider social and moral dilemmas [for example, how the choices they make as consumers affect other people's economies and environments] h   find information and advice [for example, about the risks of early sexual activity, drug misuse, self-defence for keeping safe]

i   prepare for change [for example, by anticipating problems caused by changing family relationships and friendships, and by preparing for new styles of learning at key stage 4].

The following are non-statutory guidelines

Key stage 4

During key stage 4 pupils use the knowledge, skills and understanding that they have gained in earlier key stages and their own experience to take new and more adult roles in school and the wider community. They develop the self-awareness and confidence needed for adult life, further learning and work. They have opportunities to show that they can take responsibility for their own learning and career choices by setting personal targets and planning to meet them. They develop their ability to weigh up alternative courses of action for health and well-being. They gain greater knowledge and understanding of spiritual, moral, social and cultural issues through increased moral reasoning, clarifying their opinions and attitudes in discussions with their peers and informed adults and considering the consequences of their decisions. They learn to understand and value relationships with a wide range of people and gain the knowledge and skills to seek advice about these and other personal issues. They learn to respect the views, needs and rights of people of all ages.

PSHE opportunity in science
2 → Sc2/2 (single and double).

PSHE opportunity in physical education
2c → PE/4.

Note for 2h
See health and safety in the general teaching requirements.

Knowledge, skills and understanding

Developing confidence and responsibility and making the most of their abilities

1   Pupils should be taught:

a   to be aware of and assess their personal qualities, skills, achievements and potential, so that they can set personal goals

b   to have a sense of their own identity and present themselves confidently in a range of situations

c   to be aware of how others see them, manage praise and criticism, and success and failure in a positive way and learn from the experience

d   to recognise influences, pressures and sources of help and respond to them appropriately

e   to use a range of financial tools and services, including budgeting and saving, in managing personal money

f   about the options open to them post-16, including employment and continuing education and training, and about their financial implications

g   to use the careers service to help them choose their next steps, negotiate and plan their post-16 choices with parents and others, develop career management skills, and prepare and put into practice personal action plans.

Developing a healthy, safer lifestyle

2   Pupils should be taught:

a   to think about the alternatives and long- and short-term consequences when making decisions about personal health

b   to use assertiveness skills to resist unhelpful pressure

c   the causes, symptoms and treatments for stress and depression, and to identify strategies for prevention and management

d   about the link between eating patterns and self-image, including eating disorders

e   about the health risks of alcohol, tobacco and other drug use, early sexual activity and pregnancy, different food choices and sunbathing, and about safer choices they can make

f   in the context of the importance of relationships, how different forms of contraception work, and where to get advice, in order to inform future choices

g   to seek professional advice confidently and find information about health

h   to recognise and follow health and safety requirements and develop the skills to cope with emergency situations that require basic aid procedures, including resuscitation techniques.

Developing good relationships and respecting the differences between people

3 Pupils should be taught:

a about the diversity of different ethnic groups and the power of prejudice

b to be aware of exploitation in relationships

c to challenge offending behaviour, prejudice, bullying, racism and discrimination assertively and take the initiative in giving and receiving support

d to work cooperatively with a range of people who are different from themselves

e to be able to talk about relationships and feelings

f to deal with changing relationships in a positive way, showing goodwill to others and using strategies to resolve disagreements peacefully

g about the nature and importance of marriage for family life and bringing up children

h about the role and responsibilities of a parent, and the qualities of good parenting and its value to family life

i about the impact of separation, divorce and bereavement on families and how to adapt to changing circumstances

j to know about the statutory and voluntary organisations that support relationships in crisis

k to develop working relationships with a range of adults, including people they meet during work experience, personal guidance and community activities.

Breadth of opportunities

4 During the key stage, pupils should be taught the **Knowledge, skills and understanding** through opportunities to:

a take responsibility [for example, by representing the school to visitors and at outside events]

b feel positive about themselves [for example, by gaining recognition for the role they play in school life, such as organising activities for younger pupils or working in a resource centre]

c participate [for example, in an initiative to improve their local community; in challenging activities involving physical performance, public performance or organised events outside the school]

d make real choices and decisions [for example, about their priorities, plans and use of time; about their choices post-16, with regular review and support]

e meet and work with people [for example, through activities such as work experience and industry days; through having an employer as a mentor]

f develop relationships [for example, by discussing relationships in single and mixed sex groups] g   consider social and moral dilemmas [for example, young parenthood, genetic engineering, attitudes to the law]

h   find information and provide advice [for example, by providing peer support services to other pupils]

i   prepare for change [for example, in relation to progression to further education and training].

Statement of values by the National Forum for Values in Education and the Community

An extract from the preamble to the statement

- The remit of the Forum was to decide whether there are any values that are commonly agreed upon across society, not whether there are any values that should be agreed upon across society. The only authority claimed for these values is the authority of consensus.

- These values are not exhaustive. They do not, for example, include religious beliefs, principles or teachings, though these are often the source of commonly held values. The statement neither implies nor entails that these are the only values that should be taught in schools. There is no suggestion that schools should confine themselves to these values.

- Agreement on the values outlined below is compatible with disagreement on their source. Many believe that God is the ultimate source of value, and that we are accountable to God for our actions; others that values have their source only in human nature, and that we are accountable only to our consciences. The statement of values is consistent with these and other views on the source of value.

- Agreement on these values is compatible with different interpretations and applications of them. It is for schools to decide, reflecting the range of views in the wider community, how these values should be interpreted and applied. For example, the principle 'we support the institution of marriage' may legitimately be interpreted as giving rise to positive promotion of marriage as an ideal, of the responsibilities of parenthood, and of the duty of children to respect their parents.

- The ordering of the values does not imply any priority or necessary preference. The ordering reflects the belief of many that values in the context of the self must precede the development of the other values.

- These values are so fundamental that they may appear unexceptional. Their demanding nature is demonstrated both by our collective failure consistently to live up to them, and the moral challenge which acting on them in practice entails.

Schools and teachers can have confidence that there is general agreement in society upon these values. They can therefore expect the support and encouragement of society if they base their teaching and the school ethos on these values.

The statement of values

The self

We value ourselves as unique human beings capable of spiritual, moral, intellectual and physical growth and development.

On the basis of these values, we should:

- develop an understanding of our own characters, strengths and weaknesses
- develop self-respect and self-discipline
- clarify the meaning and purpose in our lives and decide, on the basis of this, how we believe that our lives should be lived
- make responsible use of our talents, rights and opportunities
- strive, throughout life, for knowledge, wisdom and understanding
- take responsibility, within our capabilities, for our own lives.

Relationships

We value others for themselves, not only for what they have or what they can do for us. We value relationships as fundamental to the development and fulfilment of ourselves and others, and to the good of the community.

On the basis of these values, we should:

- respect others, including children
- care for others and exercise goodwill in our dealings with them
- show others they are valued
- earn loyalty, trust and confidence
- work cooperatively with others
- respect the privacy and property of others
- resolve disputes peacefully.

Society

We value truth, freedom, justice, human rights, the rule of law and collective effort for the common good. In particular, we value families as sources of love and support for all their members, and as the basis of a society in which people care for others.

On the basis of these values, we should:

- understand and carry out our responsibilities as citizens
- refuse to support values or actions that may be harmful to individuals or communities
- support families in raising children and caring for dependants
- support the institution of marriage
- recognise that the love and commitment required for a secure and happy childhood can also be found in families of different kinds

- help people to know about the law and legal processes
- respect the rule of law and encourage others to do so
- respect religious and cultural diversity
- promote opportunities for all
- support those who cannot, by themselves, sustain a dignified life-style
- promote participation in the democratic process by all sectors of the community
- contribute to, as well as benefit fairly from, economic and cultural resources
- make truth, integrity, honesty and goodwill priorities in public and private life.

The environment

We value the environment, both natural and shaped by humanity, as the basis of life and a source of wonder and inspiration.

On the basis of these values, we should:
- accept our responsibility to maintain a sustainable environment for future generations
- understand the place of human beings within nature
- understand our responsibilities for other species
- ensure that development can be justified
- preserve balance and diversity in nature wherever possible
- preserve areas of beauty and interest for future generations
- repair, wherever possible, habitats damaged by human development and other means.

This handbook:

- sets out the legal requirements of the National Curriculum in England for pupils aged 11 to 16
- provides information to help teachers implement the National Curriculum in their schools.

It has been written for secondary teachers. Parents, governors and all those with an interest in education will also find it useful.

The National Curriculum for pupils aged five to 11 is set out in the handbook for primary teachers. There are also separate booklets for the 12 National Curriculum subjects.

All these publications and related materials can be found on the National Curriculum web site at www.nc.uk.net.

Published by The Stationery Office and available from:

The Publications Centre
(mail, telephone and fax orders only)
PO Box 276, London SW8 5DT
Telephone orders/General enquiries 0870 600 5522
Fax orders 0870 600 5533

www.tso-online.co.uk

The Stationery Office Bookshops
123 Kingsway, London WC2B 6PQ
020 7242 6393 Fax 020 7242 6412
68–69 Bull Street, Birmingham B4 6AD
0121 236 9696 Fax 0121 236 9699
33 Wine Street, Bristol BS1 2BQ
0117 926 4306 Fax 0117 929 4515
9–21 Princess Street, Manchester M60 8AS
0161 834 7201 Fax 0161 833 0634
16 Arthur Street, Belfast BT1 4GD
028 9023 8451 Fax 028 9023 5401
The Stationery Office Oriel Bookshop
18–19 High Street, Cardiff CF1 2BZ
029 2039 5548 Fax 029 2038 4347
71 Lothian Road, Edinburgh EH3 9AZ
0870 606 5566 Fax 0870 606 5588

The Stationery Office's Accredited Agents
(see Yellow Pages)

and through good booksellers

£24.95

ISBN 0-11-370067-9

**Department for
Education and Employment**

QCA

About the attainment targets

An attainment target sets out the 'knowledge, skills and understanding that pupils of different abilities and maturities are expected to have by the end of each key stage'[1]. Except in the case of citizenship[2], attainment targets consist of eight level descriptions of increasing difficulty, plus a description for exceptional performance above level 8. Each level description describes the types and range of performance that pupils working at that level should characteristically demonstrate.

The level descriptions provide the basis for making judgements about pupils' performance at the end of key stages 1, 2 and 3. At key stage 4, national qualifications are the main means of assessing attainment in National Curriculum subjects.

Range of levels within which the great majority of pupils are expected to work		Expected attainment for the majority of pupils at the end of the key stage	
Key stage 1	1–3	at age 7	2
Key stage 2	2–5	at age 11	4
Key stage 3	3–7	at age 14	5/6[3]

Assessing attainment at the end of a key stage

In deciding on a pupil's level of attainment at the end of a key stage, teachers should judge which description best fits the pupil's performance. When doing so, each description should be considered alongside descriptions for adjacent levels.

Arrangements for statutory assessment at the end of each key stage are set out in detail in QCA's annual booklets about assessment and reporting arrangements.

Examples in the level descriptions

The examples in grey type are not statutory.

[1] As defined by the Education Act 1996, section 353a.
[2] In citizenship, expected performance for the majority of pupils at the end of key stages 3 and 4 is set out in end of key stage descriptions.
[3] Including modern foreign languages.

Attainment target 1: speaking and listening

Level 1

Pupils talk about matters of immediate interest. They listen to others and usually respond appropriately. They convey simple meanings to a range of listeners, speaking audibly, and begin to extend their ideas or accounts by providing some detail.

Level 2

Pupils begin to show confidence in talking and listening, particularly where the topics interest them. On occasions, they show awareness of the needs of the listener by including relevant detail. In developing and explaining their ideas they speak clearly and use a growing vocabulary. They usually listen carefully and respond with increasing appropriateness to what others say. They are beginning to be aware that in some situations a more formal vocabulary and tone of voice are used.

Level 3

Pupils talk and listen confidently in different contexts, exploring and communicating ideas. In discussion, they show understanding of the main points. Through relevant comments and questions, they show they have listened carefully. They begin to adapt what they say to the needs of the listener, varying the use of vocabulary and the level of detail. They are beginning to be aware of standard English and when it is used.

Level 4

Pupils talk and listen with confidence in an increasing range of contexts. Their talk is adapted to the purpose: developing ideas thoughtfully, describing events and conveying their opinions clearly. In discussion, they listen carefully, making contributions and asking questions that are responsive to others' ideas and views. They use appropriately some of the features of standard English vocabulary and grammar.

Level 5

Pupils talk and listen confidently in a wide range of contexts, including some that are of a formal nature. Their talk engages the interest of the listener as they begin to vary their expression and vocabulary. In discussion, they pay close attention to what others say, ask questions to develop ideas and make contributions that take account of others' views. They begin to use standard English in formal situations.

Level 6

Pupils adapt their talk to the demands of different contexts with increasing confidence. Their talk engages the interest of the listener through the variety of its vocabulary and expression. Pupils take an active part in discussion, showing understanding of ideas and sensitivity to others. They are usually fluent in their use of standard English in formal situations.

Level 7

Pupils are confident in matching their talk to the demands of different contexts. They use vocabulary precisely and organise their talk to communicate clearly. In discussion, pupils make significant contributions, evaluating others' ideas and varying how and when they participate. They show confident use of standard English in situations that require it.

Level 8

Pupils maintain and develop their talk purposefully in a range of contexts. They structure what they say clearly, using apt vocabulary and appropriate intonation and emphasis. They make a range of contributions which show that they have listened perceptively and are sensitive to the development of discussion. They show confident use of standard English in a range of situations, adapting as necessary.

Exceptional performance

Pupils select and use structures, styles and registers appropriately in a range of contexts, varying their vocabulary and expression confidently for a range of purposes. They initiate and sustain discussion through the sensitive use of a variety of contributions. They take a leading role in discussion and listen with concentration and understanding to varied and complex speech. They show assured and fluent use of standard English in a range of situations and for a variety of purposes.

Attainment target 2: reading

Level 1

Pupils recognise familiar words in simple texts. They use their knowledge of letters and sound–symbol relationships in order to read words and to establish meaning when reading aloud. In these activities they sometimes require support. They express their response to poems, stories and non-fiction by identifying aspects they like.

Level 2

Pupils' reading of simple texts shows understanding and is generally accurate. They express opinions about major events or ideas in stories, poems and non-fiction. They use more than one strategy, such as phonic, graphic, syntactic and contextual, in reading unfamiliar words and establishing meaning.

Level 3

Pupils read a range of texts fluently and accurately. They read independently, using strategies appropriately to establish meaning. In responding to fiction and non-fiction they show understanding of the main points and express preferences. They use their knowledge of the alphabet to locate books and find information.

Level 4

In responding to a range of texts, pupils show understanding of significant ideas, themes, events and characters, beginning to use inference and deduction. They refer to the text when explaining their views. They locate and use ideas and information.

Level 5

Pupils show understanding of a range of texts, selecting essential points and using inference and deduction where appropriate. In their responses, they identify key features, themes and characters and select sentences, phrases and relevant information to support their views. They retrieve and collate information from a range of sources.

Level 6

In reading and discussing a range of texts, pupils identify different layers of meaning and comment on their significance and effect. They give personal responses to literary texts, referring to aspects of language, structure and themes in justifying their views. They summarise a range of information from different sources.

Level 7

Pupils show understanding of the ways in which meaning and information are conveyed in a range of texts. They articulate personal and critical responses to poems, plays and novels, showing awareness of their thematic, structural and linguistic features. They select and synthesise a range of information from a variety of sources.

Level 8

Pupils' response is shown in their appreciation of, and comment on, a range of texts, and they evaluate how authors achieve their effects through the use of linguistic, structural and presentational devices. They select and analyse information and ideas, and comment on how these are conveyed in different texts.

Exceptional performance

Pupils confidently sustain their responses to a demanding range of texts, developing their ideas and referring in detail to aspects of language, structure and presentation. They make apt and careful comparison between texts, including consideration of audience, purpose and form. They identify and analyse argument, opinion and alternative interpretations, making cross-references where appropriate.

Attainment target 3: writing

Level 1

Pupils' writing communicates meaning through simple words and phrases. In their reading or their writing, pupils begin to show awareness of how full stops are used. Letters are usually clearly shaped and correctly orientated.

Level 2

Pupils' writing communicates meaning in both narrative and non-narrative forms, using appropriate and interesting vocabulary, and showing some awareness of the reader. Ideas are developed in a sequence of sentences, sometimes demarcated by capital letters and full stops. Simple, monosyllabic words are usually spelt correctly, and where there are inaccuracies the alternative is phonetically plausible. In handwriting, letters are accurately formed and consistent in size.

Level 3

Pupils' writing is often organised, imaginative and clear. The main features of different forms of writing are used appropriately, beginning to be adapted to different readers. Sequences of sentences extend ideas logically and words are chosen for variety and interest. The basic grammatical structure of sentences is usually correct. Spelling is usually accurate, including that of common, polysyllabic words. Punctuation to mark sentences – full stops, capital letters and question marks – is used accurately. Handwriting is joined and legible.

Level 4

Pupils' writing in a range of forms is lively and thoughtful. Ideas are often sustained and developed in interesting ways and organised appropriately for the purpose of the reader. Vocabulary choices are often adventurous and words are used for effect. Pupils are beginning to use grammatically complex sentences, extending meaning. Spelling, including that of polysyllabic words that conform to regular patterns, is generally accurate. Full stops, capital letters and question marks are used correctly, and pupils are beginning to use punctuation within the sentence. Handwriting style is fluent, joined and legible.

Level 5

Pupils' writing is varied and interesting, conveying meaning clearly in a range of forms for different readers, using a more formal style where appropriate. Vocabulary choices are imaginative and words are used precisely. Simple and complex sentences are organised into paragraphs. Words with complex regular patterns are usually spelt correctly. A range of punctuation, including commas, apostrophes and inverted commas, is usually used accurately. Handwriting is joined, clear and fluent and, where appropriate, is adapted to a range of tasks.

Level 6

Pupils' writing often engages and sustains the reader's interest, showing some adaptation of style and register to different forms, including using an impersonal style where appropriate. Pupils use a range of sentence structures and varied vocabulary to create effects. Spelling is generally accurate, including that of irregular words. Handwriting is neat and legible. A range of punctuation is usually used correctly to clarify meaning, and ideas are organised into paragraphs.

Level 7

Pupils' writing is confident and shows appropriate choices of style in a range of forms. In narrative writing, characters and settings are developed and, in non-fiction, ideas are organised and coherent. Grammatical features and vocabulary are accurately and effectively used. Spelling is correct, including that of complex irregular words. Work is legible and attractively presented. Paragraphing and correct punctuation are used to make the sequence of events or ideas coherent and clear to the reader.

Level 8

Pupils' writing shows the selection of specific features or expressions to convey particular effects and to interest the reader. Narrative writing shows control of characters, events and settings, and shows variety in structure. Non-fiction writing is coherent and gives clear points of view. The use of vocabulary and grammar enables fine distinctions to be made or emphasis achieved. Writing shows a clear grasp of the use of punctuation and paragraphing.

Exceptional performance

Pupils' writing has shape and impact and shows control of a range of styles maintaining the interest of the reader throughout. Narratives use structure as well as vocabulary for a range of imaginative effects, and non-fiction is coherent, reasoned and persuasive. A variety of grammatical constructions and punctuation is used accurately and appropriately and with sensitivity. Paragraphs are well constructed and linked in order to clarify the organisation of the writing as a whole.

Attainment target 1: using and applying mathematics

Teachers should expect attainment at a given level in this attainment target to be demonstrated through activities in which the mathematics from the other attainment targets is at, or very close to, the same level.

Level 1

Pupils use mathematics as an integral part of classroom activities. They represent their work with objects or pictures and discuss it. They recognise and use a simple pattern or relationship.

Level 2

Pupils select the mathematics they use in some classroom activities. They discuss their work using mathematical language and are beginning to represent it using symbols and simple diagrams. They explain why an answer is correct.

Level 3

Pupils try different approaches and find ways of overcoming difficulties that arise when they are solving problems. They are beginning to organise their work and check results. Pupils discuss their mathematical work and are beginning to explain their thinking. They use and interpret mathematical symbols and diagrams. Pupils show that they understand a general statement by finding particular examples that match it.

Level 4

Pupils are developing their own strategies for solving problems and are using these strategies both in working within mathematics and in applying mathematics to practical contexts. They present information and results in a clear and organised way. They search for a solution by trying out ideas of their own.

Level 5

In order to carry through tasks and solve mathematical problems, pupils identify and obtain necessary information. They check their results, considering whether these are sensible. Pupils show understanding of situations by describing them mathematically using symbols, words and diagrams. They draw simple conclusions of their own and give an explanation of their reasoning.

Level 6

Pupils carry through substantial tasks and solve quite complex problems by independently breaking them down into smaller, more manageable tasks. They interpret, discuss and synthesise information presented in a variety of mathematical forms. Pupils' writing explains and informs their use of diagrams. Pupils are beginning to give mathematical justifications.

Level 7

Starting from problems or contexts that have been presented to them, pupils progressively refine or extend the mathematics used to generate fuller solutions. They give a reason for their choice of mathematical presentation, explaining features they have selected. Pupils justify their generalisations, arguments or solutions, showing some insight into the mathematical structure of the problem. They appreciate the difference between mathematical explanation and experimental evidence.

Level 8

Pupils develop and follow alternative approaches. They reflect on their own lines of enquiry when exploring mathematical tasks; in doing so they introduce and use a range of mathematical techniques. Pupils convey mathematical or statistical meaning through precise and consistent use of symbols that is sustained throughout the work. They examine generalisations or solutions reached in an activity, commenting constructively on the reasoning and logic or the process employed, or the results obtained, and make further progress in the activity as a result.

Exceptional performance

Pupils give reasons for the choices they make when investigating within mathematics itself or when using mathematics to analyse tasks; these reasons explain why particular lines of enquiry or procedures are followed and others rejected. Pupils apply the mathematics they know in familiar and unfamiliar contexts. Pupils use mathematical language and symbols effectively in presenting a convincing reasoned argument. Their reports include mathematical justifications, explaining their solutions to problems involving a number of features or variables.

Attainment target 2: number and algebra

Level 1

Pupils count, order, add and subtract numbers when solving problems involving up to 10 objects. They read and write the numbers involved.

Level 2

Pupils count sets of objects reliably, and use mental recall of addition and subtraction facts to 10. They begin to understand the place value of each digit in a number and use this to order numbers up to 100. They choose the appropriate operation when solving addition and subtraction problems. They use the knowledge that subtraction is the inverse of addition. They use mental calculation strategies to solve number problems involving money and measures. They recognise sequences of numbers, including odd and even numbers.

Level 3

Pupils show understanding of place value in numbers up to 1000 and use this to make approximations. They begin to use decimal notation and to recognise negative numbers, in contexts such as money and temperature. Pupils use mental recall of addition and subtraction facts to 20 in solving problems involving larger numbers. They add and subtract numbers with two digits mentally and numbers with three digits using written methods. They use mental recall of the 2, 3, 4, 5 and 10 multiplication tables and derive the associated division facts. They solve whole-number problems involving multiplication or division, including those that give rise to remainders. They use simple fractions that are several parts of a whole and recognise when two simple fractions are equivalent.

Level 4

Pupils use their understanding of place value to multiply and divide whole numbers by 10 or 100. In solving number problems, pupils use a range of mental methods of computation with the four operations, including mental recall of multiplication facts up to 10×10 and quick derivation of corresponding division facts. They use efficient written methods of addition and subtraction and of short multiplication and division. They add and subtract decimals to two places and order decimals to three places. In solving problems with or without a calculator, pupils check the reasonableness of their results by reference to their knowledge of the context or to the size of the numbers. They recognise approximate proportions of a whole and use simple fractions and percentages to describe these. Pupils recognise and describe number patterns, and relationships including multiple, factor and square. They begin to use simple formulae expressed in words. Pupils use and interpret coordinates in the first quadrant.

Level 5

Pupils use their understanding of place value to multiply and divide whole numbers and decimals by 10, 100 and 1000. They order, add and subtract negative numbers in context. They use all four operations with decimals to two places. They reduce a fraction to its simplest form by cancelling common factors and solve simple problems involving ratio and direct proportion. They calculate fractional or percentage parts of quantities and measurements, using a calculator where appropriate. Pupils understand and use an appropriate non-calculator method for solving problems that involve multiplying and dividing any three-digit number by any two-digit number. They check their solutions by applying inverse operations or estimating using approximations. They construct, express in symbolic form, and use simple formulae involving one or two operations. They use brackets appropriately. Pupils use and interpret coordinates in all four quadrants.

Level 6

Pupils order and approximate decimals when solving numerical problems and equations [for example, $x^3 + x = 20$], using trial-and-improvement methods. Pupils are aware of which number to consider as 100 per cent, or a whole, in problems involving comparisons, and use this to evaluate one number as a fraction or percentage of another. They understand and use the equivalences between fractions, decimals and percentages, and calculate using ratios in appropriate situations. They add and subtract fractions by writing them with a common denominator. When exploring number sequences, pupils find and describe in words the rule for the next term or nth term of a sequence where the rule is linear. They formulate and solve linear equations with whole-number coefficients. They represent mappings expressed algebraically, and use Cartesian coordinates for graphical representation interpreting general features.

Level 7

In making estimates, pupils round to one significant figure and multiply and divide mentally. They understand the effects of multiplying and dividing by numbers between 0 and 1. Pupils solve numerical problems involving multiplication and division with numbers of any size, using a calculator efficiently and appropriately. They understand and use proportional changes, calculating the result of any proportional change using only multiplicative methods. Pupils find and describe in symbols the next term or nth term of a sequence where the rule is quadratic; they multiply two expressions of the form $(x + n)$; they simplify the corresponding quadratic expressions. Pupils use algebraic and graphical methods to solve simultaneous linear equations in two variables. They solve simple inequalities.

Level 8

Pupils solve problems involving calculating with powers, roots and numbers expressed in standard form, checking for correct order of magnitude. They choose to use fractions or percentages to solve problems involving repeated proportional changes or the calculation of the original quantity given the result of a proportional change. They evaluate algebraic formulae, substituting fractions, decimals and negative numbers. They calculate one variable, given the others, in formulae such as $V = \pi r^2 h$. Pupils manipulate algebraic formulae, equations and expressions, finding common factors and multiplying two linear expressions. They know that $a^2 - b^2 = (a+b)(a-b)$. They solve inequalities in two variables. Pupils sketch and interpret graphs of linear, quadratic, cubic and reciprocal functions, and graphs that model real situations.

Exceptional performance

Pupils understand and use rational and irrational numbers. They determine the bounds of intervals. Pupils understand and use direct and inverse proportion. In simplifying algebraic expressions, they use rules of indices for negative and fractional values. In finding formulae that approximately connect data, pupils express general laws in symbolic form. They solve simultaneous equations in two variables where one equation is linear and the other is quadratic. They solve problems using intersections and gradients of graphs.

Attainment target 3: shape, space and measures

Level 1

When working with 2-D and 3-D shapes, pupils use everyday language to describe properties and positions. They measure and order objects using direct comparison, and order events.

Level 2

Pupils use mathematical names for common 3-D and 2-D shapes and describe their properties, including numbers of sides and corners. They distinguish between straight and turning movements, understand angle as a measurement of turn, and recognise right angles in turns. They begin to use everyday non-standard and standard units to measure length and mass.

Level 3

Pupils classify 3-D and 2-D shapes in various ways using mathematical properties such as reflective symmetry for 2-D shapes. They use non-standard units, standard metric units of length, capacity and mass, and standard units of time, in a range of contexts.

Level 4

Pupils make 3-D mathematical models by linking given faces or edges, draw common 2-D shapes in different orientations on grids. They reflect simple shapes in a mirror line. They choose and use appropriate units and instruments, interpreting, with appropriate accuracy, numbers on a range of measuring instruments. They find perimeters of simple shapes and find areas by counting squares.

Level 5

When constructing models and when drawing or using shapes, pupils measure and draw angles to the nearest degree, and use language associated with angle. Pupils know the angle sum of a triangle and that of angles at a point. They identify all the symmetries of 2-D shapes. They know the rough metric equivalents of imperial units still in daily use and convert one metric unit to another. They make sensible estimates of a range of measures in relation to everyday situations. Pupils understand and use the formula for the area of a rectangle.

Level 6

Pupils recognise and use common 2-D representations of 3-D objects. They know and use the properties of quadrilaterals in classifying different types of quadrilateral. They solve problems using angle and symmetry properties of polygons and angle properties of intersecting and parallel lines, and explain these properties. They devise instructions for a computer to generate and transform shapes and paths. They understand and use appropriate formulae for finding circumferences and areas of circles, areas of plane rectilinear figures and volumes of cuboids when solving problems. They enlarge shapes by a positive whole-number scale factor.

Level 7

Pupils understand and apply Pythagoras' theorem when solving problems in two dimensions. They calculate lengths, areas and volumes in plane shapes and right prisms. Pupils enlarge shapes by a fractional scale factor, and appreciate the similarity of the resulting shapes. They determine the locus of an object moving according to a rule. Pupils appreciate the imprecision of measurement and recognise that a measurement given to the nearest whole number may be inaccurate by up to one half in either direction. They understand and use compound measures, such as speed.

Level 8

Pupils understand and use congruence and mathematical similarity. They use sine, cosine and tangent in right-angled triangles when solving problems in two dimensions. They distinguish between formulae for perimeter, area and volume, by considering dimensions.

Exceptional performance

Pupils sketch the graphs of sine, cosine and tangent functions for any angle, and generate and interpret graphs based on these functions. Pupils use sine, cosine and tangent of angles of any size, and Pythagoras' theorem when solving problems in two and three dimensions. They use the conditions for congruent triangles in formal geometric proofs [for example, to prove that the base angles of an isosceles triangle are equal]. They calculate lengths of circular arcs and areas of sectors, and calculate the surface area of cylinders and volumes of cones and spheres. Pupils appreciate the continuous nature of scales that are used to make measurements.

Attainment target 4: handling data

Level 1

Pupils sort objects and classify them, demonstrating the criterion they have used.

Level 2

Pupils sort objects and classify them using more than one criterion. When they have gathered information, pupils record results in simple lists, tables and block graphs, in order to communicate their findings.

Level 3

Pupils extract and interpret information presented in simple tables and lists. They construct bar charts and pictograms, where the symbol represents a group of units, to communicate information they have gathered, and they interpret information presented to them in these forms.

Level 4

Pupils collect discrete data and record them using a frequency table. They understand and use the mode and range to describe sets of data. They group data, where appropriate, in equal class intervals, represent collected data in frequency diagrams and interpret such diagrams. They construct and interpret simple line graphs.

Level 5

Pupils understand and use the mean of discrete data. They compare two simple distributions, using the range and one of the mode, median or mean. They interpret graphs and diagrams, including pie charts, and draw conclusions. They understand and use the probability scale from 0 to 1. Pupils find and justify probabilities, and approximations to these, by selecting and using methods based on equally likely outcomes and experimental evidence, as appropriate. They understand that different outcomes may result from repeating an experiment.

Level 6

Pupils collect and record continuous data, choosing appropriate equal class intervals over a sensible range to create frequency tables. They construct and interpret frequency diagrams. They construct pie charts. Pupils draw conclusions from scatter diagrams, and have a basic understanding of correlation. When dealing with a combination of two experiments, pupils identify all the outcomes, using diagrammatic, tabular or other forms of communication. In solving problems, they use their knowledge that the total probability of all the mutually exclusive outcomes of an experiment is 1.

Level 7

Pupils specify hypotheses and test them by designing and using appropriate methods that take account of variability or bias. They determine the modal class and estimate the mean, median and range of sets of grouped data, selecting the statistic most appropriate to their line of enquiry. They use measures of average and range, with associated frequency polygons, as appropriate, to compare distributions and make inferences. They draw a line of best fit on a scatter diagram, by inspection. Pupils understand relative frequency as an estimate of probability and use this to compare outcomes of experiments.

Level 8

Pupils interpret and construct cumulative frequency tables and diagrams, using the upper boundary of the class interval. They estimate the median and interquartile range and use these to compare distributions and make inferences. They understand how to calculate the probability of a compound event and use this in solving problems.

Exceptional performance

Pupils interpret and construct histograms. They understand how different methods of sampling and different sample sizes may affect the reliability of conclusions drawn. They select and justify a sample and method to investigate a population. They recognise when and how to work with probabilities associated with independent mutually exclusive events.

Attainment target 1: scientific enquiry

Level 1

Pupils describe or respond appropriately to simple features of objects, living things and events they observe, communicating their findings in simple ways [for example, talking about their work, through drawings, simple charts].

Level 2

Pupils respond to suggestions about how to find things out and, with help, make their own suggestions about how to collect data to answer questions. They use simple texts, with help, to find information. They use simple equipment provided and make observations related to their task. They observe and compare objects, living things and events. They describe their observations using scientific vocabulary and record them, using simple tables when appropriate. They say whether what happened was what they expected.

Level 3

Pupils respond to suggestions and put forward their own ideas about how to find the answer to a question. They recognise why it is important to collect data to answer questions. They use simple texts to find information. They make relevant observations and measure quantities, such as length or mass, using a range of simple equipment. Where appropriate, they carry out a fair test with some help, recognising and explaining why it is fair. They record their observations in a variety of ways. They provide explanations for observations and for simple patterns in recorded measurements. They communicate in a scientific way what they have found out and suggest improvements in their work.

Level 4

Pupils recognise that scientific ideas are based on evidence. In their own investigative work, they decide on an appropriate approach [for example, using a fair test] to answer a question. Where appropriate, they describe, or show in the way they perform their task, how to vary one factor while keeping others the same. Where appropriate, they make predictions. They select information from sources provided for them. They select suitable equipment and make a series of observations and measurements that are adequate for the task. They record their observations, comparisons and measurements using tables and bar charts. They begin to plot points to form simple graphs, and use these graphs to point out and interpret patterns in their data. They begin to relate their conclusions to these patterns and to scientific knowledge and understanding, and to communicate them with appropriate scientific language. They suggest improvements in their work, giving reasons.

Level 5

Pupils describe how experimental evidence and creative thinking have been combined to provide a scientific explanation [for example, Jenner's work on vaccination at key stage 2, Lavoisier's work on burning at key stage 3]. When they try to answer a scientific question, they identify an appropriate approach. They select from a range of sources of information. When the investigation involves a fair test, they identify key factors to be considered. Where appropriate, they make predictions based on their scientific knowledge and understanding. They select apparatus for a range of tasks and plan to use it effectively. They make a series of observations, comparisons or measurements with precision appropriate to the task. They begin to repeat observations and measurements and to offer simple explanations for any differences they encounter. They record observations and measurements systematically and, where appropriate, present data as line graphs. They draw conclusions that are consistent with the evidence and begin to relate these to scientific knowledge and understanding. They make practical suggestions about how their working methods could be improved. They use appropriate scientific language and conventions to communicate quantitative and qualitative data.

Level 6

Pupils describe evidence for some accepted scientific ideas and explain how the interpretation of evidence by scientists leads to the development and acceptance of new ideas. In their own investigative work, they use scientific knowledge and understanding to identify an appropriate approach. They select and use sources of information effectively. They make enough measurements, comparisons and observations for the task. They measure a variety of quantities with precision, using instruments with fine-scale divisions. They choose scales for graphs and diagrams that enable them to show data and features effectively. They identify measurements and observations that do not fit the main pattern shown. They draw conclusions that are consistent with the evidence and use scientific knowledge and understanding to explain them. They make reasoned suggestions about how their working methods could be improved. They select and use appropriate methods for communicating qualitative and quantitative data using scientific language and conventions.

Level 7

Pupils describe some predictions based on scientific theories and give examples of the evidence collected to test these predictions. In their own work, they use scientific knowledge and understanding to decide on appropriate approaches to questions. They identify the key factors in complex contexts and in contexts in which variables cannot readily be controlled, and plan appropriate procedures. They synthesise information from a range of sources, and identify possible limitations in secondary data. They make systematic observations and measurements with precision, using a wide range of apparatus. They identify when they need to repeat measurements, comparisons and observations in order to obtain reliable data. Where appropriate, they represent data in graphs, using lines of best fit. They draw conclusions that are consistent with the evidence and explain these using scientific knowledge and understanding. They begin to consider whether the data they have collected are sufficient for the conclusions they have drawn. They communicate what they have done using a wide range of scientific and technical language and conventions, including symbols and flow diagrams.

Level 8

Pupils give examples of scientific explanations or models that have had to be changed in the light of additional scientific evidence. They evaluate and synthesise data from a range of sources. They recognise that investigating different kinds of scientific questions requires different strategies, and use scientific knowledge and understanding to select an appropriate strategy in their own work. They decide which observations are relevant in qualitative work and include suitable detail in their records. They decide the level of precision needed in comparisons or measurements, and collect data enabling them to test relationships between variables. They identify and begin to explain anomalous observations and measurements and allow for these when they draw graphs. They use scientific knowledge and understanding to draw conclusions from their evidence. They consider graphs and tables of results critically. They communicate findings and arguments using appropriate scientific language and conventions, showing awareness of a range of views.

Exceptional performance

Pupils give examples of scientific explanations and models that have been challenged by subsequent experiments and explain the significance of the evidence in modifying scientific theories. They evaluate and synthesise data from a range of sources. They recognise that investigating different kinds of scientific questions requires different strategies, and use scientific knowledge and understanding to select an appropriate strategy in their own work. They make records of relevant observations and comparisons, clearly identifying points of particular significance. They decide the level of precision needed in measurements and collect data that satisfy these requirements. They use their data to test relationships between variables. They identify and explain anomalous observations and measurements, allowing for these when they draw graphs. They use scientific knowledge and understanding to interpret trends and patterns and to draw conclusions from their evidence. They consider graphs and tables of results critically and give reasoned accounts of how they could collect additional evidence. They communicate findings and arguments using appropriate scientific language and conventions, showing their awareness of the degree of uncertainty and a range of alternative views.

Attainment target 2: life processes and living things

Level 1

Pupils recognise and name external parts of the body [for example, head, arm] and of plants [for example, leaf, flower]. They communicate observations of a range of animals and plants in terms of features [for example, colour of coat, size of leaf]. They recognise and identify a range of common animals [for example, fly, goldfish, robin].

Level 2

Pupils use their knowledge about living things to describe the basic conditions [for example, a supply of food, water, air, light] that animals and plants need in order to survive. They recognise that living things grow and reproduce. They sort living things into groups, using simple features. They describe the basis for their groupings [for example, number of legs, shape of leaf]. They recognise that different living things are found in different places [for example, ponds, woods].

Level 3

Pupils use their knowledge and understanding of basic life processes [for example, growth, reproduction] when they describe differences between living and non-living things. They provide simple explanations for changes in living things [for example, diet affecting the health of humans or other animals, lack of light or water altering plant growth]. They identify ways in which an animal is suited to its environment [for example, a fish having fins to help it swim].

Level 4

Pupils demonstrate knowledge and understanding of life processes and living things drawn from the key stage 2 or key stage 3 programme of study. They use scientific names for some major organs of body systems [for example, the heart at key stage 2, the stomach at key stage 3] and identify the position of these organs in the human body. They identify organs [for example, stamen at key stage 2, stigma, root hairs at key stage 3] of different plants they observe. They use keys based on observable external features to help them to identify and group living things systematically. They recognise that feeding relationships exist between plants and animals in a habitat, and describe these relationships using food chains and terms [for example, predator and prey].

Level 5
Pupils demonstrate an increasing knowledge and understanding of life processes and living things drawn from the key stage 2 or key stage 3 programme of study. They describe the main functions of organs of the human body [for example, the heart at key stage 2, stomach at key stage 3], and of the plant [for example, the stamen at key stage 2, root hairs at key stage 3]. They explain how these functions are essential to the organism. They describe the main stages of the life cycles of humans and flowering plants and point out similarities. They recognise that there is a great variety of living things and understand the importance of classification. They explain that different organisms are found in different habitats because of differences in environmental factors [for example, the availability of light or water].

Level 6
Pupils use knowledge and understanding drawn from the key stage 3 programme of study to describe and explain life processes and features of living things. They use appropriate scientific terminology when they describe life processes [for example, respiration, photosynthesis] in animals and plants. They distinguish between related processes [for example, pollination, fertilisation]. They describe simple cell structure and identify differences between simple animal and plant cells. They describe some of the causes of variation between living things. They explain that the distribution and abundance of organisms in habitats are affected by environmental factors [for example, the availability of light or water].

Level 7
Pupils use knowledge and understanding of life processes and living things drawn from the key stage 3 programme of study to make links between life processes in animals and plants and the organ systems involved. They explain the processes of respiration and photosynthesis in terms of the main underlying chemical change. They use their knowledge of cell structure to explain how cells [for example, ovum, sperm, root hair] are adapted to their functions. They identify common variations between individuals, including some features [for example, eye colour] that are inherited and others [for example, height] that can also be affected by environmental factors. They construct models [for example, food webs, pyramids of numbers] to show feeding relationships, and explain how these relationships affect population size.

Level 8
Pupils demonstrate an extensive knowledge and understanding of life processes and living things drawn from the key stage 3 programme of study by describing and explaining how biological systems function. They relate the cellular structure of organs to the associated life processes [for example, the absorption of food in the digestive system, gas exchange in the lungs]. They recognise, predict and explain changes in biological systems [for example, the effect of increased carbon dioxide concentration on the growth of greenhouse crops, the consequences of smoking for organ systems]. They explain how characteristics can be inherited by individuals and apply their knowledge [for example, in relation to selective breeding]. They predict the short-term and long-term effects of environmental change on ecosystems and use their understanding of such systems to justify their predictions.

Exceptional performance
Pupils demonstrate both breadth and depth of knowledge and understanding drawn from the key stage 3 programme of study when they describe and explain how biological systems function. They recognise that organisms respond to change, and describe ways in which this is achieved. They relate their understanding of internal and external cellular structures to life processes [for example, the increased surface areas of cells in the digestive system]. They relate their understanding of cellular structure to inheritance and variation and explain how this leads to new varieties [for example, how genetic engineering is a modern form of selective breeding]. They recognise the importance of quantitative data [for example, related to populations in an environment] when they describe and explain patterns of change within an ecosystem.

Attainment target 3: materials and their properties

Level 1

Pupils know about a range of properties [for example, texture, appearance] and communicate observations of materials in terms of these properties.

Level 2

Pupils identify a range of common materials and know about some of their properties. They describe similarities and differences between materials. They sort materials into groups and describe the basis for their groupings in everyday terms [for example, shininess, hardness, smoothness]. They describe ways in which some materials are changed by heating or cooling or by processes such as bending or stretching.

Level 3

Pupils use their knowledge and understanding of materials when they describe a variety of ways of sorting them into groups according to their properties. They explain simply why some materials are particularly suitable for specific purposes [for example, glass for windows, copper for electrical cables]. They recognise that some changes [for example, the freezing of water] can be reversed and some [for example, the baking of clay] cannot, and they classify changes in this way.

Level 4

Pupils demonstrate knowledge and understanding of materials and their properties drawn from the key stage 2 or key stage 3 programme of study. They describe differences between the properties of different materials and explain how these differences are used to classify substances [for example, as solids, liquids, gases at key stage 2, as acids, alkalis at key stage 3]. They describe some methods [for example, filtration, distillation] that are used to separate simple mixtures. They use scientific terms [for example, evaporation, condensation] to describe changes. They use knowledge about some reversible and irreversible changes to make simple predictions about whether other changes are reversible or not.

Level 5

Pupils demonstrate an increasing knowledge and understanding of materials and their properties drawn from the key stage 2 or key stage 3 programme of study. They describe some metallic properties [for example, good electrical conductivity] and use these properties to distinguish metals from other solids. They identify a range of contexts in which changes [for example, evaporation, condensation] take place. They use knowledge about how a specific mixture [for example, salt and water, sand and water] can be separated to suggest ways in which other similar mixtures might be separated.

Level 6

Pupils use knowledge and understanding of the nature and behaviour of materials drawn from the key stage 3 programme of study to describe chemical and physical changes, and how new materials can be made. They recognise that matter is made up of particles, and describe differences between the arrangement and movement of particles in solids, liquids and gases. They identify and describe similarities between some chemical reactions [for example, the reactions of acids with metals, the reactions of a variety of substances with oxygen]. They use word equations to summarise simple reactions. They relate changes of state to energy transfers in a range of contexts [for example, the formation of igneous rocks].

Level 7

Pupils use knowledge and understanding drawn from the key stage 3 programme of study to make links between the nature and behaviour of materials and the particles of which they are composed. They use the particle model of matter in explanations of phenomena [for example, changes of state]. They explain differences between elements, compounds and mixtures in terms of their constituent particles. They recognise that elements and compounds can be represented by symbols and formulae. They apply their knowledge of physical and chemical processes to explain the behaviour of materials in a variety of contexts [for example, the way in which natural limestone is changed through the action of rainwater, ways in which rocks are weathered]. They use patterns of reactivity [for example, those associated with a reactivity series of metals] to make predictions about other chemical reactions.

Level 8

Pupils demonstrate an extensive knowledge and understanding drawn from the key stage 3 programme of study, which they use to describe and explain the behaviour of, and changes to, materials. They use the particle model in a wide range of contexts. They describe what happens in a range of chemical reactions and classify some [for example, oxidation, neutralisation]. They represent common compounds by chemical formulae and use these formulae to form balanced symbol equations for reactions [for example, those of acids with metals, carbonates or oxides]. They apply their knowledge of patterns in chemical reactions to suggest how substances [for example, salts] could be made.

Exceptional performance

Pupils demonstrate both breadth and depth of knowledge and understanding drawn from the key stage 3 programme of study when they describe and explain the nature and behaviour of materials. They use particle theory in a wider range of contexts, recognising that differences in the properties of materials relate to the nature of the particles within them. They recognise, and give explanations for, examples of chemical behaviour that do not fit expected patterns. They routinely use balanced symbol equations for reactions. They interpret quantitative data about chemical reactions, suggesting explanations for patterns identified.

Attainment target 4: physical processes

Level 1

Pupils communicate observations of changes in light, sound or movement that result from actions [for example, switching on a simple electrical circuit, pushing and pulling objects]. They recognise that sound and light come from a variety of sources and name some of these.

Level 2

Pupils know about a range of physical phenomena and recognise and describe similarities and differences associated with them. They compare the way in which devices [for example, bulbs] work in different electrical circuits. They compare the brightness or colour of lights, and the loudness or pitch of sounds. They compare the movement of different objects in terms of speed or direction.

Level 3

Pupils use their knowledge and understanding of physical phenomena to link cause and effect in simple explanations [for example, a bulb failing to light because of a break in an electrical circuit, the direction or speed of movement of an object changing because of a push or a pull]. They begin to make simple generalisations about physical phenomena [for example, explaining that sounds they hear become fainter the further they are from the source].

Level 4

Pupils demonstrate knowledge and understanding of physical processes drawn from the key stage 2 or key stage 3 programme of study. They describe and explain physical phenomena [for example, how a particular device may be connected to work in an electrical circuit, how the apparent position of the Sun changes over the course of a day]. They make generalisations about physical phenomena [for example, motion is affected by forces, including gravitational attraction, magnetic attraction and friction]. They use physical ideas to explain simple phenomena [for example, the formation of shadows, sounds being heard through a variety of materials].

Level 5

Pupils demonstrate knowledge and understanding of physical processes drawn from the key stage 2 or key stage 3 programme of study. They use ideas to explain how to make a range of changes [for example, altering the current in a circuit, altering the pitch or loudness of a sound]. They use some abstract ideas in descriptions of familiar phenomena [for example, objects are seen when light from them enters the eye at key stage 2, forces are balanced when an object is stationary at key stage 3]. They use simple models to explain effects that are caused by the movement of the Earth [for example, the length of a day or year].

Level 6

Pupils use and apply knowledge and understanding of physical processes drawn from the key stage 3 programme of study. They use abstract ideas in some descriptions and explanations [for example, electric current as a way of transferring energy, the sum of several forces determining changes in the direction or the speed of movement of an object, wind and waves as energy resources available for use]. They recognise, and can give examples of, the wide application of many physical concepts [for example, the transfer of energy by light, sound or electricity, the refraction and dispersion of light]. They give explanations of phenomena in which a number of factors have to be considered [for example, the relative brightness of planets and stars].

Level 7

Pupils use knowledge and understanding of physical processes drawn from the key stage 3 programme of study to make links between different phenomena. They make connections between electricity and magnetism when explaining phenomena [for example, the strength of electromagnets]. They use some quantitative definitions [for example, speed, pressure] and perform calculations, using the correct units. They apply abstract ideas in explanations of a range of physical phenomena [for example, the appearance of objects in different colours of light, the relationship between the frequency of vibration and the pitch of a sound, the role of gravitational attraction in determining the motion of bodies in the solar system, the dissipation of energy during energy transfers].

Level 8

Pupils demonstrate an extensive knowledge and understanding of the physical processes in the key stage 3 programme of study. They use models to describe and explain phenomena [for example, the magnetic field of an electromagnet, the passage of sound waves through a medium]. They use quantitative relationships between physical quantities in calculations that may involve more than one step. They offer detailed and sometimes quantitative interpretations of graphs [for example, speed–time graphs]. They consider ways of obtaining data [for example, of the solar system] and they use their knowledge of physical processes to explain patterns that they find. They consider physical phenomena from different perspectives [for example, relating the dissipation of energy during energy transfer to the need to conserve limited energy resources].

Exceptional performance

Pupils demonstrate both breadth and depth of knowledge and understanding of the physical processes in the key stage 3 programme of study when they describe and explain physical phenomena. They make effective use of a range of quantitative relationships between physical quantities. They understand how models [for example, the particle model] are useful in explaining physical phenomena [for example, how sweating causes cooling]. They apply their understanding of physical phenomena to a wide range of systems [for example, recognising the role of gravitational attraction in determining the movement of satellites, planets and stars]. They recognise the importance of quantitative data and make effective use of this when they consider questions such as energy efficiency.

Attainment target for design and technology

Level 1

Pupils generate ideas and recognise characteristics of familiar products. Their plans show that, with help, they can put their ideas into practice. They use pictures and words to describe what they want to do. They explain what they are making and which tools they are using. They use tools and materials with help, where needed. They talk about their own and other people's work in simple terms and describe how a product works.

Level 2

Pupils generate ideas and plan what to do next, based on their experience of working with materials and components. They use models, pictures and words to describe their designs. They select appropriate tools, techniques and materials, explaining their choices. They use tools and assemble, join and combine materials and components in a variety of ways. They recognise what they have done well as their work progresses, and suggest things they could do better in the future.

Level 3

Pupils generate ideas and recognise that their designs have to meet a range of different needs. They make realistic plans for achieving their aims. They clarify ideas when asked and use words, labelled sketches and models to communicate the details of their designs. They think ahead about the order of their work, choosing appropriate tools, equipment, materials, components and techniques. They use tools and equipment with some accuracy to cut and shape materials and to put together components. They identify where evaluation of the design and make process and their products has led to improvements.

Level 4

Pupils generate ideas by collecting and using information. They take users' views into account and produce step-by-step plans. They communicate alternative ideas using words, labelled sketches and models, showing that they are aware of constraints. They work with a variety of materials and components with some accuracy, paying attention to quality of finish and to function. They select and work with a range of tools and equipment. They reflect on their designs as they develop, bearing in mind the way the product will be used. They identify what is working well and what could be improved.

Level 5

Pupils draw on and use various sources of information. They clarify their ideas through discussion, drawing and modelling. They use their understanding of the characteristics of familiar products when developing and communicating their own ideas. They work from their own detailed plans, modifying them where appropriate. They work with a range of tools, materials, equipment, components and processes with some precision. They check their work as it develops and modify their approach in the light of progress. They test and evaluate their products, showing that they understand the situations in which their designs will have to function and are aware of resources as a constraint. They evaluate their products and their use of information sources.

Level 6

Pupils draw on and use a range of sources of information, and show that they understand the form and function of familiar products. They make models and drawings to explore and test their design thinking, discussing their ideas with users. They produce plans that outline alternative methods of progressing and develop detailed criteria for their designs and use these to explore design proposals. They work with a range of tools, materials, equipment, components and processes and show that they understand their characteristics. They check their work as it develops and modify their approach in the light of progress. They evaluate how effectively they have used information sources, using the results of their research to inform their judgements when designing and making. They evaluate their products as they are being used, and identify ways of improving them.

Level 7

Pupils use a wide range of appropriate sources of information to develop ideas. They investigate form, function and production processes before communicating ideas, using a variety of media. They recognise the different needs of a range of users and develop fully realistic designs. They produce plans that predict the time needed to carry out the main stages of making products. They work with a range of tools, materials, equipment, components and processes, taking full account of their characteristics. They adapt their methods of manufacture to changing circumstances, providing a sound explanation for any change from the design proposal. They select appropriate techniques to evaluate how their products would perform when used and modify their products in the light of the evaluation to improve their performance.

Level 8

Pupils use a range of strategies to develop appropriate ideas, responding to information they have identified. When planning, they make decisions on materials and techniques based on their understanding of the physical properties and working characteristics of materials. They identify conflicting demands on their design, explain how their ideas address these demands and use this analysis to produce proposals. They organise their work so that they can carry out processes accurately and consistently, and use tools, equipment, materials and components with precision. They identify a broad range of criteria for evaluating their products, clearly relating their findings to the purpose for which the products were designed and the appropriate use of resources.

Exceptional performance

Pupils seek out information to help their design thinking, and recognise the needs of a variety of client groups. They are discriminating in their selection and use of information sources to support their work. They work from formal plans that make the best use of time and resources. They work with tools, equipment, materials and components to a high degree of precision. They make products that are reliable and robust and that fully meet the quality requirements given in the design proposal.

Attainment target for information and communication technology capability

Level 1

Pupils explore information from various sources, showing they know that information exists in different forms. They use ICT to work with text, images and sound to help them share their ideas. They recognise that many everyday devices respond to signals and instructions. They make choices when using such devices to produce different outcomes. They talk about their use of ICT.

Level 2

Pupils use ICT to organise and classify information and to present their findings. They enter, save and retrieve work. They use ICT to help them generate, amend and record their work and share their ideas in different forms, including text, tables, images and sound. They plan and give instructions to make things happen and describe the effects. They use ICT to explore what happens in real and imaginary situations. They talk about their experiences of ICT both inside and outside school.

Level 3

Pupils use ICT to save information and to find and use appropriate stored information, following straightforward lines of enquiry. They use ICT to generate, develop, organise and present their work. They share and exchange their ideas with others. They use sequences of instructions to control devices and achieve specific outcomes. They make appropriate choices when using ICT-based models or simulations to help them find things out and solve problems. They describe their use of ICT and its use outside school.

Level 4

Pupils understand the need for care in framing questions when collecting, finding and interrogating information. They interpret their findings, question plausibility and recognise that poor-quality information leads to unreliable results. They add to, amend and combine different forms of information from a variety of sources. They use ICT to present information in different forms and show they are aware of the intended audience and the need for quality in their presentations. They exchange information and ideas with others in a variety of ways, including using e-mail. They use ICT systems to control events in a predetermined manner and to sense physical data. They use ICT-based models and simulations to explore patterns and relationships, and make predictions about the consequences of their decisions. They compare their use of ICT with other methods and with its use outside school.

Level 5

Pupils select the information they need for different purposes, check its accuracy and organise it in a form suitable for processing. They use ICT to structure, refine and present information in different forms and styles for specific purposes and audiences. They exchange information and ideas with others in a variety of ways, including using e-mail. They create sequences of instructions to control events, and understand the need to be precise when framing and sequencing instructions. They understand how ICT devices with sensors can be used to monitor and measure external events. They explore the effects of changing the variables in an ICT-based model. They discuss their knowledge and experience of using ICT and their observations of its use outside school. They assess the use of ICT in their work and are able to reflect critically in order to make improvements in subsequent work.

Level 6

Pupils develop and refine their work to enhance its quality, using information from a range of sources. Where necessary, they use complex lines of enquiry to test hypotheses. They present their ideas in a variety of ways and show a clear sense of audience. They develop, try out and refine sequences of instructions to monitor, measure and control events, and show efficiency in framing these instructions. They use ICT-based models to make predictions and vary the rules within the models. They assess the validity of these models by comparing their behaviour with information from other sources. They discuss the impact of ICT on society.

Level 7

Pupils combine information from a variety of ICT-based and other sources for presentation to different audiences. They identify the advantages and limitations of different information-handling applications. They select and use information systems suited to their work in a variety of contexts, translating enquiries expressed in ordinary language into the form required by the system. They use ICT to measure, record and analyse physical variables and control events. They design ICT-based models and procedures with variables to meet particular needs. They consider the benefits and limitations of ICT tools and information sources and of the results they produce, and they use these results to inform future judgements about the quality of their work. They take part in informed discussions about the use of ICT and its impact on society.

Level 8

Pupils independently select appropriate information sources and ICT tools for specific tasks, taking into account ease of use and suitability. They design successful ways to collect and prepare information for processing. They design and implement systems for others to use. When developing systems that respond to events, they make appropriate use of feedback. They take part in informed discussions about the social, economic, ethical and moral issues raised by ICT.

Exceptional performance

Pupils evaluate software packages and ICT-based models, analysing the situations for which they were developed and assessing their efficiency, ease of use and appropriateness. They suggest refinements to existing systems and design, implement and document systems for others to use, predicting some of the consequences that could arise from the use of such systems. When discussing their own and others' use of ICT, they use their knowledge and experience of information systems to inform their views on the social, economic, political, legal, ethical and moral issues raised by ICT.

Attainment target for history

Level 1

Pupils recognise the distinction between present and past in their own and other people's lives. They show their emerging sense of chronology by placing a few events and objects in order, and by using everyday terms about the passing of time. They know and recount episodes from stories about the past. They find answers to some simple questions about the past from sources of information.

Level 2

Pupils show their developing sense of chronology by using terms concerned with the passing of time, by placing events and objects in order, and by recognising that their own lives are different from the lives of people in the past. They show knowledge and understanding of aspects of the past beyond living memory, and of some of the main events and people they have studied. They are beginning to recognise that there are reasons why people in the past acted as they did. They are beginning to identify some of the different ways in which the past is represented. They observe or handle sources of information to answer questions about the past on the basis of simple observations.

Level 3

Pupils show their developing understanding of chronology by their realisation that the past can be divided into different periods of time, their recognition of some of the similarities and differences between these periods, and their use of dates and terms. They show knowledge and understanding of some of the main events, people and changes studied. They are beginning to give a few reasons for, and results of, the main events and changes. They identify some of the different ways in which the past is represented. They use sources of information in ways that go beyond simple observations to answer questions about the past.

Level 4

Pupils show factual knowledge and understanding of aspects of the history of Britain and the wider world. They use this to describe characteristic features of past societies and periods, and to identify changes within and across different periods. They describe some of the main events, people and changes. They give some reasons for, and results of, the main events and changes. They show some understanding that aspects of the past have been represented and interpreted in different ways. They are beginning to select and combine information from different sources. They are beginning to produce structured work, making appropriate use of dates and terms.

Level 5

Pupils show increasing depth of factual knowledge and understanding of aspects of the history of Britain and the wider world. They use this to describe features of past societies and periods and to begin to make links between them. They describe events, people and changes. They describe and make links between events and changes and give reasons for, and results of, these events and changes. They know that some events, people and changes have been interpreted in different ways and suggest possible reasons for this. Using their knowledge and understanding, pupils are beginning to evaluate sources of information and identify those that are useful for particular tasks. They select and organise information to produce structured work, making appropriate use of dates and terms.

Level 6

Pupils use their factual knowledge and understanding of the history of Britain and the wider world to describe past societies and periods, and to make links between features within and across different periods. They examine and explain the reasons for, and results of, events and changes. Pupils describe, and begin to analyse, why there are different historical interpretations of events, people and changes. Using their knowledge and understanding, they identify and evaluate sources of information, which they use critically to reach and support conclusions. They select, organise and deploy relevant information to produce structured work, making appropriate use of dates and terms.

Level 7

Pupils make links between their factual knowledge and understanding of the history of Britain and the wider world. They use these links to analyse relationships between features of a particular period or society, and to analyse reasons for, and results of, events and changes. They explain how and why different historical interpretations have been produced. Pupils show some independence in following lines of enquiry, using their knowledge and understanding to identify, evaluate and use sources of information critically. They sometimes reach substantiated conclusions independently. They select, organise and use relevant information to produce well-structured narratives, descriptions and explanations, making appropriate use of dates and terms.

Level 8

Pupils use their factual knowledge and understanding of the history of Britain and the wider world to analyse the relationships between events, people and changes, and between the features of different past societies and cultures. Their explanations of reasons for, and results of, events and changes are set in a wider historical context. They analyse and explain different historical interpretations and are beginning to evaluate them. Drawing on their historical knowledge and understanding, they use sources of information critically, carry out historical enquiries, and reach substantiated conclusions independently. They select, organise and deploy relevant information to produce consistently well-structured narratives, descriptions and explanations, making appropriate use of dates and terms.

Exceptional performance

Pupils use their extensive and detailed factual knowledge and understanding of the history of Britain and the wider world to analyse relationships between a wide range of events, people, ideas and changes and between the features of different past societies and cultures. Their explanations and analyses of reasons for, and results of, events and changes, are well substantiated and set in their wider historical context. They analyse links between events and developments that took place in different countries and in different periods. They make balanced judgements based on their understanding of the historical context about the value of different interpretations of historical events and developments. Drawing on their historical knowledge and understanding, they use sources of information critically, carry out historical enquiries, develop, maintain and support an argument and reach and sustain substantiated and balanced conclusions independently. They select, organise and deploy a wide range of relevant information to produce consistently well-structured narratives, descriptions and explanations, making appropriate use of dates and terms.

Attainment target for geography

Level 1

Pupils show their knowledge, skills and understanding in studies at a local scale. They recognise and make observations about physical and human features of localities. They express their views on features of the environment of a locality. They use resources that are given to them, and their own observations, to ask and respond to questions about places and environments.

Level 2

Pupils show their knowledge, skills and understanding in studies at a local scale. They describe physical and human features of places, and recognise and make observations about those features that give places their character. They show an awareness of places beyond their own locality. They express views on the environment of a locality and recognise how people affect the environment. They carry out simple tasks and select information using resources that are given to them. They use this information and their own observations to help them ask and respond to questions about places and environments. They begin to use appropriate geographical vocabulary.

Level 3

Pupils show their knowledge, skills and understanding in studies at a local scale. They describe and compare the physical and human features of different localities and offer explanations for the locations of some of those features. They are aware that different places may have both similar and different characteristics. They offer reasons for some of their observations and for their views and judgements about places and environments. They recognise how people seek to improve and sustain environments. They use skills and sources of evidence to respond to a range of geographical questions, and begin to use appropriate vocabulary to communicate their findings.

Level 4

Pupils show their knowledge, skills and understanding in studies of a range of places and environments at more than one scale and in different parts of the world. They begin to recognise and describe geographical patterns and to appreciate the importance of wider geographical location in understanding places. They recognise and describe physical and human processes. They begin to understand how these can change the features of places, and how these changes affect the lives and activities of people living there. They understand how people can both improve and damage the environment. They explain their own views and the views that other people hold about an environmental change. Drawing on their knowledge and understanding, they suggest suitable geographical questions, and use a range of geographical skills from the key stage 2 or 3 programme of study to help them investigate places and environments. They use primary and secondary sources of evidence in their investigations and communicate their findings using appropriate vocabulary.

Level 5

Pupils show their knowledge, skills and understanding in studies of a range of places and environments at more than one scale and in different parts of the world. They describe and begin to explain geographical patterns and physical and human processes. They describe how these processes can lead to similarities and differences in the environments of different places and in the lives of people who live there. They recognise some of the links and relationships that make places dependent on each other. They suggest explanations for the ways in which human activities cause changes to the environment and the different views people hold about them. They recognise how people try to manage environments sustainably. They explain their own views and begin to suggest relevant geographical questions and issues. Drawing on their knowledge and understanding, they select and use appropriate skills and ways of presenting information from the key stage 2 or 3 programme of study to help them investigate places and environments. They select information and sources of evidence, suggest plausible conclusions to their investigations and present their findings both graphically and in writing.

Level 6

Pupils show their knowledge, skills and understanding in studies of a wide range of places and environments at various scales, from local to global, and in different parts of the world. They describe and explain a range of physical and human processes and recognise that these processes interact to produce the distinctive characteristics of places. They describe ways in which physical and human processes operating at different scales create

geographical patterns and lead to changes in places. They appreciate the many links and relationships that make places dependent on each other. They recognise how conflicting demands on the environment may arise and describe and compare different approaches to managing environments. They appreciate that different values and attitudes, including their own, result in different approaches that have different effects on people and places. Drawing on their knowledge and understanding, they suggest relevant geographical questions and issues and appropriate sequences of investigation. They select a range of skills and sources of evidence from the key stage 3 programme of study and use them effectively in their investigations. They present their findings in a coherent way and reach conclusions that are consistent with the evidence.

Level 7

Pupils show their knowledge, skills and understanding in studies of a wide range of places and environments at various scales, from local to global, and in different parts of the world. They describe interactions within and between physical and human processes, and show how these interactions create geographical patterns and help change places and environments. They understand that many factors, including people's values and attitudes, influence the decisions made about places and environments, and use this understanding to explain the resulting changes. They appreciate that the environment in a place and the lives of the people who live there are affected by actions and events in other places. They recognise that human actions, including their own, may have unintended environmental consequences and that change sometimes leads to conflict. They appreciate that considerations of sustainable development affect the planning and management of environments and resources. With growing independence, they draw on their knowledge and understanding to identify geographical questions and issues and establish their own sequence of investigation. They select and use accurately a wide range of skills from the key stage 3 programme of study. They evaluate critically sources of evidence, present well-argued summaries of their investigations and begin to reach substantiated conclusions.

Level 8

Pupils show their knowledge, skills and understanding in studies of a wide range of places and environments at various scales, from local to global, and in different parts of the world. They offer explanations for interactions within and between physical and human processes. They explain changes in the characteristics of places over time, in terms of location, physical and human processes, and interactions with other places. They begin to account for disparities in development and understand the range and complexity of factors that contribute to the quality of life in different places. They recognise the causes and consequences of environmental issues and understand a range of views about them and different approaches to tackling them. They understand how considerations of sustainable development can affect their own lives as well as the planning and management of environments and resources. They use examples to illustrate this. Drawing on their knowledge and understanding, they show independence in identifying appropriate geographical questions and issues, and in using an effective sequence of investigation. They select a wide range of skills from the key stage 3 programme of study and use them effectively and accurately. They evaluate critically sources of evidence before using them in their investigations. They present full and coherently argued summaries of their investigations and reach substantiated conclusions.

Exceptional performance

Pupils show their knowledge, skills and understanding in studies of a wide range of places and environments at the full range of scales, from local to global, and in different parts of the world. They explain complex interactions within and between physical and human processes. They refer to a wide range of geographical factors to explain and predict change in the characteristics of places over time. They understand alternative approaches to development and the implications of these for the quality of life in different places. They assess the relative merits of different ways of tackling environmental issues and justify their views about these different approaches. They understand how considerations of sustainable development can affect their own lives as well as the planning and management of environments and resources. They illustrate this with a full range of examples. They draw selectively on geographical ideas and theories, and use accurately a wide range of appropriate skills and sources of evidence from the key stage 3 programme of study. They carry out geographical investigations independently at different scales. They evaluate critically sources of evidence and present coherent arguments and effective, accurate and well-substantiated conclusions. They evaluate their work by suggesting improvements in approach and further lines of enquiry.

Attainment target 1: listening and responding

Level 1

Pupils show that they understand simple classroom commands, short statements and questions. They understand speech spoken clearly, face-to-face or from a good-quality recording, with no background noise or interference. They may need a lot of help, such as repetition and gesture.

Level 2

Pupils show that they understand a range of familiar statements and questions [for example, everyday classroom language and instructions for setting tasks]. They respond to a clear model of standard language, but may need items to be repeated.

Level 3

Pupils show that they understand short passages made up of familiar language that is spoken at near normal speed without interference. These passages include instructions, messages and dialogues. Pupils identify and note main points and personal responses [for example, likes, dislikes and feelings], but may need short sections to be repeated.

Level 4

Pupils show that they understand longer passages, made up of familiar language in simple sentences, that are spoken at near normal speed with little interference. They identify and note main points and some details, but may need some items to be repeated.

Level 5

Pupils show that they understand extracts of spoken language made up of familiar material from several topics, including present and past or future events. They cope with language spoken at near normal speed in everyday circumstances that has little or no interference or hesitancy. They identify and note main points and specific details, including opinions, and may need some repetition.

Level 6

Pupils show that they understand short narratives and extracts of spoken language, which cover various past, present and future events and include familiar language in unfamiliar contexts. They cope with language spoken at normal speed and with some interference and hesitancy. They identify and note main points and specific details, including points of view, and need little repetition.

Level 7

Pupils show that they understand a range of material that contains some complex sentences and unfamiliar language. They understand language spoken at normal speed, including brief news items and non-factual material taken from radio or television, and need little repetition.

Level 8

Pupils show that they understand different types of spoken material from a range of sources [for example, news items, interviews, documentaries, films and plays]. When listening to familiar and less familiar material they draw inferences, recognise attitudes and emotions, and need little repetition.

Exceptional performance

Pupils show that they understand a wide range of factual and imaginative speech, some of which expresses different points of view, issues and concerns. They summarise in detail, report, and explain extracts, orally and in writing. They develop their independent listening by selecting from and responding to recorded sources according to their interests.

Attainment target 2: speaking

Level 1

Pupils respond briefly, with single words or short phrases, to what they see and hear. Their pronunciation may be approximate, and they may need considerable support from a spoken model and from visual cues.

Level 2

Pupils give short, simple responses to what they see and hear. They name and describe people, places and objects. They use set phrases [for example, to ask for help and permission]. Their pronunciation may still be approximate and the delivery hesitant, but their meaning is clear.

Level 3

Pupils take part in brief prepared tasks of at least two or three exchanges, using visual or other cues to help them initiate and respond. They use short phrases to express personal responses [for example, likes, dislikes and feelings]. Although they use mainly memorised language, they occasionally substitute items of vocabulary to vary questions or statements.

Level 4

Pupils take part in simple structured conversations of at least three or four exchanges, supported by visual or other cues. They are beginning to use their knowledge of grammar to adapt and substitute single words and phrases. Their pronunciation is generally accurate and they show some consistency in their intonation.

Level 5

Pupils take part in short conversations, seeking and conveying information and opinions in simple terms. They refer to recent experiences or future plans, as well as everyday activities and interests. Although there may be some mistakes, pupils make themselves understood with little or no difficulty.

Level 6

Pupils take part in conversations that include past, present and future actions and events. They apply their knowledge of grammar in new contexts. They use the target language to meet most of their routine needs for information and explanations. Although they may be hesitant at times, pupils make themselves understood with little or no difficulty.

Level 7

Pupils initiate and develop conversations and discuss matters of personal or topical interest. They improvise and paraphrase. Their pronunciation and intonation are good, and their language is usually accurate.

Level 8

Pupils give and justify opinions and discuss facts, ideas and experiences. They use a range of vocabulary, structures and time references. They adapt language to deal with unprepared situations. They speak confidently with good pronunciation and intonation, and their language is largely accurate with few mistakes of any significance.

Exceptional performance

Pupils discuss a wide range of factual and imaginative topics, giving and seeking personal views and opinions in informal and formal situations. They deal confidently with unpredictable elements in conversations, or with people who are unfamiliar. They speak fluently, with consistently accurate pronunciation, and can vary intonation. They give clear messages and make few errors.

Attainment target 3: reading and responding

Level 1
Pupils show that they understand single words presented in clear script in a familiar context. They may need visual cues.

Level 2
Pupils show that they understand short phrases presented in a familiar context. They match sound to print by reading aloud single familiar words and phrases. They use books or glossaries to find out the meanings of new words.

Level 3
Pupils show that they understand short texts and dialogues, made up of familiar language, printed in books or word processed. They identify and note main points and personal responses [for example, likes, dislikes and feelings]. They are beginning to read independently, selecting simple texts and using a bilingual dictionary or glossary to look up new words.

Level 4
Pupils show that they understand short stories and factual texts, printed or clearly handwritten. They identify and note main points and some details. When reading on their own, as well as using a bilingual dictionary or glossary, they are beginning to use context to work out what unfamiliar words mean.

Level 5
Pupils show that they understand a range of written material, including texts covering present and past or future events. They identify and note main points and specific details, including opinions. Their independent reading includes authentic materials [for example, information leaflets, newspaper extracts, letters, databases]. They are generally confident in reading aloud, and in using reference materials.

Level 6
Pupils show that they understand a variety of texts that cover past, present and future events and include familiar language in unfamiliar contexts. They identify and note main points and specific details, including points of view. They scan written material, for stories or articles of interest, and choose books or texts to read on their own, at their own level. They are more confident in using context and their knowledge of grammar to work out the meaning of language they do not know.

Level 7
Pupils show that they understand a range of material, imaginative and factual, that includes some complex sentences and unfamiliar language. They use new vocabulary and structures found in their reading to respond in speech or in writing. They use reference materials when these are helpful.

Level 8
Pupils show that they understand a wide variety of types of written material. When reading for personal interest and for information, they consult a range of reference sources where appropriate. They cope readily with unfamiliar topics involving more complex language, and recognise attitudes and emotions.

Exceptional performance
Pupils show that they understand a wide range of factual and imaginative texts, some of which express different points of view, issues and concerns, and which include official and formal material. They summarise in detail, report, and explain extracts, orally and in writing. They develop their independent reading by choosing stories, articles, books and plays according to their interests, and responding to them.

Attainment target 4: writing

Level 1
Pupils copy single familiar words correctly. They label items and select appropriate words to complete short phrases or sentences.

Level 2
Pupils copy familiar short phrases correctly. They write or word process items [for example, simple signs and instructions] and set phrases used regularly in class. When they write familiar words from memory their spelling may be approximate.

Level 3
Pupils write two or three short sentences on familiar topics, using aids [for example, textbooks, wallcharts and their own written work]. They express personal responses, [for example, likes, dislikes and feelings]. They write short phrases from memory and their spelling is readily understandable.

Level 4
Pupils write individual paragraphs of about three or four simple sentences, drawing largely on memorised language. They are beginning to use their knowledge of grammar to adapt and substitute individual words and set phrases. They are beginning to use dictionaries or glossaries to check words they have learnt.

Level 5
Pupils produce short pieces of writing, in simple sentences, that seek and convey information and opinions. They refer to recent experiences or future plans, as well as to everyday activities. Although there may be some mistakes, the meaning can be understood with little or no difficulty. They use dictionaries or glossaries to check words they have learnt and to look up unknown words.

Level 6
Pupils write in paragraphs, using simple descriptive language, and refer to past, present and future actions and events. They apply grammar in new contexts. Although there may be a few mistakes, the meaning is usually clear.

Level 7
Pupils produce pieces of writing of varying lengths on real and imaginary subjects, using an appropriate register. They link sentences and paragraphs, structure ideas and adapt previously learnt language for their own purposes. They edit and redraft their work, using reference sources to improve their accuracy, precision and variety of expression. Although there may be occasional mistakes, the meaning is clear.

Level 8
Pupils express and justify ideas, opinions or personal points of view, and seek the views of others. They develop the content of what they have read, seen or heard. Their spelling and grammar are generally accurate, and the style is appropriate to the content. They use reference materials to extend their range of language and improve their accuracy.

Exceptional performance
Pupils write coherently and accurately about a wide range of factual and imaginative topics. They choose the appropriate form of writing for a particular task, and use resources to help them vary the style and scope of their writing.

Modifications for pupils studying Chinese (Cantonese or Mandarin) or Japanese

Chinese (Cantonese or Mandarin)

The level descriptions for **listening and responding** assume that Chinese may be spoken at a slower speed than indicated and that the range of topics may be more limited.

The level descriptions for **reading and responding** and **writing** assume that, as well as using pinyin, pupils can work with an approximate number of characters as indicated below. These should mainly be simple and frequently occurring characters that are relevant to the contexts for learning. It is expected that pupils can understand compound phrases and four character phrases (idioms).

	Reading and responding	Writing
Level 1:	20–30 characters	10–20 characters
Level 2:	30–60 characters	20–30 characters
Level 3:	60–100 characters	30–50 characters
Level 4:	100–150 characters	50–100 characters
Level 5:	150–250 characters	100–150 characters
Level 6:	250–350 characters	150–250 characters
Level 7:	350–450 characters	250–350 characters
Level 8:	450–600 characters	350–500 characters
Exceptional performance:	600 or more characters	500 or more characters

The level descriptions for **reading and responding** assume that characters that are beyond the level of pupils' development but appear in authentic materials may be glossed using pinyin or a similar romanised transcription.

Japanese

The level descriptions for levels 1 to 4 for **reading and responding** and **writing** assume that pupils' script capability has developed so that they can work with the following:

Level 1: hiragana symbols
Level 2: hiragana symbols and modifications [for example, nigori]
Level 3: hiragana and katakana symbols and modifications
Level 4: hiragana, katakana and 20–40 kanji

The level descriptions for level 5 and above for **reading and responding** and **writing** assume that, as well as using hiragana and katakana and any modifications, pupils can work with an approximate number of kanji as indicated below. These should mainly be simple and frequently occurring kanji that are relevant to the contexts for learning.

	Reading and responding	Writing
Level 5:	40–90 kanji	40–60 kanji
Level 6:	90–140 kanji	60–90 kanji
Level 7:	140–200 kanji	90–140 kanji
Level 8:	200–270 kanji	140–220 kanji
Exceptional performance:	270 or more kanji	220 or more kanji

The level descriptions for **reading and responding** assume that kanji that are beyond the level of pupils' development but appear in authentic materials may be glossed using kana.

Attainment target for art and design

Level 1

Pupils respond to ideas. They use a variety of materials and processes to communicate their ideas and meanings, and design and make images and artefacts. They describe what they think or feel about their own and others' work.

Level 2

Pupils explore ideas. They investigate and use a variety of materials and processes to communicate their ideas and meanings, and design and make images and artefacts. They comment on differences in others' work, and suggest ways of improving their own.

Level 3

Pupils explore ideas and collect visual and other information for their work. They investigate visual and tactile qualities in materials and processes, communicate their ideas and meanings, and design and make images and artefacts for different purposes. They comment on similarities and differences between their own and others' work, and adapt and improve their own.

Level 4

Pupils explore ideas and collect visual and other information to help them develop their work. They use their knowledge and understanding of materials and processes to communicate ideas and meanings, and make images and artefacts, combining and organising visual and tactile qualities to suit their intentions. They compare and comment on ideas, methods and approaches used in their own and others' work, relating these to the context in which the work was made. They adapt and improve their work to realise their own intentions.

Level 5

Pupils explore ideas and select visual and other information. They use this in developing their work, taking account of the purpose. They manipulate materials and processes to communicate ideas and meanings and make images and artefacts, matching visual and tactile qualities to their intentions. They analyse and comment on ideas, methods and approaches used in their own and others' work, relating these to its context. They adapt and refine their work to reflect their own view of its purpose and meaning.

Level 6

Pupils explore ideas and assess visual and other information, including images and artefacts from different historical, social and cultural contexts. They use this information to develop their ideas, taking account of purpose and audience. They manipulate materials and processes and analyse outcomes. They interpret visual and tactile qualities to communicate ideas and meanings, and realise their intentions. They analyse and comment on how ideas and meanings are conveyed in their own and others' work. They explain how their understanding of the context affects their views and practice.

Level 7

Pupils explore ideas and assess visual and other information, analysing codes and conventions used in different genres, styles and traditions. They select, organise and present information in visual and other ways, taking account of purpose and audience. They extend their understanding of materials and processes and interpret visual and tactile qualities. They show increasing independence in the way in which they develop ideas and meanings and realise their intentions. They analyse and comment on the contexts of their own and others' work. They explain how their own ideas, experiences and values affect their views and practice.

Level 8

Pupils explore ideas and evaluate relevant visual and other information, analysing how codes and conventions are used to represent ideas, beliefs and values in different genres, styles and traditions. They research, document and present information in visual and other ways appropriate to their purpose and audience. They exploit the potential of materials and processes to develop ideas and meanings, realise their intentions and sustain their investigations. They evaluate the contexts of their own and others' work, articulating similarities and differences in their views and practice. They further develop their ideas and their work in the light of insights gained from others.

Exceptional performance

Pupils explore ideas, critically evaluate relevant visual and other information and make connections between representations in different genres, styles and traditions. They initiate research, and document and interpret information in visual and other ways appropriate to their purpose and audience. They exploit the characteristics of materials and processes to develop ideas and meanings and realise their intentions. They extend their ideas and sustain their investigations by responding to new possibilities and meanings. They identify why ideas and meanings in others' work are subject to different interpretations, using their understanding to extend their thinking and practical work. They communicate their own ideas, insights and views.

Attainment target for music

Level 1

Pupils recognise and explore how sounds can be made and changed. They use their voices in different ways such as speaking, singing and chanting, and perform with awareness of others. They repeat short rhythmic and melodic patterns and create and choose sounds in response to given starting points. They respond to different moods in music and recognise well-defined changes in sounds, identify simple repeated patterns and take account of musical instructions.

Level 2

Pupils recognise and explore how sounds can be organised. They sing with a sense of the shape of the melody, and perform simple patterns and accompaniments keeping to a steady pulse. They choose carefully and order sounds within simple structures such as beginning, middle, end, and in response to given starting points. They represent sounds with symbols and recognise how the musical elements can be used to create different moods and effects. They improve their own work.

Level 3

Pupils recognise and explore the ways sounds can be combined and used expressively. They sing in tune with expression and perform rhythmically simple parts that use a limited range of notes. They improvise repeated patterns and combine several layers of sound with awareness of the combined effect. They recognise how the different musical elements are combined and used expressively and make improvements to their own work, commenting on the intended effect.

Level 4

Pupils identify and explore the relationship between sounds and how music reflects different intentions. While performing by ear and from simple notations they maintain their own part with awareness of how the different parts fit together and the need to achieve an overall effect. They improvise melodic and rhythmic phrases as part of a group performance and compose by developing ideas within musical structures. They describe, compare and evaluate different kinds of music using an appropriate musical vocabulary. They suggest improvements to their own and others' work, commenting on how intentions have been achieved.

Level 5

Pupils identify and explore musical devices and how music reflects time and place. They perform significant parts from memory and from notations with awareness of their own contribution such as leading others, taking a solo part and/or providing rhythmic support. They improvise melodic and rhythmic material within given structures, use a variety of notations and compose music for different occasions using appropriate musical devices such as melody, rhythms, chords and structures. They analyse and compare musical features. They evaluate how venue, occasion and purpose affects the way music is created, performed and heard. They refine and improve their work.

Level 6

Pupils identify and explore the different processes and contexts of selected musical genres and styles. They select and make expressive use of tempo, dynamics, phrasing and timbre. They make subtle adjustments to fit their own part within a group performance. They improvise and compose in different genres and styles, using harmonic and non-harmonic devices where relevant, sustaining and developing musical ideas and achieving different intended effects. They use relevant notations to plan, revise and refine material. They analyse, compare and evaluate how music reflects the contexts in which it is created, performed and heard. They make improvements to their own and others' work in the light of the chosen style.

Level 7

Pupils discriminate and explore musical conventions in, and influences on, selected genres, styles and traditions. They perform in different styles, making significant contributions to the ensemble and using relevant notations. They create coherent compositions drawing on internalised sounds and adapt, improvise, develop, extend and discard musical ideas within given and chosen musical structures, genres, styles and traditions. They evaluate, and make critical judgements about, the use of musical conventions and other characteristics and how different contexts are reflected in their own and others' work.

Level 8

Pupils discriminate and exploit the characteristics and expressive potential of selected musical resources, genres, styles and traditions. They perform, improvise and compose extended compositions with a sense of direction and shape, both within melodic and rhythmic phrases and overall form. They explore different styles, genres and traditions, working by ear and by making accurate use of appropriate notations and both following and challenging conventions. They discriminate between musical styles, genres and traditions, commenting on the relationship between the music and its cultural context, making and justifying their own judgements.

Exceptional performance

Pupils discriminate and develop different interpretations. They express their own ideas and feelings in a developing personal style exploiting instrumental and/or vocal possibilities. They give convincing performances and demonstrate empathy with other performers. They produce compositions that demonstrate a coherent development of musical ideas, consistency of style and a degree of individuality. They discriminate and comment on how and why changes occur within selected traditions including the particular contribution of significant performers and composers.

Attainment target for physical education

Level 1

Pupils copy, repeat and explore simple skills and actions with basic control and coordination. They start to link these skills and actions in ways that suit the activities. They describe and comment on their own and others' actions. They talk about how to exercise safely, and how their bodies feel during an activity.

Level 2

Pupils explore simple skills. They copy, remember, repeat and explore simple actions with control and coordination. They vary skills, actions and ideas and link these in ways that suit the activities. They begin to show some understanding of simple tactics and basic compositional ideas. They talk about differences between their own and others' performance and suggest improvements. They understand how to exercise safely, and describe how their bodies feel during different activities.

Level 3

Pupils select and use skills, actions and ideas appropriately, applying them with coordination and control. They show that they understand tactics and composition by starting to vary how they respond. They can see how their work is similar to and different from others' work, and use this understanding to improve their own performance. They give reasons why warming up before an activity is important, and why physical activity is good for their health.

Level 4

Pupils link skills, techniques and ideas and apply them accurately and appropriately. Their performance shows precision, control and fluency, and that they understand tactics and composition. They compare and comment on skills, techniques and ideas used in their own and others' work, and use this understanding to improve their performance. They explain and apply basic safety principles in preparing for exercise. They describe what effects exercise has on their bodies, and how it is valuable to their fitness and health.

Level 5

Pupils select and combine their skills, techniques and ideas and apply them accurately and appropriately, consistently showing precision, control and fluency. When performing, they draw on what they know about strategy, tactics and composition. They analyse and comment on skills and techniques and how these are applied in their own and others' work. They modify and refine skills and techniques to improve their performance. They explain how the body reacts during different types of exercise, and warm up and cool down in ways that suit the activity. They explain why regular, safe exercise is good for their fitness and health.

Level 6

Pupils select and combine skills, techniques and ideas. They apply them in ways that suit the activity, with consistent precision, control and fluency. When planning their own and others' work, and carrying out their own work, they draw on what they know about strategy, tactics and composition in response to changing circumstances, and what they know about their own and others' strengths and weaknesses. They analyse and comment on how skills, techniques and ideas have been used in their own and others' work, and on compositional and other aspects of performance, and suggest ways to improve. They explain how to prepare for, and recover from, the activities. They explain how different types of exercise contribute to their fitness and health and describe how they might get involved in other types of activities and exercise.

Level 7

Pupils select and combine advanced skills, techniques and ideas, adapting them accurately and appropriately to the demands of the activities. They consistently show precision, control, fluency and originality. Drawing on what they know of the principles of advanced tactics and compositional ideas, they apply these in their own and others' work. They modify them in response to changing circumstances and other performers. They analyse and comment on their own and others' work as individuals and team members, showing that they understand how skills, tactics or composition and fitness relate to the quality of the performance. They plan ways to improve their own and others' performance. They explain the principles of practice and training, and apply them effectively. They explain the benefits of regular, planned activity on health and fitness and plan their own appropriate exercise and activity programme.

Level 8

Pupils consistently distinguish and apply advanced skills, techniques and ideas, consistently showing high standards of precision, control, fluency and originality. Drawing on what they know of the principles of advanced tactics or composition, they apply these principles with proficiency and flair in their own and others' work. They adapt it appropriately in response to changing circumstances and other performers. They evaluate their own and others' work, showing that they understand the impact of skills, strategy and tactics or composition, and fitness on the quality and effectiveness of performance. They plan ways in which their own and others' performance could be improved. They create action plans and ways of monitoring improvement. They use their knowledge of health and fitness to plan and evaluate their own and others' exercise and activity programme.

Exceptional performance

Pupils consistently use advanced skills, techniques and ideas with precision and fluency. Drawing on what they know of the principles of advanced strategies and tactics or composition, they consistently apply these principles with originality, proficiency and flair in their own and others' work. They evaluate their own and others' work, showing that they understand how skills, strategy and tactics or composition, and fitness relate to and affect the quality and originality of performance. They reach judgements independently about how their own and others' performance could be improved, prioritising aspects for further development. They consistently apply appropriate knowledge and understanding of health and fitness in all aspects of their work.

Attainment target for citizenship

The following descriptions describe the types and range of performance that the majority of pupils should characteristically demonstrate by the end of the key stage, having been taught the relevant programme of study. The descriptions are designed to help teachers judge the extent to which their pupils' attainment relates to this expectation. The expectations match the level of demand in other subjects and are broadly equivalent to levels 5 and 6 at key stage 3.

Key stage 3

Pupils have a broad knowledge and understanding of the topical events they study; the rights, responsibilities and duties of citizens; the role of the voluntary sector; forms of government; provision of public services; and the criminal and legal systems. They show how the public gets information and how opinion is formed and expressed, including through the media. They show understanding of how and why changes take place in society. Pupils take part in school and community-based activities, demonstrating personal and group responsibility in their attitudes to themselves and others.

Key stage 4

Pupils have a comprehensive knowledge and understanding of the topical events they study; the rights, responsibilities and duties of citizens; the role of the voluntary sector; forms of government; and the criminal and civil justice, legal and economic systems. They obtain and use different kinds of information, including the media, to form and express an opinion. They evaluate the effectiveness of different ways of bringing about change at different levels of society. Pupils take part effectively in school and community-based activities, showing a willingness and commitment to evaluate such activities critically. They demonstrate personal and group responsibility in their attitudes to themselves and others.

The National Curriculum attainment targets

Acknowledgements

About the work used in this document
The artwork and photographs used in this book are the result of a national selection organised by QCA and the Design Council. We would like to thank all 3,108 pupils who took part and especially the following pupils and schools whose work has been used throughout the National Curriculum.

Pupils Frankie Allen, Sarah Anderson, Naomi Ball, Kristina Battleday, Ashley Boyle, Martin Broom, Katie Brown, Alex Bryant, Tania Burnett, Elizabeth Burrows, Caitie Calloway, Kavandeep Chahal, Donna Clarke, Leah Cliffe, Megan Coombs, Andrew Cornford, Samantha Davidoff, Jodie Evans, Holly Fowler, Rachel Fort, Christopher Fort, Hannah Foster, Ruth Fry, Nicholas Furlonge, Tasleem Ghanchi, Rebecca Goodwin, Megan Goodwin, Joanna Gray, Alisha Grazette, Emma Habbeshon, Zoe Hall, Kay Hampshire, Jessica Harris, Aimee Howard, Amy Hurst, Katherine Hymers, Safwan Ismael, Tamaszina Jacobs-Abiola, Tomi Johnson, Richard Jones, Bruno Jones, Thomas Kelleher, Sophie Lambert, Gareth Lloyd, Ope Majekodunmi, Sophie Manchester, Alex Massie, Amy McNair, Dale Meachen, Katherine Mills, Rebecca Moore, Andrew Morgán, Amber Murrell, Sally O'Connor, Rosie O'Reilly, Antonia Pain, Daniel Pamment, Jennie Plant, Christopher Prest, Megan Ramsay, Alice Ross, David Rowles, Amy Sandford, Zeba Saudagar, Nathan Scarfe, Daniel Scully, Bilal Shakoor, Sandeep Sharma, Morrad Siyahla, Daryl Smith, Catriona Statham, Scott Taylor, Amy Thornton, Jessica Tidmarsh, Alix Tinkler, Lucy Titford, Marion Tulloch, Charlotte Ward, Kaltuun Warsame, Emily Webb, Bradley West, Daniel Wilkinson, Soriah Williams, Susan Williamson, Helen Williamson, Charlotte Windmill, Ryan Wollan, Olivia Wright.

Schools Adam's Grammar School, Almondbury Junior School, Bishops Castle Community College, Bolton Brow Junior and Infant School, Boxford C of E Voluntary Controlled Primary School, Bugbrooke School, Cantell School, Charnwood Primary School, Cheselbourne County First School, Chester Catholic High School, Dales Infant School, Deanery C of E High School, Driffield C of E Infants' School, Dursley Primary School, Fourfields County Primary School, Furze Infants School, Gosforth High School, Grahame Park Junior School, Green Park Combined School, Gusford Community Primary School, Hartshill School, Headington School, Holyport Manor School, Jersey College for Girls Preparatory School, King Edward VI School, King James's School, Kingsway Junior School, Knutsford High School, Leiston Primary School, Maltby Manor Infant School, Mullion Comprehensive School, North Marston C of E First School, Norton Hill School, Penglais School, Priory Secondary School, Redknock School, Richard Whittington Primary School, Ringwood School, Sarah Bonnell School, Sedgemoor Manor Infants School, Selly Park Technology College for Girls, Southwark Infant School, St Albans High School for Girls, St Denys C of E Infant School, St Helen's C of E (Aided) Primary School, St John's Infants School, St Joseph's RC Infant School, St Laurence School, St Mary Magdalene School, St Matthews C of E Aided Primary School, St Michael's C of E School, St Saviour's and St Olave's School, St Thomas The Martyr C of E Primary School, Sawtry Community College, The Duchess's High School, Tideway School, Torfield School, Trinity C of E Primary School, Upper Poppelton School, Walton High School.

QCA and the Design Council would also like to thank the figures from public life who contributed their ideas about the value of each curriculum subject.

Excellence in schools